Climbing
THE LADDER OF
READING & WRITING

Meeting the Needs of ALL Learners

Edited by
Nancy Young, Ed.D.
Jan Hasbrouck, Ph.D.

Foreword by
Maryanne Wolf, Ed.D.

TABLE OF CONTENTS

| PART I | UNDERSTANDING THE BIG PICTURE |

FOREWORD

BY Maryanne Wolf

Educators are the guardians of knowledge. Unfortunately, they are insufficiently acknowledged as such, making the book, *Climbing the Ladder of Reading & Writing: Meeting the Needs of All Learners*, even more important. Supporting educators and families who encounter a wide range of ease in children as they learn to read and write represents one of the primary goals of this book and one of the most important responsibilities of society.

Nancy Young and Jan Hasbrouck disseminate the work of some of our field's most respected scholars and practitioners. Each of the contributors unpacks an area of critical importance in the teaching and learning of reading and writing. The result is a tremendous resource that gives any reader the knowledge needed to make research-based decisions that propel all children toward better literacy outcomes.

The very impetus for this book has its origins in Nancy Young's efforts to visually depict what educators need to know to teach reading and writing. The power of her infographic is its basis in research and its central goal: to ensure that regardless of where a child is on the continuum of ease, they receive the instruction and support they need. This entire volume reflects this goal through multiple lenses.

Although my particular lens is grounded in cognitive neuroscience, I share that goal with the authors. Indeed, it was my use of neuroscience research in creating the first RAVE-O Intervention program that formed the basis of my friendship with Nancy Young. Her insights then and now are a prime example of the *reciprocity between teacher and researcher* that should always guide our work together.

Maryanne Wolf

Director of the UCLA Center for Dyslexia,
Diverse Learners, and Social Justice

From a slightly different perspective, I have worked side-by-side with Jan Hasbrouck for several years. We are both long committed to building and implementing the science of reading. We are also similarly committed to an evolving conceptualization of science. Such a view incorporates past research and propels new directions that should never be narrowly constrained to one particular emphasis in teaching or one hypothesis about learning to read and write.

I want to end this Foreword with my debt to the teachers I have known. Specifically, Merryl Pischa, who taught my son, Ben, and other children with dyslexia. To the children she said, "I want you to know that the hardest thing you will ever learn is the first thing you will learn: how to read. And you will learn!" To colleagues and parents, she said, "How can we teach all children to read if we don't give them the bottom rungs of the Ladder and just expect them to leap to the middle?" As conveyed throughout, this timely volume is accessible for all who care about fostering young readers and writers. The authors skillfully capture both the scientific research and classroom applications needed to empower literacy instruction.

I salute the authors of this book, educators like Merryl Pischa, and all who teach children to climb the difficult, beautiful, always ascending rungs of the Ladder that lead to deep readers, writers, and thinkers—the citizens of tomorrow. Godspeed!

CONTRIBUTING AUTHORS

PART I

CH 1: THE MESSAGE
Laura Stewart, M.F.A., M.S.
Chief Academic Officer, 95 Percent Group LLC
Geneva, IL, United States

CH 2: A CLOSER LOOK
Nancy Young, Ed.D.
Educational Consultant
Creator of *The Ladder of Reading & Writing* infographic
Nanoose Bay, British Columbia, Canada

CH 3: INSTRUCTIONAL IMPLICATIONS
Margie Gillis, Ed.D.
President, Literacy How, Inc.
Trumbull, CT, United States

Nancy Young, Ed.D.
Educational Consultant
Creator of *The Ladder of Reading & Writing* infographic
Nanoose Bay, British Columbia, Canada

CH 4: DATA-INFORMED INSTRUCTION
Jan Hasbrouck, Ph.D.
Researcher/Consultant, JH Educational Services, Inc.
Seattle, WA, United States

CH 5: MANAGING DIFFERENTIATED INSTRUCTION
Vicki Gibson, Ph.D.
Founding Director, Charlotte Sharp Children's Center
Dean of Education Excellence Professorship, Texas A & M University
School of Education and Human Development
College Station, TX, United States

PART II

CH 6: DYSLEXIA
Jan Hasbrouck, Ph.D.
Researcher/Consultant, JH Educational Services, Inc.
Seattle, WA, United States

CH 7: SPECIFIC READING COMPREHENSION DISABILITY (SRCD)
Nathan H. Clemens Ph.D., NCSP, LSSP
Associate Professor, The University of Texas
Department of Special Education
Austin, TX, United States

Katherine E. O'Donnell, Ph.D.
Assistant Professor, The University of Utah
Department of Educational Psychology
Salt Lake City, UT, United States

CH 8: WRITTEN EXPRESSION DIFFICULTIES (WD)
Jan Hasbrouck, Ph.D.
Researcher/Consultant, JH Educational Services, Inc.
Seattle, WA, United States

Nancy Young, Ed.D.
Educational Consultant
Creator of *The Ladder of Reading & Writing* infographic
Nanoose Bay, British Columbia, Canada

CH 9: DEVELOPMENTAL LANGUAGE DISORDER (DLD)
Maura Curran, Ph.D., CCC-SLP
Clinical Speech-Language Pathologist
Boston, MA, United States

Tiffany Hogan, Ph.D., CCC-SLP
Professor, MGH Institute of Health Professions
Boston, MA, United States

CH 10: ATTENTION DEFICIT/HYPERACTIVITY DISORDER (ADHD)
Carolyn A. Denton, Ph.D.
Educational Consultant
Port Townsend, WA, United States

CH 11: INTELLECTUAL DISABILITY (ID)

Jennifer Stewart, Ph.D.
Postdoctoral Research Fellow, University of Virginia
Center for Advanced Study of Teaching and Learning (CASTL)
School of Education and Human Development
Charlottesville, VA, United States

Carlin Conner, Ph.D.
Senior Research Scientist, University of Virginia
School of Education and Human Development
Charlottesville, VA, United States

Stephanie Al Otaiba, Ph.D.
Professor and Patsy Ray Caldwell Centennial Chair
Southern Methodist University
Harold Simmons School of Education and Human Development
Dallas, TX, United States

CH 12: DEAF OR HARD OF HEARING (D/HH)

Erica W. Jones, M.Ed., LSL Cert. AVEd.
Program Director/Teacher, Katherine Hamm Center
Atlanta Speech School
Atlanta, GA, United States

CH 13: ADVANCED IN READING (AIR)

Nancy Young, Ed.D.
Educational Consultant
Creator of *The Ladder of Reading & Writing* infographic
Nanoose Bay, British Columbia, Canada

PART III

CH 14: OLDER STUDENTS

Christy R. Austin, Ph.D.
Assistant Professor, Educational Psychology
University of Utah
Salt Lake City, UT, United States

Elizabeth A. Stevens, Ph.D.
Assistant Professor of Special Education
The University of Kansas
Lawrence, KS, United States

Sharon Vaughn, Ph.D.
Manuel J. Justiz Endowed Chair in Education, The University of Texas
Executive Director, Meadows Center for Preventing Educational Risk
Austin, TX, United States

CH 15: VARIATIONS OF ENGLISH

Kymyona Burk, Ed.D.
Senior Policy Fellow, Early Literacy
Foundation for Excellence in Education (ExcelinEd)
Tallahassee, FL, United States

Casey Sullivan Taylor, Ed.S.
Policy Director, Early Literacy
Foundation for Excellence in Education (ExcelinEd)
Tallahassee, FL, United States

CH 16: MULTILINGUAL LEARNERS

Gairan Pamei, M.A., M.Phil.
Doctoral Student, The Chinese University of Hong Kong
Department of Psychology
Hong Kong, China

Zebedee Cheah, M.Phil.
Doctoral Student, The Chinese University of Hong Kong
Department of Psychology
Hong Kong, China

Jing Tong Ong, M.Ed.
Lab Manager, Purdue University
Department of Human Development and Family Science
West Lafayette, IN, United States

Catherine (Cammie) McBride, Ph.D.
Professor, Purdue University
Department of Human Development and Family Science
West Lafayette, IN, United States

CH 17: SOCIOECONOMIC FACTORS

Steven P. Dykstra Ph.D.
Clinical Psychologist
Milwaukee County, WI, United States

CH 18: HOME-SCHOOL CONNECTIONS

Amy Fleisher, M.I.T.
General Education Classroom and Intervention Teacher
Seattle, WA, United States

Julie Bedell, M.S.
Reading Specialist and General Education Classroom Teacher
Seattle, WA, United States

CH 19: TECHNOLOGY

Kathleen Puckett, Ph.D.
Associate Professor, MLF Teachers College
Arizona State University
Tempe, AZ, United States

CH 20: TEACHER DEVELOPMENT

Tiffany Peltier, Ph.D.
Lead Learning and Delivery Specialist in Literacy at NWEA
A division of HMH
Boston, MA, United States

Erin K. Washburn, Ph.D.
Associate Professor of Reading Education
University of North Carolina
Charlotte, NC, United States

WHY WE CREATED THIS BOOK
FROM Nancy Young

The first version of my infographic, entitled *The Ladder of Reading*, was created in 2012 as part of a Master's course assignment. My goal was to visually represent the continuum of ease in reading acquisition and implications for instruction and practice. Once created, the infographic became my standby tool to explain reading challenges as I worked with families and schools.

 The infographic became my standby tool to explain reading challenges as I worked with families and schools.

As I began to provide professional development further afield, and used my infographic during conference presentations, many people told me how helpful it was to understand the range of ease in reading skill mastery in order to address reading difficulties. When I joined the world of social media, to my amazement, my infographic went "viral"!

Over the years, I was glad to see schools abandoning the teaching of strategies (such as "guessing") that research has shown to be ineffective. Yet an unexpected result of this shift was that I also observed schools now implementing whole-class instruction during which all students were being directly taught the same way using the same materials—every day. It seemed the differentiation that had been integral to previous reading instruction was being abandoned, too.

The shift to "one-sized-fits-all" that I saw happening greatly concerned me. As an educator, differentiation had been integral to my practice. As the mother of two children who were reading before Kindergarten, I also worried about the unmet learning needs of students who were more advanced in reading skills.

Nancy Young
Educational Consultant
Creator of *The Ladder of Reading & Writing*
Nanoose Bay, British Columbia, Canada

Along the way, I had made occasional revisions to my infographic. I realized I needed to make clearer my original intent that *every* student deserves to grow in their reading and writing skills, and that it is the responsibility of schools to provide the appropriate instruction and related support for this to happen.

The idea of a book to bring even greater clarity to the importance of needs-based instruction was simmering when I reached out to Dr. Jan Hasbrouck in 2021. Thus began our exciting collaboration which not only led to a major revision of my infographic later that year, becoming *The Ladder of Reading & Writing*, but also to the co-editing this very book you are reading. (A few further tweaks to the wording in *The Ladder of Reading & Writing* happened along the way; the 2023 update with those changes was released ahead of the publication of this book.)

For more than two years now, I have communicated daily with Jan as we've shared thoughts, dug into the research, reached out to experts, and questioned constantly (always smiling!) in our journey to create a book about the infographic I created many years ago, never dreaming it might positively impact students, teachers, and parents/caregivers across the globe. I will be forever grateful to Jan for this amazing learning adventure!

The Ladder of Reading & Writing

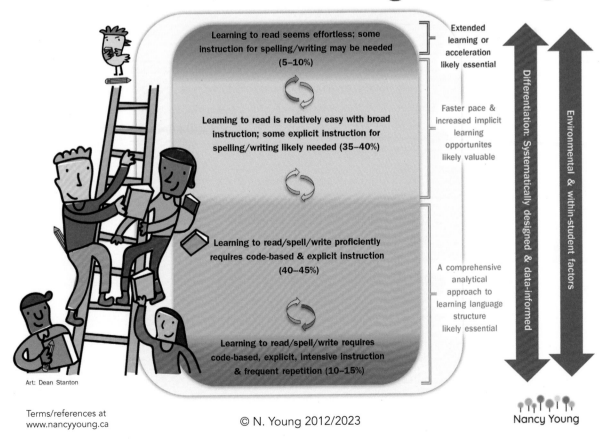

Terms/references at www.nancyyoung.ca

© N. Young 2012/2023

FROM Jan Hasbrouck

don't remember when or where I first saw Nancy's *The Ladder of Reading* infographic, but I do remember thinking it was wonderful! I immediately recognized that it would be a valuable addition to my toolkit in working with educators.

I have worked in the field of reading instruction my entire professional career, first as a reading specialist and coach, then as a university professor and researcher and, more recently, collaborating with colleagues around the world to help translate the ever-growing and evolving body of research now referred to as "the science of reading," or SOR, into effective classroom practice. It was clear to me that the image of happy students climbing a ladder to represent the journey of learning to read, combined with accurate information about the continuum of ease and the instructional considerations for each group, would help educators think deeply about the incredibly complex processes involved in teaching students to read and write.

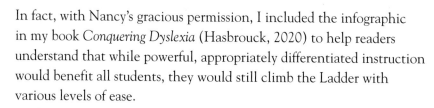

> We started on a joyful and intense period of thinking about, discussing, and drafting versions as *The Ladder of Reading* expanded into *The Ladder of Reading & Writing*.

In fact, with Nancy's gracious permission, I included the infographic in my book *Conquering Dyslexia* (Hasbrouck, 2020) to help readers understand that while powerful, appropriately differentiated instruction would benefit all students, they would still climb the Ladder with various levels of ease.

I finally had a chance to meet Nancy in person at a reading conference and so began our professional collaboration. I was honored when she reached out to me in 2021 as she first started thinking about the idea of a book about her infographic, along with a major update of the infographic itself, and asked if I would join her in that work. I agreed, and we started on a joyful and intense period of thinking about, discussing, and drafting versions as *The Ladder of Reading* expanded into *The Ladder of Reading & Writing*. Once that was released, the joy continued as the book became our focus! More thinking and many fun discussions, along with extensive reading, collaborative writing, and co-editing as the content of the book evolved to what you see here (and, along the way, a few more tweaks to the infographic, too!).

Jan Hasbrouck
Researcher/Consultant
JH Educational Services, Inc.
Seattle, WA, United States

x

FROM Nancy & Jan

Throughout the creation of this book, we have strived to include varying perspectives about reading and writing instruction. We are both mothers who have worn the shoes of parents concerned about our children's learning needs not being met; Jan's daughter has dyslexia and Nancy's children were both reading before the start of Kindergarten. We have both spent decades in various teaching roles serving a wide range of learning needs (both for students and their teachers) in North America and around the world. Jan brought to the table her knowledge as a researcher and university professor. Nancy brought her knowledge of the field of giftedness. We have seen the gaps, and we are all too aware of the social-emotional ramifications that can stem from unmet academic needs.

Early on, we realized how beneficial it would be to invite subject-area experts to write specific parts of the book that related to their areas of professional expertise. Their voices would enable us to not only provide clarity in our goal of helping educators, parents/caregivers, and community members better understand how to interpret and apply certain parts of the infographic, but such expertise would clarify terms and concepts in an easy-to-understand way grounded in solid research.

Over the many months of working with our amazing contributing authors, we have been continuously grateful for their time, expertise, and flexibility as the book evolved into what all of us hope will help move the field forward to better serve all students. We had an idea; our authors embraced our idea and became a part of the adventure as we worked with our publisher to create a unique book around a unique infographic. Teamwork in its truest sense!

As we extend our sincere thanks to our contributing authors for their time, dedication, and expertise, we also thank you, the reader of this book. We hope that the combined voices in this book will help you, whatever your role, lend your own voice to improving the teaching of reading and writing to better serve the wide range of needs within today's classroom. It is truly our wish that *The Ladder of Reading & Writing* will build bridges of understanding in the field as educators, parents, and community members work together in positive ways to address the reading and writing needs of ALL students!

PUTTING IT IN PERSPECTIVE

The Ladder of Reading & Writing infographic illustrates what we know from research: that learning to read and write in English is a complex process influenced by multiple internal and external factors. Therefore, instruction cannot be "one size fits all." Rather, students vary widely in the ease with which they master the interwoven skills of reading and writing. It is the responsibility of educators to provide appropriate, differentiated instruction to support each student wherever they are on their learning journey. Navigating the delivery of appropriate, differentiated instruction for all students, however, can be overwhelming. This book serves to shed light on efficient and effective ways to approach that very task.

WHO IS THIS BOOK FOR?

This book is primarily written for *teachers*, those who carry the precious responsibility day in and day out of teaching all students to read and write. Today's classrooms are arguably more diverse than ever. Or at least research has made us more aware than ever of this diversity as well as the vast complexities involved in rewiring the brain for literacy. This book explores the nuances and instructional implications of *The Ladder of Reading & Writing* infographic. It serves to provide a perspective for understanding students' diverse instructional needs.

This book is also for *school administrators* and the many *other professionals* who support teachers, whether in the classroom or through ongoing professional development. Understanding the diverse exceptionalities and environmental considerations that affect student learning can help all members of the team work collaboratively to provide appropriate support as teachers differentiate instruction and practice for their students.

Finally, this book is for *parents*, *caregivers* and other *community members* who love and care for children as they climb the Ladder. Truly, it takes a village ... and the better we can communicate and coordinate our support for specific students, the more effective those efforts will be.

WHAT IS THE BEST WAY TO USE THIS BOOK?

Consider using this book in the following ways:

If you are a teacher ...	If you are an administrator or professional leader ...	If you are a parent or caregiver ...
• Read through Part 1 to gain a thorough understanding of the concepts presented in the infographic.	• Read through Part 1 to gain a thorough understanding of the concepts presented in the infographic.	• Read through Part 1 to gain a thorough understanding of the concepts presented in the infographic.
• Consider your own classroom and students to determine what recommendations from Part 1 will have the most impact on improving your efficiency or effectiveness when delivering appropriate, differentiated instruction for students.	• Consider your role in helping teachers understand and apply these concepts, which may mean dialoguing with specific teachers to identify next steps for application.	• Consider where your child is on their climb up the Ladder.
• Use Parts 2 and 3 for reference as you consider how to address specific students' needs.	• Be sure to read Chapter 20 Teacher Development and use Parts 2 and 3 for reference.	• Be sure to read Chapter 18 Home-School Connections and use Parts 2 and 3 for reference.
• As needed, consult and/or create instructional goals and plans for individual or small groups of students with related needs to access grade-level content or advance in their climb up the Ladder.	• Write down actionable steps to support teachers as they implement specific recommendations from Part 1 to enhance their delivery of appropriate, differentiated instruction.	• Collect and study any available information or data to help you understand your child's instructional needs.
		• Reach out to teachers, administrators, or professionals working with your child to plan and/or monitor your child's progress.
		• Engage your child in frequent conversation about their learning, interests, and goals.

HOW IS THIS BOOK ORGANIZED?

PART I expands on concepts illustrated in *The Ladder of Reading & Writing* infographic. Chapter 1 explores the message behind the infographic that ALL students deserve appropriate instruction differentiated to their unique needs. Chapter 2 unpacks each of the features in the infographic, and Chapter 3 explores the instructional implications of those features. Chapters 4 and 5 expound on the importance of using data to inform instructional decision-making and managing the classroom environment to create a structure in which effective differentiated instruction may occur.

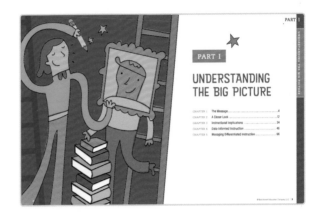

PART II explores a range of exceptionalities that students may bring to the classroom. This part of the book is intended for reference as you address the needs of specific students. These exceptional needs include dyslexia, specific reading comprehension disability (SRCD), attention deficit/hyperactivity disorder (ADHD), deaf or hard of hearing (d/hh), and others. These affect how students learn and what types of scaffolding may be best to support their climb up the Ladder.

PART III addresses other issues related to student learning including age, language, and home environment. As we are all aware, students' learning does not take place in a vacuum and these issues must also be considered when planning and providing appropriate instruction. You may use this part also as a reference to quickly access information applicable to individual students or your current planning needs.

Scan this QR code for additional book resources

The Ladder of

Nancy's infographic has been adapted to fit onto two pages.

A PDF of this infographic can be downloaded from Nancy's website *www.nancyyoung.ca*

Learning to read seems effortless; some instruction for spelling/writing may be needed

Learning to read is relatively easy with broad instruction; some explicit instruction for spelling/writing likely needed

Learning to read/spell/write proficiently requires code-based & explicit instruction

Learning to read/spell/write requires code-based, explicit, intensive instruction & frequent repetition

Art: Dean Stanton

Reading & Writing

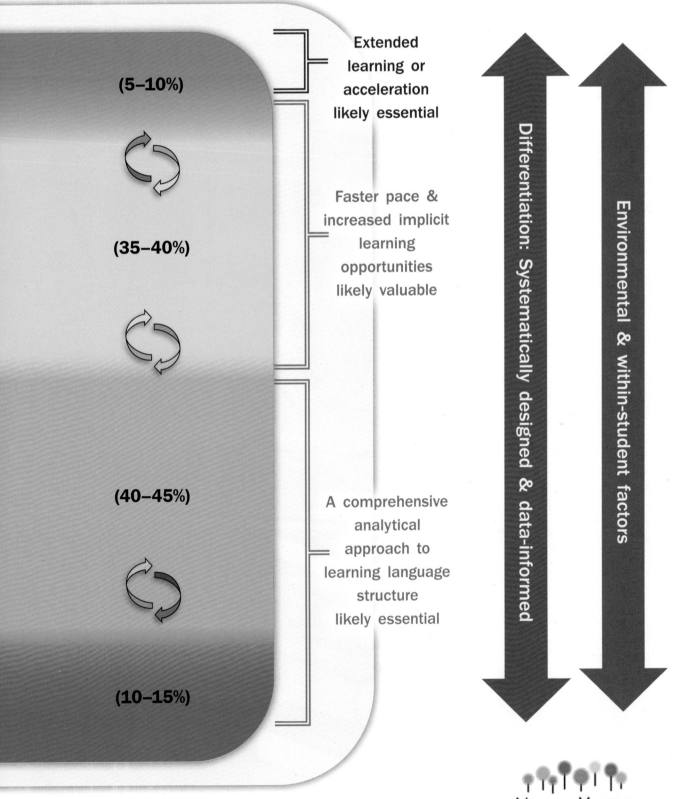

(5–10%)

Extended learning or acceleration likely essential

(35–40%)

Faster pace & increased implicit learning opportunities likely valuable

(40–45%)

A comprehensive analytical approach to learning language structure likely essential

(10–15%)

Differentiation: Systematically designed & data-informed

Environmental & within-student factors

Nancy Young

PART I

UNDERSTANDING THE BIG PICTURE

THE MESSAGE

The magic of reading your first storybook. The satisfaction of understanding the directions for a building project. The empathy of learning about others different from yourself. The poignancy of a resonant passage. The tenderness of lap-reading with your grand-baby. The power of writing a journal entry that captures a memorable experience.

The gifts of a literate life are many. Learning to read and write is the gateway to these gifts, and for the majority of us, instruction is required. While the research is clear that nearly all students (90–95%) can be taught to read (Goldberg & Goldenberg, 2022; Moats, 2020; Vaughn & Fletcher, 2020–2021), there are many students who are not mastering this fundamental life skill.

> " The gifts of a literate life are many. Learning to read and write is the gateway to these gifts ... "

AUTHOR **Laura Stewart**
Chief Academic Officer
95 Percent Group LLC
Geneva, IL, USA

" *The Ladder of Reading & Writing* infographic was created to support the vital efforts of educators everywhere. "

As a result, these gifts are denied to a significant number of our fellow citizens. *The Ladder of Reading & Writing* infographic was created to support the vital efforts of educators everywhere who are committed to providing instruction to help ALL students become joyful and accomplished readers and writers!

A CONCERNING DECLINE

Recent data from the National Assessment of Educational Progress (NCES, 2022) shows that only 33% of U.S. public-school fourth graders and 31% of eight graders are performing at or above proficient levels on the 2019 reading assessment. While these data have been relatively flat over several decades, the newest data show a concerning decline, most pronounced in our lowest-performing students, likely due to the impact of COVID-19 (NCES, 2022). These figures are alarming, especially when the consequences of illiteracy are so severe.

 Only 33 percent of U.S. public-school fourth graders and 31 percent of eight graders are performing at or above proficient levels.

Long-Term Ramifications of Illiteracy

Individuals with the lowest levels of literacy face a myriad of potentially compromising life consequences. Elementary students who struggle with reading face a potential downward spiral as the gap expands between where they are and the increasing complexity of text demands. About 16 percent of students who are not reading proficiently by the end of third grade do not graduate from high school, a rate four times greater than that for proficient readers (The Annie E. Casey Foundation, 2012).

Eighty-five percent of juveniles who are involved in the juvenile court system are functionally low literate; furthermore, juvenile incarceration reduces the possibility of high school graduation and increases the probability of incarceration later in life (Aizer & Doyle, 2015).

Many adults with low literacy levels and their families live in a cycle of poverty, which has far-reaching effects on health, security, housing, food, and access to education. Childhood poverty can affect brain development, making individuals less able to learn (Noble, 2017).

 Low literacy is an issue of health and safety; from reading instructions for a dosage of medicine, to understanding directions and warnings, to interpreting maps and diagrams. People with low literacy skills are often marginalized and disenfranchised. As a result, our society misses out on the talents and skills of people whose voices go unheard.

Important U.S. Public School Statistics

- 33 percent of 4th graders are performing at or above proficient reading level expectations.

- 31 percent of 8th graders are performing at or above proficient reading level expectations.

- 37 percent of 12th graders are performing at or above proficient reading level expectations.

- 16 percent of students who are not reading proficiently by the end of Grade 3 do not graduate from high school (4x higher than proficient readers).

- 85 percent of all juveniles in the court system are functionally low literate (which reduces the likelihood of high school graduation and increases the probability of future incarceration).

The Promise of Appropriate Instruction

This all seems very grim. Where is the hope and promise in all of this? Appropriate instruction. The gap between where we are now and where we can be is the opportunity for instruction. Instruction matters. As Maryanne Wolf (2007) reminds us, "We were never born to read" (p. 3), and those neural connections necessary for reading can be developed through the right instruction at the right time for almost everyone.

Fortunately, we know a great deal from the current body of research around reading. The past 50+ years have yielded powerful interdisciplinary insights about reading acquisition and instruction from developmental psychology, cognitive neuropsychology, developmental linguistics, neuroscience, intervention studies, and the educational research community.

Major research syntheses have drawn similar conclusions about the process of learning to read and the impact of instruction (National Early Literacy Panel, 2008; NICHD, 2000; Rose, 2006; Rowe & National Inquiry into the Teaching of Literacy, 2005) including the fact that despite the many differences between individual learners, all brains have similar constraints and follow a predictable neurological pattern when processing language (Dehaene, 2009).

Learn More!

Wolf, M. (2007). *Proust and the squid: The story and science of the reading brain*. Harper Collins.

Dehaene, S. (2009) *Reading in the brain: The science and evolution of a human invention*. Viking.

Petscher, Y., Cabell, S., Catts, H. W., Compton, D., Foorman, B., Hart, S. A., Lonigan, C., Phillips, B., Schatschneider, C., Steacy, L., Terry, N., & Wagner, R. (2020). How the science of reading informs 21st century education. *Reading Research Quarterly, 55*(S1).

Early Instruction Matters

Most importantly, early instruction matters. Looking at the NAEP data, it is clear that when students struggle to learn to read, that struggle can be pervasive and long-term. Yet according to Moats (2011, p. 51), "A large body of research evidence shows that with appropriate, intensive instruction, all but the most severe reading disabilities can be ameliorated in the early grades and students can get on track toward academic success." A prevention-oriented approach is necessary to mitigate the potential for repeated cycles of intervention.

If instruction is key, and we know much about the effective principles of that instruction, why are so many students still struggling? Many educators in their teacher preparation and ongoing professional development have not been provided this knowledge base (Seidenberg, 2017; Solari et al., 2020). Educators can't teach what they don't know, and yet a knowledgeable teacher is the critical factor in student achievement (Lyon & Weiser, 2009). Although more research is undoubtedly needed about the most effective implementation of the science of reading, the role of the teacher is key.

WHERE TO BEGIN

Where does a novice educator begin? Where can a seasoned teacher look for clarity? That is where *The Ladder of Reading & Writing* infographic comes in. The infographic acts as a visual road map, an instructional anchor of core principles, or an at-a-glance guidepost. As one teacher put it (Young, 2021):

> Your *Ladder of Reading & Writing* creates a type of instantaneous psychological relief for teachers. Most of us teacher folk are committed to ALL our students. Nature and its marvelous diversity of abilities can make teachers feel like instruction for all will make us lose our minds. Your infographic rapidly helps teachers feel that all the joys AND frustrations of our daily, teaching lives can be captured on one page; can be comprehended. Between the ever-changing schedules, continuous interruptions and life events of our students, our families and ourselves—at least we have a literacy map to anchor our purpose. What a psychological relief!
>
> — *Lorraine Yamin, Learning Specialist, New York City, NY*

Check Your Understanding

Check all that apply.

Appropriate early instruction:

___ can ameliorate all but the most severe reading disabilities

___ mitigates the potential for repeated cycles of intervention

___ does not need to be explicitly taught in professional development

___ is most effective when led by a knowledgeable teacher

A Powerful Tool

Why is *The Ladder of Reading & Writing* infographic such a powerful tool? First, it provides us with these **operating principles**:

• All students need and deserve appropriate and effective instruction.

• Needs-based instruction is vital to reach all students, whether they are progressing as expected, are at risk and need early intervention, have an exceptionality requiring support, or are progressing at an advanced rate and need opportunities for acceleration.

• Appropriate data must be used to guide needs-based instruction that is differentiated and systematically designed.

• Instruction needs to be *proactive* rather than *reactive*. Evidence-aligned instruction from the first day of school gets all students off to a strong start rather than relying on intervention to "catch them up."

• Environmental (e.g., home language and economic circumstances) and within-student factors (i.e., ADHD and learning challenges) vary among individuals and may affect learning.

An Evolving Understanding

The Ladder of Reading & Writing infographic is effective in helping us move away from either/or thinking about reading and writing instruction. The gradation of colors in the continuum of the infographic clearly indicates the wide range of explicitness and nuances of instruction that need to be considered.

Another important feature of the Ladder in the infographic is the inclusion of the 5–10 percent of students for whom learning to read and write seems effortless and challenging content is likely needed. Oftentimes, we focus our attention on those students at risk of failure, and given the grim statistics cited above, it is not surprising educators feel the pressure to do so. However, the infographic reminds us that advanced students also need—and deserve—instruction that is differentiated to ensure their continued progress.

Finally, the Ladder infographic is not static, as it reflects new insights from the science around reading. Education's greatest gift is that learning never ceases. Taking that into account, we expect that the infographic will continue to evolve. For example, we need to know more about "what works for whom under what conditions" (Petscher et al., 2020, p. 17). Another likely area to pursue is research on advanced readers. And, of course, we will continue to explore the translation of science to practice.

Conclusion

As educators, we came into the profession to make a difference, to deliver on the promise of literacy for all students. Parents, caregivers, and community members also care deeply about the success of our students. We aren't there yet. There is work to be done, and we must act—together—with urgency and conviction. The Ladder infographic is a visual guide that encourages all of us to "believe in the possible."

 Every young child deserves classroom instruction and support differentiated for their intellectual ability and academic readiness . . . provided in ways that are both effective and FUN!
—*Nancy Young, 2021*

KEY TAKEAWAYS

- Currently, many students are not proficient in literacy skills, with potentially lifelong consequences.

- Needs-based instruction is crucial and entails serving a wide range of needs, from challenged to advanced learners.

- *The Ladder of Reading & Writing* is a visual guide for understanding and providing needs-based instruction.

A CLOSER LOOK

The Ladder of Reading & Writing infographic was created to help educators, parents/caregivers, and community members better understand the wide "range of ease" in learning to read and write the English language, a journey of skill development likened to climbing the rungs of a ladder. The colored continuum in the infographic represents the variations of ease in skill mastery and instructional implications. Throughout the infographic are additional, carefully selected images and descriptors that draw attention to important factors for consideration.

AUTHOR **Nancy Young**

Educational Consultant
Creator of *The Ladder of Reading & Writing*
Nanoose Bay, British Columbia, Canada

> " The infographic illustrates that literacy instruction cannot be construed as "one-size-fits-all." "

The use of an infographic to understand the range of needs more easily does not diminish the complexity of serving our students. Rather, the infographic illustrates that literacy instruction cannot be construed as "one-size-fits-all." Educators must consider who is learning, what they need, and why they need it, so that instruction can be systematically designed to ensure that it is appropriately differentiated for each student.

This chapter unpacks the visual features and wording on *The Ladder of Reading & Writing* to build greater understanding of the important messages the infographic represents.

THE LADDER OF READING & WRITING

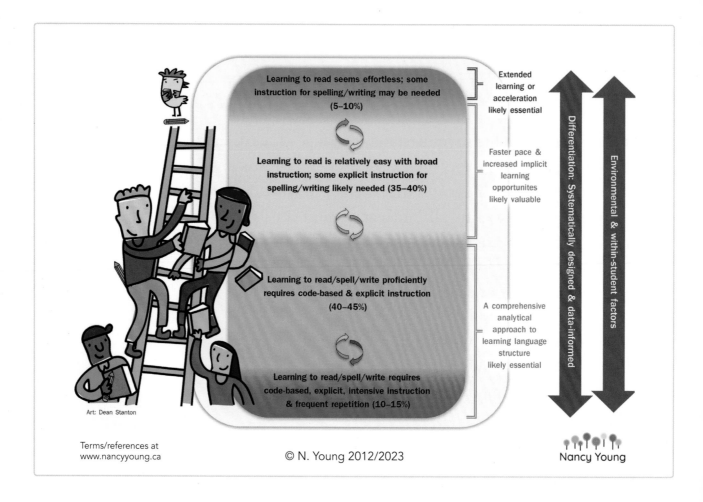

Learning to read seems effortless; some instruction for spelling/writing may be needed (5–10%)

Learning to read is relatively easy with broad instruction; some explicit instruction for spelling/writing likely needed (35–40%)

Learning to read/spell/write proficiently requires code-based & explicit instruction (40–45%)

Learning to read/spell/write requires code-based, explicit, intensive instruction & frequent repetition (10–15%)

Extended learning or acceleration likely essential

Faster pace & increased implicit learning opportunites likely valuable

A comprehensive analytical approach to learning language structure likely essential

Differentiation: Systematically designed & data-informed

Environmental & within-student factors

Art: Dean Stanton

Terms/references at www.nancyyoung.ca

© N. Young 2012/2023

Nancy Young

The title of the infographic, *The Ladder of Reading & Writing*, represents that becoming literate entails both learning to read and write. Both skills are necessary, and they are reciprocal—learning one enhances the other.

On the left side of the infographic, the image of the Ladder portrays the journey of learning to read and write as climbing the rungs of a ladder. Although not a strictly linear process, the journey to becoming literate is often thought of as reaching a series of milestones, from the initial excitement of reading or writing a single word independently to the satisfaction of reading or writing a lengthy and complex text. As we think of repurposing the brain's wiring to do something none of us were born to do, we can imagine climbing rungs of this Ladder. With mastery of each rung, there is celebration that the learner is closer to being able to "fly," or read and write independently, although the learning never ends!

THE SMILING CLIMBERS

The journey to becoming a fluent reader and writer varies in difficulty. The smiling students climbing the Ladder send a crucial message to the adults helping students learn to read and write: Climbing the Ladder should be joyful for every learner! Some students will leap up each rung, while others will take much longer and require extensive support to progress. Whether a beginning reader learning a new skill, or an advanced reader building knowledge of more complex text or expressing their thoughts in writing, it is the responsibility of adults to ensure that every learner is smiling as each rung is mastered.

Books and Pencils

Look closely and you will see that the students are bringing along books as they climb the Ladder. Even the little bird at the top of the Ladder, ready to fly, is holding a book. The student in the green shirt halfway up the Ladder on the right loves reading so much that her pack is overloaded with books and they are falling out! Books are featured in the art not just to remind adults that exposure to a wide variety of texts in various ways should happen at all stages of the climb (Shanahan, 2016), but that our goal is to instill a love of reading. We want our readers to treasure various forms of text and the riches of knowledge they contain.

Similarly, pencils represent writing. Both reading and writing are important for academic success (Fletcher et al., 2019; Graham, 2020). Writing improves reading and reading improves writing (Graham, 2020; Graham & Hebert, 2010). Students need to be writing throughout the journey, from practicing letter formation at the foundational stages to the acquisition of skills that enable them to organize and express their ideas as well as demonstrate knowledge (Graham, Bollinger et al., 2018).

Learn More!

Castles, A., Rastle, K., & Nation, K. (2018). Ending the reading wars: Reading acquisition from novice to expert. *Psychological Science in the Public Interest, 19*(1), 5–51.

Hoover, W. A., & Tunmer, W. E. (2020). Summary of the cognitive foundations framework. In *The cognitive foundations of reading and its acquisition: A framework with applications connecting teaching and learning* (Vol. 20, pp. 85–88). Springer Cham.

Graham, S. (2020). The sciences of reading and writing must become more fully integrated. *Reading Research Quarterly, 55*(S1), S35–S44.

THE CONTINUUM OF EASE

The colors in the middle of the infographic, the continuum of red, orange, light green, and dark green colors, represent the wide range of ease in learning to read. This range of ease is sometimes described by researchers as a "continuous distribution" of reading ability (Boada et al., 2002; Fletcher & Miciak, 2019; Shaywitz et al., 1992). Mastery of writing also ranges in ease (Gentry & Graham, 2010; Graham et al., 2018). Addressing the range of ease for both reading and writing requires that instructional approaches and materials be differentiated (Fletcher et al., 2019). Therefore, a needs-based approach is central to the message of the infographic.

As areas of the continuum are summarized, note that the instructional implications are addressed more fully in Chapter 3, along with additional citations of supporting research.

Learning to read seems effortless; some instruction for spelling/writing may be needed (5–10%)

Learning to read is relatively easy with broad instruction; some explicit instruction for spelling/writing likely needed (35–40%)

Learning to read/spell/write proficiently requires code-based & explicit instruction (40–45%)

Learning to read/spell/write requires code-based, explicit, intensive instruction & frequent repetition (10–15%)

Red Area of the Continuum

For some students, represented by the red area of the continuum, learning to read and write is challenging. They are likely to require explicit and intensive instruction with frequent repetition. Although not all students in the red area of the continuum will have difficulty learning to decode, the inclusion of the word "code-based" in the red area makes it clear that we should not teach students to guess at words (Hoover & Tunmer, 2020; Seidenberg, 2017). The specific needs, and severity of those needs, vary within the red area of the continuum, but may include students with developmental or learning exceptionalities. Students in this area of the continuum are likely to require intervention programming that involves increased frequency and intensity of instruction and practice (Tier 2 likely, Tier 3 possibly).

Orange Area of the Continuum

For students in the orange area of the continuum, the instructional methodology remains similar to the red area (code-based and explicit) but instruction is likely to be less intense and the pace will be faster than for students in the red area. Students in the orange area of the continuum will generally require fewer steps and less repetition during instruction than students in the red.

Light Green Area of the Continuum

For students within the light green area of the continuum, learning to read is far less challenging and implicit learning plays a greater role. Broad instruction enables learning at a faster pace, with earlier transition to independent practice than students in the orange area of the continuum. Spelling and writing instruction may encompass explicit instruction of strategies that enable ongoing implicit learning opportunities such as word sorting and collaborative writing.

> " For students within the light green area of the continuum, learning to read is far less challenging and implicit learning plays a greater role. "

Dark Green Area of the Continuum

Students in the dark green area of the continuum generally arrive at Kindergarten already reading. Although some of these students may be two or three (or more) years ahead in their reading skills, their abilities must be allowed to flourish through the provision of advanced learning opportunities. Any needed support for spelling or writing must consider their advanced reading skills, their ability to learn rapidly, and their need for intellectual challenge.

> " Although some of these students may be two or three (or more) years ahead in their reading skills, their abilities must be allowed to flourish through the provision of advanced learning opportunities. "

Check Your Understanding

Match each description below to the continuum color described:

(a) Red   (b) Orange   (c) Light Green   (d) Dark Green

___ These students require advanced learning opportunities to keep them moving forward.

___ These students require intensive instruction with frequent repetition.

___ These students will move forward with broad instruction, some skills taught explicitly as needed.

___ These students require code-based instruction but likely less intense and faster paced.

Words to the Right of the Continuum

To the right of the continuum, the infographic provides further guidelines for instruction.

Key Instructional Points for the Red and Orange Areas

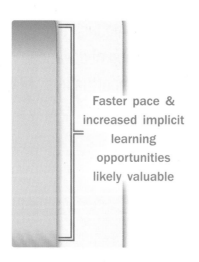

A comprehensive analytical approach to learning language structure likely essential

For children in the red and orange areas of the continuum, a comprehensive analytical approach to teaching language structure is likely essential. "Comprehensive" means that reading and writing are integrated (Graham, 2020) and instruction generally includes phonemic awareness/phonics along with fluency, vocabulary, and comprehension (including background knowledge) (Fletcher et al., 2019; Smith et al., 2021). "Analytical" represents the process whereby students learn the alphabetic principle (letters represent speech sounds), leading to the ability to strategically decode/encode as well as identify units of meaning within individual words and sentences (Castles et al., 2018; Hoover & Tunmer, 2020). A comprehensive analytical approach encompasses the elements sometimes described as the "Big 5" or "5 Pillars" (NICHD, 2000) and as "structured literacy" (Spear-Swerling, 2018).

Key Instructional Points for the Light Green Area

Faster pace & increased implicit learning opportunities likely valuable

For students in the light green area, both content and methods should be adjusted to account for the greater ease and faster pace with which they master skills. They will move more quickly from decoding to comprehension of text. Able to address more new concepts at once, they benefit from implicit learning opportunities gained through peer-collaboration and discovery-based learning.

Key Instructional Points for the Dark Green Area

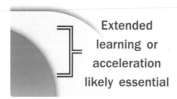

Extended learning or acceleration likely essential

The words to the right of the dark green area present ways for advanced readers to continue learning by building on their already advanced skills. This includes extended programming or acceleration. The word "essential" is here because programming that does not recognize advanced skills may delay continued skill development and lead to loss of motivation to learn, resulting in underachievement (Reis & Fogarty, 2020). Chapter 13 provides more information about advanced readers and how to support their learning needs.

Percentages and Curved Arrows

Within each of the colored areas of the continuum, percentages represent approximations as we consider the entire continuous distribution of learners (Boada et al., 2002; Fletcher & Miciak, 2019; Lyon, 2002; Vaughn & Fletcher, 2020–21). The percentages are there to support educators in understanding the variations of ease in learning to read and write.

> " The percentages are there to support educators in understanding the variations of ease in learning to read and write. "

The three sets of curved arrows bridging the colored areas of the continuum serve as reminders that learners' needs will vary even within the colors themselves. Some students may need more instruction of certain content (the *what*) delivered using specific methodology (the *how*), some less, and some none at all. For example, a student whose screening results indicate risk factors for reading difficulties in Kindergarten may have an advanced spoken vocabulary and thus not require intense vocabulary instruction but a heavier emphasis on phonics.

The curved arrows also serve to remind us that some students of high intellect may also have dyslexia and/or ADHD (or other exceptionalities). In addition to the reading and writing instruction they require, these students benefit from learning opportunities that reflect their intellectual abilities and personal interests.

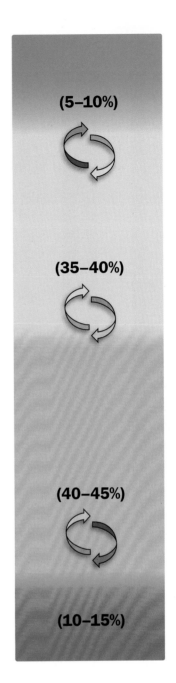

(5–10%)

(35–40%)

(40–45%)

(10–15%)

Differentiation: Systematically designed & data-informed

Environmental & within-student factors

Purple and Blue Arrows

The purple and blue arrows to the right of the colored continuum address other aspects to think about as students grow in their reading and writing skills. Notice that both arrows are pointing up and down; this means we need to consider the information in these arrows for *every* student on the continuum when defining an appropriate needs-based approach.

The words in the purple arrow emphasize that differentiated instruction applies to the whole continuum, including programs and accompanying materials systematically designed and data-informed, no matter where a student is on their climb up the Ladder.

The words in the blue arrow point out factors that can impact learning across the continuum, including environmental (e.g., teacher/school, literacy in the home, language/dialect, economic circumstances) and within-student factors (e.g., attentional and psychological disorders as well as disabilities).

Conclusion

Learning to read and write is a process that ranges in difficulty. *The Ladder of Reading & Writing* infographic visually represents the journey, including the wide range of ease in skill mastery, instructional ramifications, and factors that affect learning. It underscores that differentiation is essential to effectively meet the needs of all learners in our schools.

In Chapter 3, we will delve further into the instructional implications suggested by the continuum on the infographic and provide examples of programming designed to address specific needs. The remainder of the book expands upon specific topics that connect to the words and images on the infographic.

KEY TAKEAWAYS

- The journey of learning to read and write can be compared to climbing the rungs of a ladder.

- The colored continuum on the infographic represents the wide range of ease that students may experience when learning to read and write.

- Differentiation is essential to address the full range of students' needs, and requires systematically designed and data-informed instruction.

- Environmental and within-student factors can impact any student's journey as they climb the Ladder.

INSTRUCTIONAL IMPLICATIONS

The teaching of reading and writing continues to be under the microscope. How are these skills best taught? What instructional practices are supported by research? What may *not* be supported by research? What still needs more research? Are some practices more effective than others?

This chapter provides an overview of the instructional implications of the wide range of needs represented in the colored continuum on *The Ladder of Reading & Writing* infographic. We recognize that while we must continue to ask questions, re-examining older practices and integrating new findings from the ever-evolving science of reading, the students in our classrooms need instruction *now*. We cannot wait until we have all the answers to remaining questions.

AUTHORS

Margie Gillis
President, Literacy How, Inc.
Trumbull, CT, USA

Nancy Young
Educational Consultant
Creator of *The Ladder of Reading & Writing*
Nanoose Bay, British Columbia, Canada

Therefore, we begin by defining key terms to clarify understandings, explain the components underpinning mastery of reading and writing, and then provide examples of instructional methods and materials based on a large body of research. We hope this chapter will help educators better envisage where their students may be in terms of the continuum as well as ways to address the needs of individual students.

KEY TERMS DEFINED

Some common terms are now being debated, analyzed, and critiqued. New terms are being adopted eagerly and others are being rejected. Systematically designed? Explicit? Implicit? What do these words actually mean? Here's our take on three important terms that appear on *The Ladder of Reading & Writing* infographic.

Systematically Designed

As *The Ladder of Reading & Writing* infographic illustrates, there is a continuum of ease when it comes to learning to read and write. The purple arrow to the right of the colored continuum tells us that programming and aligned materials must be "systematically designed" to address identified student needs. What does this mean?

> Instruction is *systematic* when it is designed to:
>
> - address clearly defined *goals* for each knowledge unit,
>
> - teach a specified set of skills or strategies or a defined breadth and depth of knowledge (i.e., the scope of instruction),
>
> - follow a *logical sequence* of knowledge units (e.g., moving from easier to harder skills),
>
> - present carefully selected *examples* to deepen and extend learning, and
>
> - *distribute practice* to build fluency and retention (Carnine et al., 2010).

Using systematically designed programming helps all students on their climb up the Ladder. Research-based curricula help teachers provide consistent, appropriate instruction through efficient planning and delivery of content. However, it is important to remember that even a systematically designed program may need to be supplemented and/or modified to meet varying student needs.

Differentiation: Systematically designed & data-informed

TAKEAWAY
Systematic design supports effective instruction.

Ladder Implications
Reading and writing instruction should be systematically designed.

Explicit

Explicit instruction involves modeling and active engagement, including frequent opportunities to respond during teacher-guided practice (Archer & Hughes, 2010). Explicit instruction is deliberately planned and implemented and can take a variety of forms (Fletcher et al., 2019).

Explicit instruction has been demonstrated to benefit certain students in the early stages of skill acquisition to maximize learning and application (Carnine et al., 2010; Seidenberg, 2021). Students vary in their speed of acquisition of skills and strategies, influencing both the pace of instruction (Archer & Hughes, 2010) and the amount of explicit instruction that should be provided (Fletcher et al., 2019). As students move toward mastery of skills and strategies, the use of explicit instruction is reduced and replaced by implicit learning.

> " Explicit instruction has been demonstrated to benefit certain students in the early stages of skill acquisition to maximize learning and application. "

TAKEAWAY
The use of explicit instruction will vary depending on the needs of individual students.

Ladder Implications
Some students require intensive explicit instruction while others require less.

Implicit

Implicit learning happens every day as we absorb information from our environment, without conscious awareness. We are born to learn! Think of a toddler playing with plastic containers or a first-grade student learning to maneuver on playground equipment.

Learning to read and write changes our brain (Dehaene, 2011), but the combination of instruction and environment to make that happen will vary depending on the student. Instruction must consider that some students will absorb greater amounts of information implicitly and will benefit from learning through exposure, discovery, and problem-solving, while other students will require explicit instruction to master a skill or strategy (Fletcher et al., 2019; Seidenberg, 2021).

Understanding the role of implicit learning means recognizing that "much (if not most)" (Hoover & Tunmer, 2020, p. 203) of what is learned as students master the English alphabetic code will not be directly taught. Exposure to patterns in individual and combined words impacts the acquisition of literacy, commonly referred to as "statistical learning" (Seidenberg, 2017; Treiman & Kessler, 2022). For this reason, it is crucially important all students have early and ongoing exposure to a variety of texts (e.g., books, signs, food labels, etc.) at home and school.

TAKEAWAY
Implicit learning occurs throughout every waking hour.

Ladder Implications
The classroom setting needs to offer a learning environment and materials that support ongoing implicit learning.

INSTRUCTIONAL CONTENT AND METHODS

Planning appropriate instruction involves making decisions about both the instructional content and materials (the *what*) and the instructional methods (the *how*) used to deliver the content.

Instructional Content

Instructional content is what we teach so students achieve desired learning outcomes. Underpinning the journey to becoming a proficient reader and writer are certain components of language structure (Graham, 2020; NICHD, 2000; Spear-Swerling, 2018; Wolf, 2007; Wolf, 2013). These components are represented by *The Literacy How Reading Wheel* diagram below and defined in the text box on the following page.

Learn More!

Connor, C. M. (2014). Individualizing teaching in beginning reading. In *Better: Evidence-based education* (pp. 4–7). Institute for Effective Education at the University of York and the Center for Research and Reform in Education at Johns Hopkins School of Education.

Seidenberg, M. (2017). *Language at the speed of sight: How we read, why so many can't, and what can be done about it.* Basic Books.

Gillis, M. B., & Eberhardt, N. C. (2018). *Syntax knowledge to practice.* Literacy How.

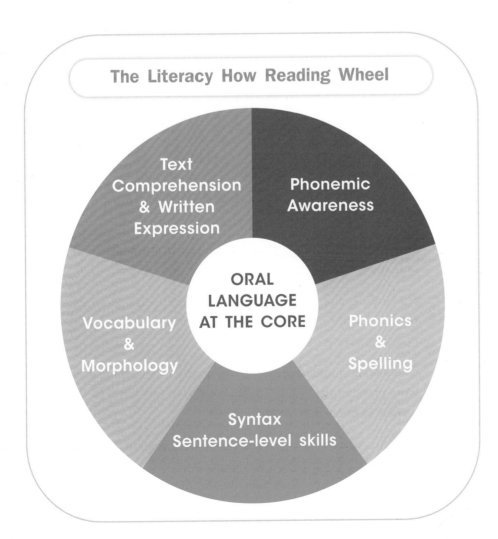

The Literacy How Reading Wheel

Text Comprehension & Written Expression — Phonemic Awareness — ORAL LANGUAGE AT THE CORE — Phonics & Spelling — Syntax Sentence-level skills — Vocabulary & Morphology

Components of Language Structure

Phonemic awareness: conscious or unconscious awareness of the sounds (phonemes) in spoken words

Phonics and spelling: the relationship between graphemes (letters) and phonemes (sounds)

Syntax: the arrangement of words, phrases, and clauses in sentences

Vocabulary: a body of words and their meanings

Morphology: the study of meaningful parts of words (morphemes) including affixes (prefixes and suffixes), root and base words

Text comprehension: the ability to process text, understand its meaning, and integrate that understanding with what the reader already knows

Written expression: a process that requires the simultaneous integration of transcription and language skills as well as cognitive processes (e.g., attention, working memory)

When considering these components, it is important to know that:

- Phonemic awareness is acquired gradually and involves learning the letters that represent speech sounds.

- Sound-symbol associations are used to identify words in print. In phonics instruction, students are taught the most common sound-spelling relationships so they can decode words to make meaning of text as well as spell/encode the words they want to write.

- Students develop syntactic awareness as they listen to, speak, read, and write a variety of sentences—simple, compound, and complex.

- Students must understand vocabulary to comprehend text and write proficiently. Vocabulary knowledge is one of the strongest predictors of reading comprehension.

- Including morphology in literacy instruction can help readers expand their vocabularies and improve spelling because many English words have more than one meaningful unit.

- Writing is complex because it requires both lower-level skills (e.g., handwriting, spelling) as well as higher-order thinking to generate ideas and express knowledge using text. When students write about what they read, their comprehension and writing skills improve.

- Decoding (print-to-speech) and encoding (speech-to-print) are reciprocal skills and, when taught together, support reading and writing accuracy and automaticity.

The purpose of reading is comprehension. Scientific research has established that a reader must have a certain level of fluency to access comprehension of text. Text reading fluency has been defined as "reasonable accuracy, at an appropriate rate, with suitable expression that leads to accurate and deep comprehension" (Hasbrouck & Glaser, 2019, p. 9). To achieve reading fluency, the many components of language structure related to reading must be effortlessly accessed by the reader, and some of them must have been learned to a level of automaticity. Fluent writing also requires automaticity of underlying foundational skills such as handwriting/transcription.

> "The purpose of reading is comprehension. Scientific research has established that a reader must have a certain level of fluency to access comprehension of text."

Instructional Methods

Enabling *every* student to move forward in their learning *every* day necessitates being proactive in selecting appropriate instructional methods. Teachers must know both the components or content (the *what*) of language structure and the methods (the *how*) to effectively teach the content—including when and to whom. How to provide instruction will vary depending on students' needs.

> Teachers must know both the components or content (the *what*) of language structure and the methods (the *how*) to effectively teach the content.

The importance of appropriate instruction is brought home by Conner et al. (2011) whose findings indicate that "Specific instructional activities that are effective for students with typical reading and language skills may be ineffective for students with weaker or above-average skills and vice versa" (p. 190). As reading and writing skills develop, content and methods must continue to align to need. *The Ladder of Reading & Writing* infographic uses carefully chosen words within the colored continuum and alongside the continuum to reflect the instructional implications of the wide range of ease in mastering reading and writing skills.

Red Area: Instructional Implications

Students in the *red* area of the continuum benefit from systematically designed and explicitly delivered instruction that includes abundant teacher-guided practice. Although the severity and causes of students' challenges within this area of the infographic will vary, systematically designed and explicitly delivered instruction is especially important for these students due to their difficulty in acquiring reading and writing skills implicitly (Fletcher et al., 2019). These challenges can be the result of neurobiological causes including dyslexia.

Educators should carefully choose a well-designed program to address these students' needs. However, they should be aware that no single program is likely to meet the needs of all students (Fletcher et al., 2019) and that an inflexible program that expects every student to learn the same skills taught exactly the same way may be ineffective and actually delay progress (Connor et al., 2004; Connor et al., 2014).

Orange Area: Instructional Implications

Students in the *orange* area of the continuum also benefit from systematically designed and explicitly delivered instruction for reading and writing. Within this area, the components of language structure receiving particular emphasis are likely to vary by student; some students may require more phonics instruction, others more vocabulary building, and others more fluency practice. With regard to writing, some students may need more explicit instruction on how to brainstorm and organize ideas while others need to focus on applying syntax and grammatical conventions.

Whatever the need, these students are likely to require somewhat less scaffolding and deliberate practice to achieve skill mastery than students in the red area of the continuum. It is important to note that without adequate instruction, some students in the orange area may appear to have a learning disability (Fletcher et al., 2019). A term widely used to describe these students is "instructional casualties" (Fletcher et al., 2013, p. 47).

Light Green Area: Instructional Implications

For students in the *light green* area of the continuum, systematic design takes into account that some skills such as decoding or encoding (spelling) may need to be explicitly taught at the foundational stages, but these students generally proceed at a faster pace and require less scaffolded instruction and less directed practice than students in the red and orange areas. The learning process for students in the light green area can offer more implicit learning opportunities, including greater amounts of discovery learning and peer collaboration with explicit instruction provided as needed in various ways (Fletcher et al., 2019; Templeton & Morris, 2000).

Dark Green Area: Instructional Implications

For students in the *dark green* area of the continuum, systematic design considers they have already mastered many foundational skills through implicit learning. Appropriate programming options include academic acceleration (e.g., receiving instruction with students in a higher grade) or extended learning in a program designed to provide greater complexity and generate more critical thinking (Hughes et al., 2014; VanTassel-Baska, 2023).

Continued progression of skill development necessitates challenging learning experiences as well as continued enjoyment of reading (Brighton et al., 2015; Reis & Fogarty, 2020). The development of writing skills, including spelling, may benefit from guided practice and feedback in a collaborative learning environment (Bass, 2020).

The colored areas on the infographic emphasize what Connor et al. (2009) noted, that "optimal patterns of instruction differ for each child across a continuum" (p. 18). Differentiation is key.

 The colored areas on the infographic emphasize… Differentiation is key.

SYSTEMATIC DESIGN ACROSS THE CONTINUUM

While there is a wide body of research on learning to read, there is less evidence about applying that science to classroom instruction (Graham, 2020; Seidenberg et al., 2020). Therefore, we must move forward based on what the research currently suggests *and* remain open to adjustment as new research becomes available.

Taking this into account, the following vignettes serve to broadly illustrate the wide range of needs typically present in early grade classrooms, and how different methods and materials might effectively be used to meet students' needs. These are not complete lessons but simply a glimpse into aspects of instruction for four students with varied needs as they climb the Ladder. In providing these snapshots, we hope to deliver the message that the components of language structure can be woven into lessons in various ways, and that *what* and *how* will be based on each student's current readiness.

Check Your Understanding

Check all that apply.

Planning differentiated reading and writing instruction involves:

___ understanding the components of language structure (the *what*)

___ selecting appropriate instructional methods (the *how*)

___ determining what content is necessary for whom

___ continually aligning content and methods to students' needs

Scenario: Emma's initial Kindergarten screening assessment revealed that she was below benchmark with key foundational skills in reading. However, her teachers observed that her oral vocabulary and background knowledge were advanced for her age. During her Kindergarten phonics lessons, Emma experienced great difficulty mastering sound-symbol correspondences. Emma also struggled with writing; her letter formation was both inaccurate and slow. Now, at the end of Grade 1, she can accurately decode and encode words with short vowels and initial and final consonants, and she has begun decoding and encoding words with digraphs, but her fluency with word identification is slow and she has acquired few sight words. Diagnostic skills assessment conducted mid-Grade 1 indicates that Emma has the characteristics of dyslexia and dysgraphia.

In the regular classroom (Tier 1): Emma receives some reading and writing instruction in her small group, knowing that she will also receive additional, targeted, supplemental intervention in Tier 2 to address her skill deficits. Emma's teacher includes handwriting in her language arts lessons.

During intervention (Tier 2): Emma receives instruction along with two of her peers, taught by a reading specialist. Based on the results of diagnostic skills assessments, the comprehensive and sequential lessons continue to develop her foundational skills. Phonemic awareness is developed as new concepts are taught during phonics instruction using letter tiles (focusing on decoding and encoding). Emma practices reading and spelling words, as well as sentence-level skills (syntax) with newly taught correspondences (e.g., *Can the black bat flap its wings in the den?*). Word meanings are discussed, and morphemes are added orally or visually depending on the spelling complexity. Words are used in sentences in various ways, such as a verb (i.e., "The flag started to *flap*.") and a noun (i.e., "Close the *flap* on that box."). Decodable texts provide practice reading words with the new concept, with an integrated focus on both fluency and comprehension. Additional "hands on" activities include interactive games focusing on each new concept. Emma also receives support from an occupational therapist (OT) three times per week to help with letter formation.

Home-school connection: Emma's mother has been provided with a practice kit containing cards for newly learned phoneme-grapheme correspondences, along with a list of words for Emma to create with her cards. The kit also includes sentences and decodable books to read aloud. In-person coaching and videos have been provided to demonstrate how to decode and encode words, and practice reading aloud using the same error-correction strategies applied at school. To encourage accurate letter and word formation, Emma's mother has been shown the pencil grip taught by the OT and provided with specially lined paper. Emma has access to free apps for practicing foundational skills in engaging game formats and an audiobook system, enabling listening to more advanced text with an option to read along.

More Info!

Read more about dyslexia in Chapter 9, dysgraphia in Chapter 8, and using data to inform instructional decision-making in Chapter 4.

Scenario: When Mateo entered Kindergarten, his family indicated they spoke Spanish at home. Mateo attended a bilingual preschool, and his English developed well. Initial screening at the beginning of Kindergarten indicated Mateo was slightly below benchmark for early foundational skills; progress monitoring that year showed steady growth. Now, in the middle of Grade 1, Mateo is making steady improvement in reading and is spelling two-syllable words. He is reading decodable texts aligned to the sequence of instruction, but sometimes lacks the vocabulary to fully comprehend the text.

In the regular classroom (Tier 1): Mateo and his small group receive comprehensive instruction encompassing explicit instruction in phonics, morphology, and syntax. A lesson might include the following:

 Sample Lesson

1. The teacher says, *"Look at these sentences as I read them to you: I rock the baby. I rocked the baby."*

2. The teacher reads a word-pair list including words with all three ways of sounding out **-ed,** the sound associated with the suffix **-ed** noted and emphasized (meanings of words discussed as needed).

3. The students highlight the action word (verb) in each sentence.

4. The teacher demonstrates how to write each of the verbs using mini lines to represent each phoneme while reinforcing the three different pronunciations for suffix **-ed**:

    rock   <u>r</u> <u>o</u> <u>ck</u> <u>ed</u>
    fill   <u>f</u> <u>i</u> <u>ll</u> <u>ed</u>
    hand   <u>h</u> <u>a</u> <u>n</u> <u>d</u> <u>e</u> <u>d</u>

5. The students are guided in spelling words with the suffix **-ed,** using mini lines.

6. The students sort past-tense verbs into three columns under headers for the different pronunciations.

7. The students each write five sentences, including at least one word with suffix **-ed.**

8. The students take turns reading aloud an assigned text (including **-ed** words) to their peers.

During intervention (Tier 2): Mateo receives Tier 2 vocabulary intervention. This includes explicit instruction in creating a semantic map to show the relationship between words. His teacher and librarian/media specialist provide resources such as translated or trans-adapted books to support Mateo's continued vocabulary and knowledge-building.

Home-school connection: Both parents have limited English, so Mateo receives books written in Spanish to decode at home for reading practice. Mateo also uses an audiobook for additional English-reading practice, to advance vocabulary and provide access to more semantically and syntactically complex text. He is encouraged to read along while listening. Mateo's family has access to apps that build vocabulary and background knowledge using the school's license.

Scenario: Aryam's Kindergarten screener indicated she was at or slightly above expected benchmarks. Throughout Kindergarten, differentiated instruction enabled her to proceed at a faster pace than most of her classmates. Her spelling and writing of sentences progressed with minimal explicit instruction. By the end of Grade 1, Aryam was reading books beyond her age level. Her spelling continued to develop, and her vocabulary and comprehension were strong.

In the regular classroom (Tier 1): The instructional focus in Aryam's small group is comprehension. Currently, they are reading an expository text that offers more complexity (both in decoding and content) than books being read by their classmates still learning to decode. Aryam and her group members take turns reading an assigned section aloud, then engage in discussion guided by comprehension questions. Upon completion of the book, they will be explicitly taught strategies for writing a book summary. For spelling, Aryam's small group engages in a word study approach, using hands-on explorative activities; following their teacher's explanation of procedures and modeling of the word sorting process, the group carries out a word sorting activity collaboratively. They address morphology as they compare, contrast, and analyze words. Assigned activities for writing include sentence combining. Reading a variety of challenging texts takes place during and after the lesson.

During intervention (Tier 2): Not applicable.

Home-school connection: Aryam's grandmother is her caregiver; although financial circumstances restrict book purchases, the two spend Saturdays at the local library. Aryam's teachers have encouraged their selecting books that are both interesting and challenging. Aryam's grandmother has access to resources via the school's website using the school's license, including apps that help build vocabulary and background knowledge.

EXAMPLE: Dark Green Area of the Continuum

Scenario: When Jamar began Kindergarten, he was not only reading above expected benchmarks (assessments indicated reading abilities beyond that expected of an eight-year-old) but also clearly advanced in many other areas. Because Jamar could already decode, he did not require phonics instruction; his learning was differentiated to focus on comprehension (including stories and expository texts). In connected writing tasks, he demonstrated the ability to master spelling and writing of sentences and paragraphs with very little individualized instruction; a letter formation chart was used to support improved handwriting. Now in the middle of Grade 2 and formally identified as gifted, Jamar is reading books typically read in Grade 5 and up, and beyond grade-level in writing. His teacher is recommending he skip Grade 3 and go directly to Grade 4.

In the regular classroom (Tier 1): Using a book study framework designed for advanced readers, Jamar and two fellow students (also advanced readers) engage with comprehension of text in deeper and broader ways than typical for their age. At the beginning of each new book study, his teacher presents an overview of planned activities and expectations. During subsequent teacher-led small-group time, the students receive guidance and feedback to complete assigned activities that encourage higher-level thinking, including peer discussion and writing activities. Additional support is provided as needed to improve spelling and writing of sentences and paragraphs.

During intervention (Tier 2): As part of gifted services, Jamar attends a pull-out enrichment program twice a week. His interest in nature has extended into researching endangered wildlife. His goal is to write a book that will teach young students about endangered animals. Explicit instruction on writing strategies will support that goal.

Home-school connection: Jamar's parents are actively involved in his academics. They communicate regularly with the classroom teacher and enrichment program coordinator, supporting Jamar's interests (i.e., extending his personal library to support current interests) as well as helping Jamar manage the social-emotional issues that sometimes stem from being academically ahead of his peers. His parents are weighing the benefits of acceleration; the school principal has arranged for the whole team to receive a consultation about acceleration from an expert in this process.

More Info!

Read more about advanced readers in Chapter 13.

INSTRUCTIONAL GROUPING

Differentiation through instructional grouping is essential to effectively address the wide range of ease with which students acquire reading and writing skills. As illustrated in the infographic, the goal for all students is to support their continued progress up the Ladder, while recognizing that each student's climb may be uniquely influenced by multiple factors.

Small-Group Instruction

Teachers are encouraged to organize instructional small groups so that groupings occur within the same grade or across grades (Crumbaugh et al., 2001; Fiedler et al., 2002; Slavin, 2013; Steenbergen-Hu et al., 2016). When teachers collaborate to organize groupings within a grade or across grades, more students of similar needs can be grouped together for differentiated instruction.

If teachers collaborate to provide within- and cross-grade grouping, those large groups should still be broken into smaller groups for more needs-based differentiation. Planning for within-grade or across-grades grouping requires collaboration between teachers and support from school leadership/administration to arrange scheduling and provide students with consistent transition procedures (Shanahan, 2010).

Small-group instruction should include a balance of time spent receiving instruction from a teacher, engagement in collaborative learning with their peers, and independent practice (Connor, 2014). Small groups can be flexible, regrouping as needed based on progress monitoring data and in consideration of students' personal strengths and interests.

Whole-Group Instruction

Given the wide range of needs in many classrooms, teachers may wonder when to utilize whole-group instruction during the literacy block. Whole-group instruction may be used to:

- explain the overall plan for the block and any changes to previously made plans or groupings

- facilitate instruction on knowledge-building topics, concepts, strategies, or tools that benefit all students

- provide writing instruction that allows for flexibility based on student need within the lesson (Harris et al., 2008)

To meet the wide range of needs, advance preparation for a whole-group lesson may include preteaching vocabulary or skills for students in the red area (enabling them to fully participate) and prepping students in the dark green so they are able to contribute their advanced skills or knowledge meaningfully (e.g., creating a semantic map or explaining the etymology of a keyword).

Conclusion

The instructional implications represented by *The Ladder of Reading & Writing* infographic are complex. Every student deserves to keep progressing in their learning, no matter where they are on their climb up the Ladder. To provide effective needs-based differentiated instruction, both the content (*what*) and the methods (*how*) must be considered.

Educators need to be familiar with the research on why reading and writing may be challenging to many students, and how best to support learners who are more advanced. The goal must be to increase learning, not delay progress by providing instruction that students do not need.

The vignettes of the students presented in this chapter illustrate the instructional implications of the continuum and demonstrate that no one program will meet the needs of all. Systematically designed instruction takes into account that not everything will be (or even can be) explicitly taught, even for students in the red area of the continuum. Within the school setting, appropriate differentiated instruction provided alongside ongoing implicit learning opportunities can enable all students to continue their climb up the Ladder.

KEY TAKEAWAYS

- Students require systematic programming differentiated for their individual needs, as indicated by *The Ladder of Reading & Writing* infographic.

- Differentiation considers both the content (*what* needs to be taught) and methods (*how* instruction will be delivered).

- Without explicit instruction, students in the red area of the continuum may not learn to read and write; students in the light green and dark green areas of the continuum learn more implicitly than students in the red and orange areas.

- There is no "one-size-fits-all" program. Inappropriate instruction is likely to delay learning.

DATA-INFORMED INSTRUCTION

The Ladder of Reading & Writing infographic offers us the positive and encouraging message that it is possible for nearly all students to become successful readers and writers. This important goal can only be achieved if the instruction students receive is appropriately designed and adequately differentiated to address their individual needs. In this chapter we discuss how to collect and use data—effectively and efficiently—to guide planning and delivery of appropriate instruction to meet individual students' needs as they journey up the Ladder. The importance of using data to inform differentiated instruction to help all students successfully climb the Ladder is represented in the purple arrow to the right of the continuum.

AUTHOR **Jan Hasbrouck**

Researcher/Consultant
JH Educational Services, Inc.
Seattle, WA, USA

> " Collecting and using data effectively and efficiently guides planning and delivery of appropriate instruction to meet individual students' needs. "

Certainly no one chooses a career in education because they care deeply about data! Like other professional fields such as nursing or music, teaching is often referred to as a "calling." Teachers do this challenging work because they care deeply about students and want to provide them with positive and valuable experiences. Forming relationships with many different students, trying to understand their needs, both academic and social-emotional, and then address those needs with too-often limited resources takes creativity, bravery, and perseverance. Furthermore, a growing body of evidence strongly suggests there is also a "science" to effective teaching, especially when we are teaching our students to read and write. Using data effectively can help teachers achieve their goals.

THE IMPORTANCE OF USING DATA

The challenge of learning to read and write varies from student to student. As described in Chapter 2, some individuals acquire these complex skills without much help, while others require extensive support. Professional educators are responsible for the academic success of *every* student, so we must be certain that we have gathered sufficient, appropriate information to plan and deliver effective instruction and targeted intervention (if required) based on students' identified needs, using systematically designed materials.

Furthermore, once instruction has started, we must collect information that lets us know whether our instruction has been effective. Although observation of student performance is essential to inform our instructional decisions, professional educators must not rely simply on "cardiac assessment," that is, "in my heart, I know what is right for my students." And we must collect and apply information as efficiently as possible to maximize the time available for instruction and intervention. Having systems and structures in place to support the efficient and effective collection and use of data can help make this possible (Grissom et al., 2021).

The information teachers use to guide key decisions can and should include their experience and professional judgment, their knowledge about their students, and even their intuition to make decisions in their classrooms, but they must also embrace the information provided by academic assessments (Bambrick-Santoyo, 2019).

Four Categories of Assessments

Research has identified four categories of assessments that provide key information for planning successful literacy instruction:

Four Categories of Assessments	
1	**Screening** to identify students performing at or above a predetermined benchmark and those performing slightly or significantly below
2	**Diagnosing** to assess specific skills or target areas to focus instruction or intervention
3	**Monitoring** to determine if the instruction is meeting the student's needs
4	**Evaluating** to assess student outcomes toward the achievement of academic standards

Learn More!

Diamond, L. (2005 Fall). Assessment-driven instruction: A systems approach. *Perspectives, on Language and Literacy, 31.*

Hamilton, L., Halverson, R., Jackson, S., Mandinach, E., Supovitz, J., & Wayman, J. (2009). *Using student achievement data to support instructional decision making: IES practice guide* (NCEE 2009–4067). What Works Clearinghouse, National Center for Education Evaluation and Regional Assistance, Institute of Education Sciences, U.S. Department of Education. https://ies.ed.gov/ncee/wwc/PracticeGuide/12

Diamond, L., Ed. (2008). *Assessing reading: Multiple measures* (2nd ed.). Consortium on Reaching Excellence.

Of these four categories, the first three are often described as "formative" assessments. They are administered during the planning and delivery of instruction and thus provide the most timely and useful information. The assessments in the fourth category are considered "summative" assessments, typically administered after a sequence of instruction has concluded. These include the state level assessments often administered at the end of a specific grade level. Although outcome assessments do provide general information, they are typically more valuable to administrators, school leaders, and the general public rather than providing information to guide ongoing instruction. However, the results of these assessments can play a role in flagging older students who may be struggling with reading and may benefit from intervention.

This chapter will focus on the assessments in the first three categories because they provide educators with the key information needed to effectively plan and monitor the impact of the differentiated instruction for reading and writing. If your school system is using MTSS (Multi-Tiered System of Support), you will likely recognize some of the following information and suggestions as they are often embedded in effective MTSS frameworks (St. Martin et al., 2020).

THE PURPOSE OF ASSESSMENTS

Some educators may shy away from trying to understand the purpose and rationale for administering the assessments they give because they mistakenly believe the topic would be too complex to understand. They may have unpleasant memories of coursework taken during their teacher preparation program that dealt with complicated psychometric assessment issues such as reliability and validity. Indeed, some aspects of assessment are quite complex. However, the good news is that it is not necessary for all educators to delve deeply into these rather heavy topics. What *is* important to understand is that assessments provide information to answer significant questions and guide key decisions. The three categories of formative academic assessments each answer a simple but important question:

Three Categories of Formative Academic Assessments	
Screening Assessments	*Who* might need help?
Diagnostic Assessments	*What* help does this student need?
Progress Monitoring Assessments	Is the work *working*?

Screening Assessments

Screening assessments are designed to help educators quickly answer this important question: Which students might need some extra assistance to be successful academically? Or more simply, **who might need help?** On the infographic, this would include students in the red or orange areas of the continuum. Schools use screening assessments to flag students, so that no student who is struggling is allowed to fall between the cracks and not receive needed instructional support. Results from these assessments can also identify students who are doing exceptionally well compared to established benchmarks—students in the light and dark green areas on the continuum—so teachers can address their academic needs more accurately.

By using screening assessments on a regular basis to determine which students are below, at, or above established benchmarks, a school systematically evaluates the instructional needs of all students. Screening assessments are often administered to every student, at least in the early grades, a critical stage for reading and writing development. However, for students who are well-above established benchmarks, it may be adequate to screen them only in the beginning of each school year. When all students are assessed, this is referred to as *universal screening*. In upper grades, and in middle or high school, there should be some system in place to regularly review the academic status of every student and identify students who may need some support. This review could include a combination of grades, credits, office referrals, and results from state-wide outcomes assessments.

 When all students are assessed, this is referred to as *universal screening.*

Often assessments from the suite of curriculum-based measures (CBM) are used to screen students (see examples on the following page). CBMs have a strong research base that establishes their reliability and validity. They are designed to quickly and accurately determine a student's skill level in several areas and answer the question, *Who* might need help? At the early stages of reading, the CBM measures of Letter Sound Fluency (LSF) and Letter Naming Fluency (LNF) are often used. Once students are receiving instruction on word-level decoding, Nonsense or Pseudoword Fluency (NWF; PWF) can help identify which students are learning to "break the code" needed for early reading success.

Once students are reading text, the assessment called Oral Reading Fluency (ORF) can be used as an effective screener until students are reading at around the sixth-grade level. After that, schools may turn to yet another CBM assessment, the Maze, where students read text and identify which word best fits, where a word has been removed, among three provided options.

Commonly Used Screening Assessments

- **Letter Sound Fluency (LSF)** is a type of CBM for students in the early stages of reading that assesses their ability to identify letter-sound correspondences.

	Skill Set 2 Letter Sounds													Score
2	/t/	/a/	/m/	/r/	/s/	/i/	/o/	/f/	/d/	/h/	/g/	/l/	/c/	/21 con /5 vow
	/n/	/b/	/u/	/k/	/e/	/j/	/w/	/p/	/y/	/qu/	/v/	/z/	/x/	/26
	Comments:													

Sample: Teacher's Copy of a Letter Sound Fluency (LSF) Assessment

- **Letter Naming Fluency (LNF)** is a type of CBM for students in the early stages of reading that assesses their ability to name letters.

	Skill Set 1 Letter Names													Score
1	m	t	a	s	i	r	d	f	o	g	l	h	u	
	c	n	b	j	k	y	e	w	p	v	q	x	z	/26
	Comments:													

Sample: Letter Naming Fluency (LNF) Assessment

- **Nonsense (NWF) or Pseudoword Fluency (PSF)** is a type of CBM in which students apply what they know about decoding to nonsensical combinations of letters.

Sample: Nonsense Word Fluency (NWF) Assessment

- **Oral Reading Fluency (ORF)** are CBM assessments that measure students' reading accuracy and rate (or automaticity), expressed in terms of the number of words read correctly per minute (wcpm). Teachers select an unfamiliar passage at the student's appropriate reading level. The teacher and student each have copies of the passage. The teacher times the student reading aloud for one minute and marks errors, such as mispronunciations or substitutions, on the teacher's copy of the passage. At the end of one minute, the teacher calculates the wcpm and may compare the student's score to established grade-level norms (see Hasbrouck & Tindal, 2017).

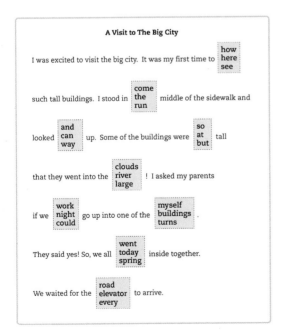

Sample: Oral Reading Fluency Assessment Passage

- **CBM Maze Assessment** is a type of CBM assessment where students read text and identify which word best fits, where a word has been removed, among three provided options.

Sample: CBM Maze Assessment

More Info!

For more information about CBM assessments, see *The ABC's of CBM* by Hosp, Hosp, & Howell (2016).

DATA-INFORMED INSTRUCTION

Considerations When Using Screeners

The majority of the research that originally validated the initial CBM assessments was conducted among students with specific learning disabilities. The original purpose of these assessments was to develop a feasible evaluation system that special education teachers could use to build more effective instructional programs (Deno, 1993). However, decades of research have now shown that CBM assessments are valuable in general education (Fuchs, 2016). More research is needed to determine the value of these assessments for providing information about advanced readers (students in the dark green area of the continuum). (See more about assessing advanced readers in Chapter 13.)

Although the focus in many schools is to screen for word reading skills (using assessments such as the LSF, LNF, ORF), we know that reading comprehension requires proficiency in both word recognition and language comprehension (Hoover & Tunmer, 2018). Many schools have significant numbers of multilingual learners; screening students to determine their needs for language development may be advisable. (See Chapter 16 for suggestions.)

Diagnostic Assessments

After schools have identified students who may need additional academic assistance, teachers turn to individually administered diagnostic skills assessments to answer the next question: What are this student's academic strengths and instructional needs? Or *what* **help does this student need?**

 Diagnostic assessments, in this context, are not the same assessments used by special educators or school psychologists to "diagnose" or identify a disability.

Diagnostic assessments, in this context, are not the same assessments used by special educators or school psychologists to "diagnose" or identify a disability. Rather these assessments are typically informal skills assessments that can be administered by classroom teachers or content specialists.

Educators know that they have no time to waste. They must design instruction that builds on what a student already knows and immediately addresses any gaps or holes in the student's skill set. Diagnostic assessments help provide specific information to plan effectively differentiated and appropriately focused instruction. Teachers should use assessments that are quick to administer and provide information about which skills a student has mastered and which are still in need of support.

Diagnostic assessments help provide specific information to plan effectively differentiated and appropriately focused instruction.

For example, to identify which reading and writing skills require targeted intervention, assessments might include determining a student's current ability to decode and encode (spell), read text fluently, and/or comprehend the text. Assessment of letter formation and writing (e.g., sentences, paragraphs) can also provide valuable information. In some cases, a student's language development should be assessed as well. Seeking the assistance of a speech and language specialist may be warranted in these situations.

Unlike universal screening assessments, diagnostic assessments are *differentiated*. Typically, only those students who did not meet benchmark on the screening assessment are assessed. And to be most effective and efficient, teachers should only administer the assessment that is appropriate for each student's age, grade, and level of skill development, wherever they are on the Ladder continuum.

For example, a student in Kindergarten who did not meet the benchmark on a screener would not be given a test focusing on reading comprehension. It would be more appropriate to assess this student's letter-sound knowledge and perhaps consider a language assessment. Similarly, it is unlikely that a Grade 2 student who is skillfully decoding text yet seems to be having trouble understanding what they have read, would need to have their phonemic awareness assessed.

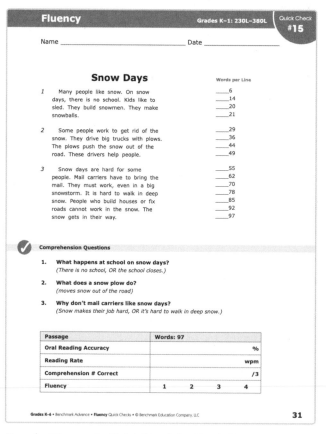

Sample: Diagnostic Quick Check for Grade 2

Progress Monitoring Assessments

Once instruction has started, educators turn to progress monitoring assessments to answer the question: Is learning happening? Is the the student acquiring targeted skills? Or **is the work *working*?** Answering this question can provide essential information about individual students, but also about the effectiveness of programs when data collected over time is analyzed across classrooms and schools (Hosp et al., 2016).

> Waiting until the end of the school year or even the end of a semester is too long to get information that can help determine if a student is actually learning.

Looking for clear answers to this important question is imperative to ensure that every student be academically successful. Using progress monitoring assessments periodically throughout the school year to measure instructional effectiveness can make a big difference in our students' success. Waiting until the end of the school year or even the end of a semester is too long to get information that can help determine if a student is actually learning. Professional educators must be prepared to ask this brave question about the effectiveness of their instruction. As Bambrick-Santoyo (2019, p. 19) states: "Effective instruction isn't about whether we taught it. It's about whether students learned it."

Like diagnostic skills assessments, progress monitoring is *differentiated*. While every student should be monitored, whether they are in the red or the dark green areas of the continuum, the type of assessments and the frequency of assessments should vary. The more intense the academic need (i.e., students in the red area of the continuum), the more assessment of progress needs to be intense, focused, and frequent. Keep in mind that some students may initially look like they are in the red area, but once they are provided with appropriate instruction they start to fly! Progress monitoring helps educators know when to slow down or when a child becomes ready for a much faster pace. Mark Seidenberg (Webinar, 2021) reminds us, "If a child's reading is advancing, there isn't a reason to grind away on the component skills just because they are in some curriculum."

> " Progress monitoring helps educators know when to slow down or when a child becomes ready for a much faster pace. "

To monitor the progress of students whose work is at expected levels, teachers can use the quizzes and chapter or unit tests that are typically included in most commercial programs along with the results from state-wide outcome assessments. To measure the progress of advanced readers and writers (students in the dark green area), monitoring may entail the use of materials that are above-grade-level. Progress monitoring information guides teachers to help every student move ahead as effectively and quickly as possible, no matter where they are in their climb up the Ladder.

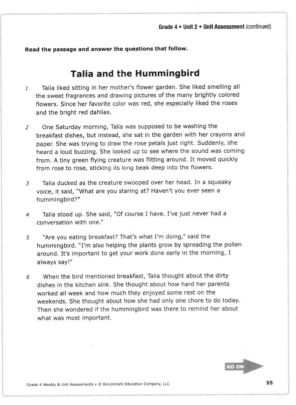

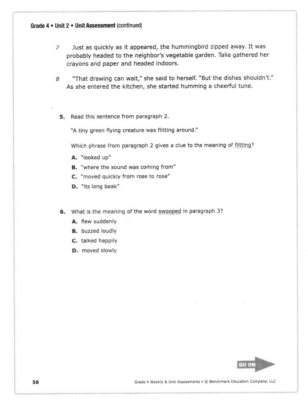

Example: Grade 4 Progress Monitoring Assessment for Reading Comprehension

Progress monitoring for all students includes regularly observing students' performance on curriculum-aligned assessments and their daily work in class, including having students periodically read aloud (in a private setting for a student reluctant to read in front of peers). For students who are receiving additional, supplementary instruction or more intensive intervention because of greater reading and writing needs, progress monitoring may also include more frequent assessments, setting specific performance goals, and graphing progress toward those goals. For this we can return to the previously discussed curriculum-based measure (CBM) of oral reading fluency (ORF).

Technology and Progress Monitoring

Increasingly, technology can support the collection and use of data for decision-making. This is especially true for assessing reading and writing. There are computer-based tools that are currently being used to instantaneously provide scores and data analysis with reporting options for classes, grade levels, and entire schools or districts. Some computerized assessments even use voice recognition software. This allows students to read aloud without a teacher or adult present and the software accurately scores for words correct per minute and overall accuracy. The evolving sophistication of these assessments includes the possibility of assessing expression or prosody of students' oral reading, and even assessing comprehension through student interactions with an avatar programmed with artificial intelligence.

Understanding the purpose of the assessments in each category is essential. Educational leaders should provide professional development to their teachers and administrators to support their understanding about why assessments are administered, which questions they answer, and how to use the information provided to make appropriate instructional decisions (Grissom et al., 2021). With this knowledge, professional educators can select and use assessments beneficially for all students wherever they are as they climb the Ladder.

Check Your Understanding

Match each type of assessment to the significant question it answers.

a. Screening Assessment

b. Diagnostic Assessment

c. Progress Monitoring Assessment

___ *What* help does this student need?

___ Is the work *working*?

___ *Who* might need help?

SHARING AND USING DATA

Along with knowing *why* certain assessments should be administered, there are at least two additional factors to consider when using data to differentiate instruction. These factors involve knowing how to *share* and then ultimately *use* student assessment data to inform instructional decision-making.

Research has shown that personnel in effective schools have learned the value of sharing the results from students' assessments (Burns & Symington, 2002; McDougal et al., 2000). To maximize the positive impact, assessment data about the needs and progress of all students should be shared in collaborative meetings that are *public, frequent,* and *nonjudgmental.*

Effective Student Data Sharing

Research has shown that personnel in effective schools review assessment data in collaborative meetings that are:

- **public**
- **frequent**
- **non-judgmental**

Public

In highly effective schools, teams of educators regularly come together to discuss student assessment results. These collaborative teams begin by analyzing results from screening assessments and then make decisions regarding appropriate "next steps" for each student, including referrals for additional assessments or placement into particular instruction or intervention programs.

Sometimes teams are organized around a specific grade level. In smaller schools, the meetings might involve all the teachers from the primary or intermediate grades. Some middle and high schools have organized themselves around the concept of "families" or "communities." Along with classroom teachers, collaborative data meetings often include other key decision-makers including the principal, special educators, and support personnel such as diagnosticians, school psychologists, content specialists, academic and behavior coaches, and even a school nurse or social worker, if needed.

Frequent

The most effective elementary schools typically universally screen most students at least three times each year—near the start of the school year, somewhere in the middle of the school year, and toward the end of the school year. Students well above benchmarks may only be assessed annually at the start of the school year. Schools at upper levels should have some system in place to regularly check the academic status of all students such as examining students' performance on state-wide outcome assessments.

Each time screening assessments are administered, the assessment team meets to examine and discuss the results. Everyone involved with an individual student or group of students should be informed about their progress and advised of changing needs.

Non-Judgmental

The tone of these assessment review meetings must be non-judgmental. They should not become meetings to sing the praises the "good" teachers and chastise or belittle the "bad" teachers. Successful assessment teams keep the meeting focused on the *students* and meeting all students' changing needs. Highly effective schools have widely reported that these positive and student-focused meetings have improved the collaboration of their staff members and the outcomes of their students (Nellis, 2012).

Using Student Data

A final way to ensure that collecting data will result in improved outcomes for students is to be sure that teachers actually *use* results to make key decisions. Far too many schools are spending significant resources (e.g., time, money, and personnel) to collect assessment data that is not effectively utilized. Spreadsheets are filled out, forms are completed, but once the "save" button is pushed and the forms are filed away, educators may turn to each other and say, "Whew … that sure took a lot of time! Now what are we supposed to do?"

> " When assessment results are not used for informing professional decisions about how to provide the best instruction for students, then these resources are essentially wasted. "

More Info!

For more information, see Burns & Symington, 2002; McDougal et al., 2000.

When assessment results are not used for informing professional decisions about how to provide the best instruction for students, then these resources are essentially wasted. We should apply data to group (and regroup) students, to decide what instruction to provide using what materials, to determine how quickly students move through a curriculum, and many more essential classroom decisions regarding the intensity and frequency of instruction.

> To help all students successfully (and joyfully!) climb the Ladder, we must efficiently collect appropriate data about our students … and collaboratively share and use that data to make accurate and effective instructional decisions.

The most effective schools, often facing enormous challenges, understand they have no time, money, or personnel to waste. To help all students successfully (and joyfully!) climb the Ladder, we must efficiently collect appropriate data about our students (i.e., to answer specific, important questions) and collaboratively share and use that data to make accurate and effective instructional decisions.

Conclusion

We know from a continuously growing body of scientific evidence that we can teach most students to be successful readers and writers. To achieve this important outcome, educators must understand how to design and successfully provide instruction that is appropriately differentiated to meet the needs of every student. The only way to accomplish this is to understand the role of data from assessments and other sources. Collecting that data and using it successfully involves understanding the different types of assessments that answer specific questions. Schools and districts play an important role in creating systems and structures to effectively and efficiently collect, analyze, and use assessment results to support appropriate instruction and intervention. When educators have this information, their instruction is more efficient and effective for all students.

KEY TAKEAWAYS

- Educators should use data from assessments and other sources to plan, deliver, and evaluate effective instruction.

- Diagnostic and progress monitoring assessments, just like instruction and intervention, should be differentiated based on student need.

- Data should be collected to address three key questions:
  - *Who* might need help?
  - *What* help does this student need?
  - Is the work *working*?

- Assessment data needs to be collected, shared, and used in the classroom to inform instruction.

MANAGING DIFFERENTIATED INSTRUCTION

To support differentiated instruction, research has shown positive benefits of small-group instruction and interactive collaborative practice (Fisher et al., 2016; Hattie, 2009; Marzano, 2003). In chapters 3 and 4, we learned that planning for differentiated instruction requires data-informed decisions about content, materials, and methods. Putting these decisions into practice can be challenging when a classroom is comprised of unique students, each on a different rung of the Ladder with their own skill sets and learning challenges. Managing the environment to support differentiated instruction enhances learning for all students, whether they are mastering foundational or advanced skills (Connor et al., 2013; Rogers, 2002; Vaughn et al., 2018).

AUTHOR **Vicki Gibson**

Founding Director, Charlotte Sharp Children's Center
Dean of Education Excellence Professorship, Texas A & M University
School of Education and Human Development
College Station, TX, USA

> " When instruction is differentiated, students feel supported and more confident. They are more likely to ask questions and seek teacher assistance in small-group settings. "

Small-group differentiated instruction allows teachers to adjust teaching in response to student needs. When instruction is differentiated, students feel supported and more confident. They are more likely to ask questions and seek teacher assistance in small-group settings that allow for both explicit instruction and collaborative learning (Fisher & Frey, 2015; Hattie, 2009).

DEFINING DIFFERENTIATION

Many theoretical frameworks for differentiating instruction were developed in the past two decades. Numerous authors created resources to help teachers manage classrooms and adjust curriculum and activities to address the increasing student variance and declining student achievement (Marzano, 2003; McLeod et al., 2003; Tomlinson, 2014). This chapter uses evidence from research and best practices to suggest tools for organizing and managing the classroom environment and student behaviors. Using these tools to structure classrooms affects *how teachers teach* and *how students learn*. Once routines are established, teachers can focus on improving instructional effectiveness and engaging students in meaningful and differentiated practice. These routines can be implemented in classrooms from Pre–K through high school and beyond with some modifications.

Practically speaking, differentiating instruction means "teaching differently" to address students' needs. Teaching differently involves managing whole-group and flexible, small-group teacher-led lessons that provide explicit instruction and immediate feedback. Independent or collaborative student practice includes student-led activities where they consolidate and apply their knowledge in interactive ways to deepen learning.

> " Practically speaking, differentiating instruction means "teaching differently" to address students' needs. "

One major challenge for differentiating instruction is implementation. Routines and procedures must be taught, practiced, and implemented consistently to engage teachers and students in whole-group and small-group activities. While one group of students participates in teacher-led, differentiated instruction, other students are engaged in collaborative or independent practice to complete assigned tasks.

FOUR TYPES OF MANAGEMENT

Four types of management work simultaneously to create order and provide structure in classrooms, so students understand and comply with expectations.

	Teaching Differently Includes Four Types of Management	
1	**Managing Time:** managing the schedules and allocating time for the various activities	
2	**Managing the Environment:** managing the use of classroom space, furniture, and supplies to create work area	
3	**Managing Behaviors:** managing teacher and student interactions by establishing routines and procedures that clarify expectations for respectful communication and collaborative participation	
4	**Managing Instruction for Differentiation:** adjusting content and methods to provide meaningful activities for teaching and practice	

Managing Time

Strategically planning and allocating time for whole-group and small-group instruction is essential for successful differentiated instruction. Several management tools may be used to maximize the use of time and communicate expectations for student participation including a posted daily schedule that identifies time periods for each group activity, and a rotation chart that visually represents assigned small-group memberships and the order of activities in which students will participate.

Allowing student choices is beneficial once routines and procedures are established and followed consistently. Teachers may use student contracts that list options for the order of participation. This helps students learn to plan and organize their time for completing assigned tasks.

Name: _____

Unit: _____

Learning Stations: Choose as directed in each category – 6 total

Content Area	Name of Learning Station	Date of Completion
ELA (choose 2)	Vocabulary Review	
	Author Study	
	Write Your Own Ending	
	Grammar Whiz	
Math (choose 2)	Computer Practice	
	Double-Digit Dominoes	
	Bank Teller (Counting Change)	
Science (choose 1)	Famous Inventors	
	Mixing Color	
	A Bug's Life	
Free Choice (choose 1)	Music Maker	
	Relaxation Station	
	Creative Expression	

Sample: Student Contract for Grade 2

Learn More!

Gibson, V. (2019b). *Classroom Management: Elementary School.* Benchmark Education.

Fisher, D., Frey, N., & Hattie, J. (2016). *Visible learning for literacy, grades K–12: Implementing practices that work best to accelerate student learning.* Corwin Literacy.

Tomlinson, C. (2014). *The differentiated classroom: Responding to the needs of all learners* (2nd ed.). Association for Supervision and Curriculum Development, ASCD.

 Strategically planning and allocating time for whole-group and small-group instruction is essential for successful differentiated instruction.

The daily schedule, rotation chart, and student contracts are tools for managing flexible grouping. Teachers establish routines for transitions, so students understand expectations and comply cooperatively.

Rotation Chart

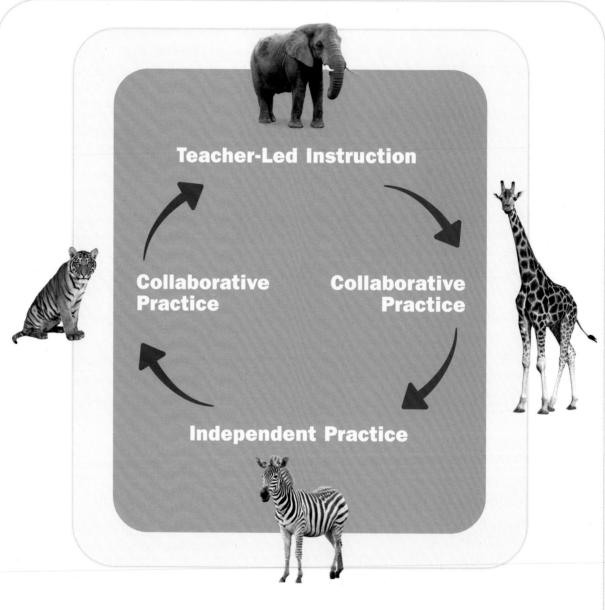

Group 1 = Elephants (Aslyn, Tori, Wen, Roberto, Afshin)

Group 2 = Giraffes (Zach, Mari, Elena, Grayson, Timmy)

Group 3 = Zebras (Ari, Franz, Myrtle, Kip, Weston)

Group 4 = Tigers (Erica, Tasha, Obi, Justin, Murray)

Sample: Rotation Chart for Grades 2–3

Teachers may also assign jobs, using a job chart, for students to complete during transitions so students remain focused and engaged in meaningful activities.

K–1 Job Chart

Absentee Substitute	Assumes the role of other students with assigned jobs who are absent or uncooperative.
Station Checker(s)	Checks stations after cleanup.
Door Holder	Holds door open for others and closes door upon departure from classroom.
Lights Monitor	Turns lights on/off when students enter or leave the classroom.
Lunch/Snack Helper	Assists the teacher or other students during snack or lunch.
Mailbox Monitor	Assists other students in retrieving or storing their mailboxes.
Rotation Chart Caller	Changes Rotation Chart to indicate small-group routines for participation.
Special Assistant	Provides assistance to other students when needed to complete a task.
Supply Monitor	Checks and replaces supplies in classroom from a supply shelf provided by teacher.
Timekeeper	Sets the timer and provides reminders to others when activities begin or end.
Trash or Environmental Monitor	Responsible for observing the general condition of the classroom, ensuring that work areas and floor are reasonably clean and orderly.

Sample: Classroom Job Descriptions for Grades K–1

Sample: Classroom Workspaces

Managing the Environment

Managing the environment entails planning where furniture and equipment will be placed to create work areas and where materials will be placed, either at point-of-use or stored for use later. Careful consideration must be given to the placement of resources and workstations intended for collaborative practice. Thoughtful planning minimizes disruptions.

Managing Behaviors

Managing behaviors requires teaching routines that clarify expectations and provide predictable order for participation in various activities. This helps students remain focused on completing their work while teachers provide differentiated instruction and feedback.

An established structure creates safe boundaries for student participation and collaboration which allows teachers to focus on teaching. While student collaboration can be a powerful tool for teaching and learning, order in the environment and clarified expectations must occur (Fisher & Frey, 2015; Hattie, 2009).

Teachers structure the classroom environment and teach routines that help students manage their emotions and behaviors. It is essential to invest sufficient time for teaching and practicing the routines to ensure that students understand expectations and develop skills for self-regulation, collaboration, and respectful communication. Failing to provide such instruction and supportive protocols will limit success for effective student collaboration and for teaching differently.

Managing Instruction for Differentiation

Differentiating instruction entails careful selection of content (*what* needs to be learned/practiced) and determining methods (*how* the content will be learned/practiced). Teachers introduce new knowledge and model skills in whole-group overviews or have quick reviews of previously taught information. In small groups, teachers differentiate teaching to extend student learning and provide feedback based on students' needs.

Collaborative practice activities completed in student-led small groups extend learning using content and skills previously taught in teacher-led groups. Separating students into small groups invites more dialogue, reflection, and peer-coaching as students exchange ideas, respond to questions, and provide feedback to each other. Work assignments are monitored for planning instruction but not always graded since the purpose is to practice and apply recently introduced content and skills.

> " It is essential to invest sufficient time for teaching and practicing the routines to ensure that students understand expectations and develop skills for self-regulation, collaboration, and respectful communication. "

GETTING STARTED

Classroom management for differentiating instruction and student practice can be implemented successfully by following five steps that work in any classroom regardless of age or grade level (Gibson, 2019a; Gibson, 2019b). Let's take a closer look at what each step entails.

Implementing Differentiated Instruction	
STEP ONE	Organize the classroom environment.
STEP TWO	Establish routines and procedures.
STEP THREE	Develop management tools.
STEP FOUR	Manage flexible grouping.
STEP FIVE	Provide differentiated instruction.

STEP ONE
Organize the Classroom Environment

Organizing the classroom environment to include workspaces for whole-group and small-group activities is a great way to initiate change for differentiating instruction including collaborative and independent student practice. Whole-group instruction usually occurs with students seated at individual or clustered desks. Teachers may also utilize floor space, furniture, and equipment to create work areas for a "teaching table" (for teacher-led explicit instruction and feedback), a "worktable" (for small-group, collaborative practice or project-based activities) and learning centers or "workstations" (for collaborative student practice). Independent practice activities may be completed at desks or assigned as homework.

Classroom Workspaces

Teacher-Led Instruction
for explicit, differentiated instruction
in small groups

Collaborative Practice

Worktable
for collaborative small-group practice,
led by another adult if available

Workstations
for collaborative practice at designated
locations or combined desks

Independent Practice
at designated locations
or individual desks

Three Types of Classroom Workspaces

Teacher-Led Instruction

One work area will be used as a **teaching table,** even though
the group may not always work at a table. Explicit instruction
differentiated to individual needs is provided at the teaching table.
The term, *teaching table*, communicates a performance expectation
for student participation. Students understand the content in the
lessons will be more challenging. Although some new content or skills
may be modeled to the whole class, teachers differentiate instruction
and provide specific feedback in small groups, where students may
ask questions to clarify understandings, and practice with scaffolded
support and feedback.

Worktable

A second work area is the **worktable**, where small groups participate in collaborative conversations and activities to enhance or extend learning. A worktable may be a collection of student desks or a designated area in the classroom where students gather to work collaboratively on assignments, helping each other to understand and apply new information. If available, another adult can provide additional scaffolded practice using materials recently introduced at the teaching table. Providing repeated exposures to new and challenging content deepens students' learning and encourages them to ask questions and affirm understandings. Worktable activities can be utilized to extend or enrich learning with or without another adult. Worktable activities can be project-based where students collaborate to apply what they are learning.

Workstations

Additional classroom work areas will be needed for **workstations**. These are designated areas where students cooperate with assigned or self-selected peers to participate in student-led collaborative practice. Workstations used to support student practice should explicitly relate to previously taught knowledge and skills and reinforce and extend learning. Additionally, workstations can be opportunities for students to begin homework assignments, thus ensuring support is accessible if needed. Workstation assignments are reviewed to inform instructional planning and may be rewarded for completion, but they are rarely graded for mastery.

Teachers can create workstations by pushing desks together and forming tabletop workspaces or simply directing students to designated areas in the room where they sit and work on the floor using clipboards or lap desks as writing surfaces. Additionally, students may have assigned roles when completing collaborative, project-based activities to ensure equitable participation. Some teachers use contracts that allow students to choose the order in which they participate in workstations to complete assignments by a designated date.

Independent Practice

After participating in teacher-led small-group instruction at a teaching table and completing multiple collaborative practice opportunities at a worktable or in workstations, students are prepared to engage in **independent practice** where they demonstrate individual progress or mastery. During independent practice, students may work at desks or tables. Assignments may be assessed or graded, and the data may be used to inform or modify instruction and practice.

Using various workspaces to assign activities provides opportunities for students to assume more agency and responsibility for their own learning and self-regulation. This helps students develop skills for time and behavioral management while working cooperatively with peers. Repeated exposures to content deepen student understanding as they apply new knowledge, skills and strategies for reading and writing.

Establish Routines and Procedures

Creating routines and procedures is essential for achieving behavioral compliance and managing flexible grouping to differentiate instruction. Classroom management tools such as a daily schedule, rotation chart, and student contracts help teachers support routines for student participation during instructional activities and transitions between activities. Classroom management tools will be discussed in the next section.

> Teachers need to think about and plan expectations for student performance, then select routines and procedures that clearly communicate expectations.

Planning, modeling, and providing frequent practice opportunities to form new habits for working together are essential to success. Teachers need to think about and plan expectations for student performance, then select routines and procedures that clearly communicate expectations so students can assume more responsibility for learning and achieving goals. Investing time practicing classroom routines helps them become well-established habits for all students.

STEP THREE
Develop Management Tools

Classroom management tools serve as visual reminders for students as they follow routines and procedures to participate as productive members in the classroom community. The tools introduced in this section will help teachers implement routines and procedures that create predictable order in classrooms. The tools include a rotation chart, daily schedule, job chart, and student contracts.

 Students use the tools with less teacher direction, saving teachers time to focus on differentiating instruction, not managing the environment or students' behaviors.

All tools can be created with inexpensive materials or pocket charts and a dry-erase or bulletin board for display. Students use the tools with less teacher direction, saving teachers time to focus on differentiating instruction, not managing the environment or students' behaviors.

Most teachers have daily schedules that include time periods for whole-group instruction along with time periods for students to complete independent activities. The suggested change involves dividing daily schedules into 10–20 minute segments, for both whole-group and small-group activities, as needed for the students in each class. This allows teachers to meet with every student every day in a small-group setting (or on alternating days for upper grades) to provide data-informed, differentiated, explicit instruction.

The management tools that follow support the creation of predictable order so teachers can teach with fewer disruptions.

Check Your Understanding

Check all that apply.

Classroom management tools:

___ are not expensive and complicated to create

___ clarify expectations for students' participation

___ empower students to self-regulate their behavior

___ provide structure for differentiated instruction to occur

Classroom Management Tools

- **Daily Schedule** includes time periods for rotations that include whole-group and small-group instruction, collaborative practice with peers to enhance understandings, and independent practice. Daily schedules are flexible and may be adapted to class, school, or district requirements as needed.

Daily Schedule

TIME	TEACHING TABLE	WORK-STATIONS	WORK-TABLE	WORK-STATIONS
8:00–8:20	Whole-Group Lesson			
8:20–8:40	G1	G2	G3	G4
8:45–9:05	G4	G1	G2	G3
9:10–9:30	Whole-Group Lesson			
9:30–9:50	G3	G4	G1	G2
10:00–10:20	G2	G3	G4	G1
10:25–10:40	Whole-Group Lesson			
10:40–11:00	Assigned Partner Practice and Technology			
11:00–11:20	Whole-Group Lesson or Review, Check, and Edit Homework			

Sample: Daily Schedule (G1 = Group 1; G2 = Group 2; G3 = Group 3; G4 = Group 4)

- **Job Chart** is used to share the work needed to sustain the classroom community, lessening the teacher's responsibility for managing many shareable tasks. Students learn accountability by sharing the work and learning to help others (i.e., social-emotional learning).

Classroom Job Descriptions for Grades 2–5

JOB	DESCRIPTION
Workstation Monitor(s)	Checks workstations after each rotation to ensure that areas are properly cleaned and all supplies replaced or restocked.
Timekeeper	Sets and monitors a wind-up or electronic timer for 15–20 minute work periods; offers a five-minute warning before transitions.
Supply Monitor(s)	Monitors use of resources and restocks as needed from a designated storage location (tissues, pencils, dry-erase markers, etc.).
Special Events Coordinator	Maintains classroom calendar and announces current or upcoming special events (e.g., birthdays, school-wide events or holidays, schedule changes).
Newsletter Reporter(s)	Gathers information from students about their accomplishments, interests, etc. Presents news to class at a designated time each week.

Sample: Classroom Jobs for Grades 2–5

- **Rotation Chart** identifies small-group memberships and the order in which students attend each workspace, with an assigned small group, partner, or individually. Teachers assign students to small groups based on instructional needs and compatibility. Small-group memberships are changed frequently depending on lesson content, instructional needs, and available materials.

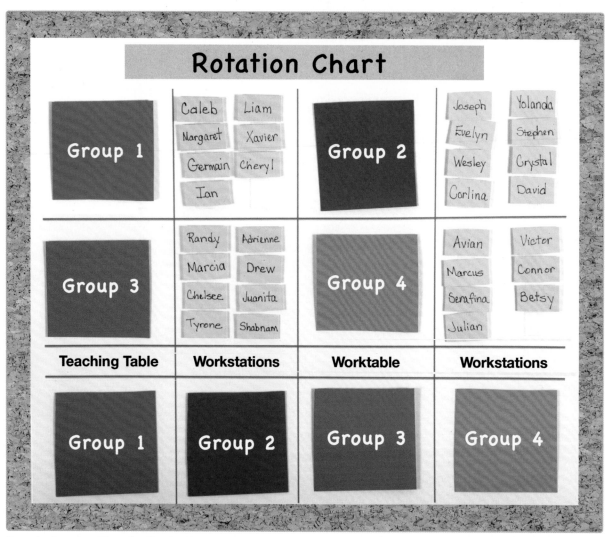

Sample: Rotation Chart for Grades K–1

" The use of the rotation chart allows teachers to flexibly adapt instruction and practice to students' needs. "

- **Student Contracts** are used to represent practice activity choices, with the understanding that students will attend all workstations and/or complete work by designated dates. Student contracts help students plan, make choices, manage their behavior, and use time efficiently to complete assignments.

Student Contract

Name: _____

Completion Date: _____   **Unit:** _____

Content/Skill/Strategy	Description of Work/Activity	Date Completed
Phonics / Word Study	Word sort focused on prefixes and suffixes	
Research and Inquiry	Private Investigator— Author Study	
Writing	Written response to the daily read-aloud	
Handwriting	Collaborative practice with whiteboards using word sort words	
Independent Reading / Fluency	Read a book related to unit's knowledge strand	

Sample: Student Contract for ELA Block, Grade 2

All management tools are posted or displayed on a surface that is easily visible from any area in the classroom. A bulletin board or dry-erase board may be labeled as the Business Center to communicate that the information displayed conveys how the "business" of teaching and learning will occur.

The Business Center and management tools help students know what to do and how to participate in various activities. Students immediately understand expectations and the order of events or how their day or class period will be conducted. This predictable order benefits students and prevents many unnecessary disruptions. Students also understand their assigned classroom responsibilities and expected contributions for that day or the week.

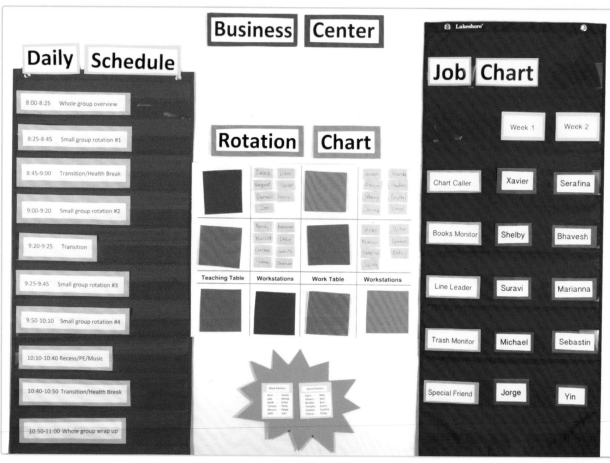

Sample: Business Center for Grades K–1

STEP FOUR
Manage Flexible Grouping

More than four decades of research supports that small-group instruction and flexible grouping practices enhance student learning (Vaughn et al., 2018). However, few teacher preparation programs include training for the classroom management necessary to support small-group differentiated instruction.

The rotation chart discussed in this chapter serves as a visual road map for managing flexible grouping and guiding students' participation in small-group activities. The top of a rotation chart indicates small-group memberships, which change frequently to accommodate students' changing instructional needs. The bottom of the chart demonstrates the order in which students in assigned small groups participate in each activity throughout the class period or class day. (Note that in upper grades worktable activities are usually replaced with independent practice.)

The use of the rotation chart allows teachers to flexibly adapt instruction and practice to students' needs. Students can also be assigned to work with peer partners within each small group. Using data to form small-group memberships or assign peer partnerships also helps with behavioral management. Students who work best apart may be assigned to different groups and activities so more teaching and learning occur with fewer disruptions.

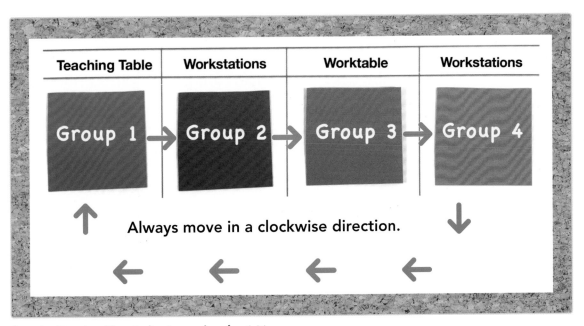

Sample: Rotation Chart indicating order of activities

Provide Differentiated Instruction

Managing the classroom environment to create predictable order and provide visual road maps for participation helps teachers and students use instructional time efficiently. Teachers can support cooperative peer relations by selecting group memberships that are compatible and capable of providing assistance to peers (mixed-skill groupings).

Modeling during whole-group lessons and providing explicit instruction at the Teaching Table prior to assigning student activities for collaborative practice will enhance understandings by developing foundational knowledge and skills before releasing responsibility to students to complete work at workstations or the worktable where there is less teacher supervision and support. Carefully selecting practice materials for workstations and worktable will increase student participation and cooperation. The content and skills required to complete practice activities should be established at the Teaching Table where feedback can be provided to enhance understandings.

The quality and quantity of instruction provided in whole and small groups is critically important for increasing student learning and achievement. However, it is managing the environment and establishing routines for behavior that create the structure within classrooms for positive change to occur. Once classroom routines with less reminders, teachers will experience less interruptions and have more time to focus on differentiating instruction.

 Scaffolding the content, activities, and student response opportunities used in a lesson are part of differentiating instruction and practice.

After teachers observe and collect data to determine students' capabilities and needs, they use data to inform groupings and to select materials for instruction and practice (see Chapters 3 and 4). Scaffolding the content, activities, and student response opportunities used in a lesson are part of differentiating instruction and practice. If the instructional approach in specific lessons is the same for all students in all small groups, then differentiating instruction is *not* occurring. While the goal for all students is access to content, the materials used and the method of delivery and/or pacing of instruction (i.e., the amount of content presented at one time or the number of practice opportunities) may differ substantially according to individual students' needs.

> " New vocabulary words may be introduced in whole group, then explicitly taught in small group where students actually use the words in connected text and discussion. "

Determining what content, skills, or activities will be presented in whole-group or small-group lessons requires reflection about student needs, time for student questions and clarification, and the level of rigor and cognitive demand required to establish understandings. Whole-group lessons may be used for introducing new understandings or reviewing previously taught content or skills. More complex understandings or new vocabulary words may be introduced in whole group, then explicitly taught in small group where students actually use the words in connected text and discussion.

BENEFITS OF DIFFERENTIATING INSTRUCTION

Differentiating instruction means teaching differently to address student variance and needs. Classroom management creates a safe environment for participation using routines and procedures that establish predictable order and clear expectations. Using management tools as visual road maps for alternating time periods for whole-group and small-group activities helps students understand what to do. Small-group lessons allow close observations for teachers to monitor students' learning and to build relationships as they participate in meaningful conversations that clarify concepts and enhance understandings.

Differentiating instruction helps teachers ...

- Develop personal relationships and trust with students.

- Closely observe and assess student capabilities and changing instructional needs.

- Provide explicit instruction that enhances student learning and achievement.

- Differentiate instruction and provide feedback and support as needed.

- Offer repeated exposures to build knowledge and skills.

- Adjust pacing for transferring responsibility from the teacher to students.

- Conduct frequent informal assessment to support progress monitoring.

- Build background knowledge to enhance comprehension based on known student interests or experiences.

More Info!

For more information about classroom management routines and tools, see *Classroom Management: Elementary School* (Gibson, 2019b).

To support teachers and students when implementing this framework in and across classrooms, stakeholders, administrators, and teachers must clearly identify and articulate how the change process will occur. Differentiated and sustained professional development will likely be needed to support teachers as they begin to change how they teach and how students practice using both whole-group and small-group instruction. Guidance may be needed to help teachers select or adjust materials and activities for teacher-led small-group lessons, as well as student-led collaborative and independent practice.

Conclusion

When teachers organize and manage their classrooms to support differentiation, optimal learning can be provided for all students no matter where they are on the Ladder. The suggestions in this chapter provide actionable steps toward change. Teachers at all grade levels can use management tools to establish routines and procedures that create predictable order in their classrooms. When they do, student engagement and performance increase while behavioral disruptions decrease. This enables teachers to focus on providing high-quality differentiated instruction that addresses students' needs.

KEY TAKEAWAYS

- Providing small-group, differentiated instruction benefits students but can be challenging to implement.

- Classroom organization involves managing time, the environment, and student behavior to support meaningful activities for teaching and practice.

- It is essential to invest time teaching and practicing routines to ensure that students understand expectations and develop skills for self-regulation, collaboration, and respectful communication.

- Once classroom routines are operating efficiently, teachers can focus on differentiating instruction.

MANAGING DIFFERENTIATED INSTRUCTION

PART II

ADDRESSING EXCEPTIONAL NEEDS

DYSLEXIA

OLIVIA was a joyful baby and toddler. She lived each day full of smiles and energy that lit up a room. She thrived in preschool where her boundless curiosity was supported by wonderful teachers. We watched her vocabulary expand daily. However, unlike her older sister who had learned to read around age 4, Olivia was not that interested.

Things began to change drastically in 1st grade. Our joyful daughter was now joyless. She hated going to school and complained of headaches every day. After school we dealt with meltdowns and homework tantrums. She was barely reading and writing by 2nd grade, yet the teacher told us, "Olivia is so smart. She'll get it eventually." We wanted to believe this, but we also knew something was not right. In 4th grade she was finally identified as having dyslexia and began receiving support.

She worked most days with a reading specialist at school and we hired tutors to work with her after school and during her summer breaks. She went on to have success in school, including college, but reading remains challenging for her. ⭐

AUTHOR Jan Hasbrouck

Researcher/Consultant
JH Educational Services, Inc.
Seattle, WA, USA

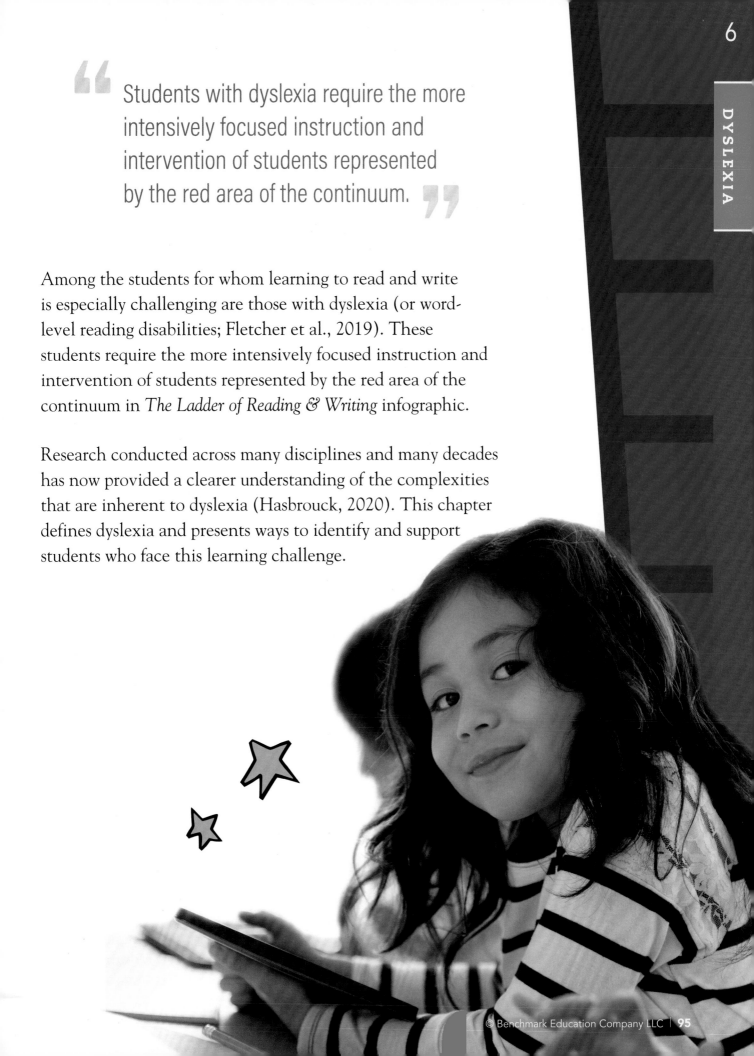

> Students with dyslexia require the more intensively focused instruction and intervention of students represented by the red area of the continuum.

Among the students for whom learning to read and write is especially challenging are those with dyslexia (or word-level reading disabilities; Fletcher et al., 2019). These students require the more intensively focused instruction and intervention of students represented by the red area of the continuum in *The Ladder of Reading & Writing* infographic.

Research conducted across many disciplines and many decades has now provided a clearer understanding of the complexities that are inherent to dyslexia (Hasbrouck, 2020). This chapter defines dyslexia and presents ways to identify and support students who face this learning challenge.

DEFINING DYSLEXIA

The International Dyslexia Association (2002) defines dyslexia as:

> a specific learning disability that is neurobiological in origin. It is characterized by difficulties with accurate and/or fluent word recognition and by poor spelling and decoding abilities.
>
> These difficulties typically result from a deficit in the phonological component of language that is often unexpected in relation to other cognitive abilities and the provision of effective classroom instruction.
>
> Secondary consequences may include problems in reading comprehension and reduced reading experience that can impede growth of vocabulary and background knowledge.

Let's discuss some of the key concepts from this definition in more detail.

Specific Learning Disability

In the United States, the term "specific learning disability" is used to describe students who are considered eligible for special education services if their disability is determined to affect their educational performance and requires specialized instruction. These regulations are part of U.S. federal law, the Individuals with Disabilities Education Act (IDEA), and applies to all states. However, different states interpret and enact IDEA differently.

In some states, students identified as having dyslexia are served within the special education program while in others there are separate services provided outside of special education. How dyslexia services are provided also varies in different countries.

Neurobiological in Origin

There is general agreement that there is some contribution of genetics in dyslexia. Somewhere between 25–60 percent of parents of children who have reading problems also display similar challenges (Fletcher et al., 2019). Dyslexia is thus considered to be neurobiological—a child is born with the brain anomalies that make learning to read more difficult than it is for their neurotypical peers. However, without adequate and appropriate early reading instruction, some older students can appear to have dyslexia.

LEARNING CHALLENGES

The brain anomalies of dyslexia result in difficulties with the *phonological component of language*; students with dyslexia may struggle to develop the metacognitive awareness or understanding that the words we hear and speak (and eventually read and spell) are comprised of speech sounds (or phonemes). In alphabetic languages such as English and Spanish, the spoken language can be divided into segments of phonemes which we have developed symbols, or letters, to represent. Learning to read and write requires understanding this connection, also known as the "alphabetic principle."

Dyslexia is characterized by mild-to-extreme difficulty in developing this foundational understanding, which results in difficulty learning to recognize, decode, and spell words. This is why students with dyslexia are often considered to be in the red area of the colored continuum on the Ladder: learning to read and write can be a challenge for them!

The *unexpected* nature of dyslexia is due to the fact that dyslexia is not related to general cognitive abilities. People with dyslexia can have levels of general intelligence ranging from extremely high (some students with dyslexia may be formally identified as gifted) to average, or even below average (Fletcher et al., 2019). When a young child has demonstrated the ability to learn many things—such as identifying colors, counting objects, riding a bike, or following the rules in a game—but then struggles as they try to learn how to read, it is "unexpected." It can be surprising and disconcerting to a parent, and frustrating and confusing to the child. Unexpected also refers to the fact that these students struggle to learn to read and write even after receiving the kind of classroom instruction that enables most of their peers to successfully master similar skills.

Learn More!

Fletcher, J. M., Lyon, G. R.,Fuchs, L. S., & Barnes, M. A. (2019). *Learning disabilities: From identification to intervention*. Guilford Press.

Hasbrouck, J. (2020). *Conquering dyslexia: A guide to early detection and intervention for teachers and families*. Benchmark Education.

International Dyslexia Association (2020). *Structured literacy: Effective instruction for students with dyslexia and other related reading difficulties*. https://dyslexiaida.org/structured-literacy-effective-instruction-for-students-with-dyslexia-and-related-reading-difficulties/

Reading Comprehension

Dyslexia, in and of itself, does not directly cause problems with reading comprehension (Fletcher et al., 2019). However, there is a relationship between dyslexia and comprehension. If a reader has difficulty reading words accurately or at a reasonable rate, both of which are defining characteristics of dyslexia, the ability to comprehend text will be impaired. And having dyslexia typically has an impact on the amount of reading a student completes.

Understandably, when reading is difficult students rarely do a lot of reading on their own and have less exposure to words. When students don't read text fluently, they are simply unable to read as much text as their on-level peers in the same amount of time. This reduced reading experience contributes to the common secondary problems related to dyslexia: lower vocabulary and background knowledge development, which then negatively affects the ability to comprehend text.

 Reduced reading experience contributes to the common secondary problems related to dyslexia: lower vocabulary and background knowledge development, which then negatively affects the ability to comprehend text. 　

Co-Occurring Challenges

Along with reading comprehension difficulties, students with dyslexia often have the co-occurring challenge of dysgraphia, a neurological anomaly that make learning to write and spell more difficult than it is for their neurotypical peers (Berninger & Wolf, 2009). While dysgraphia frequently co-occurs with dyslexia, it is considered a separate disorder (see Chapter 8). In addition to dysgraphia, both Attention Deficit/ Hyperactivity Disorder (ADHD; see Chapter 10) and Developmental Language Disorder (DLD; see Chapter 9) often co-occur in students with dyslexia, adding significant challenges to learning to read and write.

Other Considerations

Students identified as having dyslexia as well as being gifted (high IQ) are often referred to as "twice exceptional" or 2e. Although more research is needed, current evidence suggests students with co-occurring giftedness and dyslexia should receive support for their giftedness (their intellectual and academic strengths) *and* their dyslexia (instructional/remediation requirements and associated needs); they require dual differentiation (Maddocks, 2020).

Along with these academic concerns, there is sobering information regarding the social, behavioral, and emotional tolls that having dyslexia can take. Studies have connected dyslexia with sometimes long-term and serious emotional consequences including low self-esteem, anxiety, depression, and even self-harm (Haft, 2019; Hasbrouck, 2020; Hendren et al., 2018). These challenges may be exacerbated when dyslexia co-occurs with other exceptionalities. Dyslexia may impact the family as well. It is deeply painful to watch a child struggle with the basic skills that are part of everyday life in school, and later in society. Social-emotional support should be an integral part of program planning (Livingston et al., 2018).

 Studies have connected dyslexia with sometimes long-term and serious emotional consequences including low self-esteem, anxiety, depression, and even self-harm.

IDENTIFYING STUDENTS WITH DYSLEXIA

The identification of dyslexia is challenging, in part because the process of determining whether or not a student has dyslexia is defined by laws and policies that vary significantly across countries, states, districts, and even from school to school. Unfortunately, there is no one, single, universally adopted assessment that can be used definitively to determine if a student has dyslexia (Odegard, 2019). Nonetheless, early screening for defining characteristics related to foundational skills is proving helpful for identification so that appropriate instruction may be administered (Burns et al., 2022).

Universal Screening

Because it is important to identify and address dyslexia as early as possible, many U.S. states are mandating universal screening for dyslexia in the primary grades. The research regarding the accuracy of dyslexia screening is still developing (Elliott, 2020; Hall & Vaughn, 2021), but many of the screeners being recommended involve short, timed assessments of letter naming or letter sound identification. These measures have been found to be both efficient to administer and reasonably accurate in their prediction of future reading difficulties, including dyslexia (Burns et al., 2022).

Characteristics of Dyslexia

After screening for dyslexia, the next step in the process is to identify whether or not a student has the characteristics of dyslexia. Many researchers suggest relying on a *pattern* or *cluster* of concerns directly related to the specific foundational skills that are typically a challenge for students with dyslexia (Hall & Vaughn, 2021; Odegaard, 2019).

 A formal diagnosis of dyslexia would involve whatever process is required by the student's school or district.

Foundational skills that students with dyslexia
are likely to find challenging include:

- phonemic awareness (thinking consciously about the
  sounds or phonemes in spoken words)

- decoding (the relationship between graphemes/letters
  and phonemes/sounds)

- encoding/spelling (representing spoken words in print)

- reading fluency (the ability to read with reasonable
  accuracy, appropriate rate, and suitable expression)

If a student's performance of these skills is lower than expected for their
age and grade, despite having received adequate instruction, we can
reasonably conclude that a student has the "characteristics" of dyslexia.
A formal diagnosis of dyslexia would involve whatever process is
required by the student's school or district.

TEACHING STUDENTS WITH DYSLEXIA

There is now a convergence of scientific evidence that indicates approximately 95 percent of all students can achieve literacy skills at or approaching grade level, including students with dyslexia and other learning disabilities (Hasbrouck, 2020). To achieve this level of success, whether a student has been identified as having the characteristics of dyslexia or has received a more formal diagnosis, the response is the same: Design and deliver appropriate instruction (with sufficient duration and intensity) as soon as possible! The planning process should, as always, address instructional differentiation based on students' identified strengths and challenges.

Effective lessons for students with dyslexia will be *systematically designed* based on data about students' current strengths and instructional needs. Moreover, lessons will be *explicit* and *differentiated*. Let's explore what that means in classroom practice.

Systematic Design

Instruction will be carefully connected across lessons to build the essential skills student needs in a logical order. For a student with dyslexia, early intervention would likely focus on phoneme awareness, embedded within decoding and encoding (writing or spelling) instruction, and language comprehension. Moving to the sentence and text level and including a focus on reading fluency would be an appropriate sequence for instruction.

Explicit Instruction

Instruction that is *explicit* involves step-by-step teacher modeling and active engagement with frequent opportunities for students to respond. For a beginning reader with dyslexia, segmenting and blending words must be taught explicitly with ample guided practice, incorporating multimodal procedures (i.e., seeing, hearing, saying, writing).

Explicit instruction for each component must be differentiated based on the results of both diagnostic skills assessments and ongoing progress monitoring. For a beginning reader in Kindergarten or Grade 1, phoneme awareness and phonics lessons should involve explicit instruction in sound identification, blending, and segmenting using teacher modeling, guided practice, and independent practice. For example,

> Teacher: *This letter says /m/. Say it with me.*
> Your turn: *What is this letter's sound?*

For multimodal practice, you may have students write the letters and words on paper or a whiteboard. For an older student with dyslexia in Grades 3 or 4, explicit instruction might focus on decoding multisyllable words using morphemes. For example,

> Teacher: *Transport. This word has two syllables.*
> *Say the syllables (**trans-port**). Both syllables carry*
> *meaning. **Trans** means "across" or "over." **Port** means*
> *"to carry." **Transport** means "to carry across or over."*

Again, having students see, say, and write the words they are learning provides optimal multimodality practice.

More Info!

For more detailed information about systematically designed and explicit instruction of foundational skills, see Chapter 3.

Check Your Understanding

Match each type of potential learning challenge to the correct description.

a. Decoding/Encoding

b. Reduced Reading Experience

c. Co-occurring Challenge

d. Social and Emotional Impact

Students with dyslexia...

___ may experience low self-esteem or depression

___ may read less on their own with less exposure to words

___ may struggle to identify or connect phonemes in words

___ may be gifted or face other challenges like ADHD

Assistive Technology

Using assistive technology can provide significant beneficial support for students with dyslexia (see Chapter 19). Assistive technology can include the use of audiobooks to provide access to more complex text than a student with dyslexia might be able to read on their own. Many programs now provide text-to-speech options, allowing the computer to read aloud individual words or sections of written text which may help students with dyslexia successfully read and understand text independently. Apps can also be used to practice decoding words (segmenting and blending) in a game-like format.

Differentiated Instruction

Differentiation may involve adjusting the focus, duration, and/or intensity of the instruction to meet the identified needs of an individual student. Teachers and interventionists can determine if the instruction has been effective by monitoring each student's progress toward the identified instructional goals (see Chapter 4). If a goal has been reached or the student is making expected progress toward achieving the goal, teachers can conclude the skill was taught with sufficient quality and intensity. If the student is not making progress toward the goal, teachers should modify the current instruction to increase the quality or the intensity of the instruction.

Providing instruction more frequently, for a longer period of time, or one-on-one are ways to increase instructional intensity. Teachers are encouraged to include parents and caregivers as part of the process; many want to know how to support their child's progress and are eager to support practice at home (see Chapter 18).

Conclusion

Learning to read is a complex cognitive task that involves numerous interconnected and codependent linguistic processes, drawing upon a variety of skills (Hasbrouck & Glaser, 2019). For students who are in the red area of the continuum, which includes students with dyslexia, a successful journey up the Ladder is possible but it will take significant amounts of intentional, focused, and sustained effort. And many students with dyslexia face additional challenges of dysgraphia, ADHD, Developmental Language Disorder (DLD), or being intellectually gifted (2e). Appropriate instruction should begin as early as possible and follow the guidelines that research has found to be the most effective for these students. Appropriately differentiated, systematically designed, and explicit instruction that is informed by data at every step will help students dealing with the challenges of dyslexia joyfully and successfully climb the Ladder.

KEY TAKEAWAYS

- Dyslexia (word-level reading disability) affects the ease with which students become skilled readers.

- Students with dyslexia may be intellectually gifted or have co-occurring challenges such as dysgraphia, ADHD, or DLD.

- Assessments and observations can help detect the skill deficits that characterize dyslexia.

- Dyslexia can be addressed through intentional instruction and intervention that is differentiated, rigorous, and sustained over time.

SRCD
SPECIFIC READING COMPREHENSION DISABILITY

I sat down with Ms. Matthews, *a new third-grade teacher, to discuss one of her students. Jackson had recently been identified with a learning disability in reading comprehension and determined eligible for special education. I'd been a special educator for several years and was working with Jackson in a pull-out intervention for reading comprehension each day. Ms. Matthews wanted advice to support Jackson across the rest of the day, particularly in content areas like social studies and science. She also noted there were other students in her classroom who, like Jackson, appeared to be reading grade-level texts accurately but struggling to answer comprehension questions or identify the main idea.*

Together, we worked on ways to support Jackson and the other students whose difficulties were specific to reading comprehension. We discussed how to consistently provide opportunities for students to read every day with support. We also discussed ways to begin language arts, science, and social studies lessons by reviewing key background knowledge and teaching vocabulary important to understand upcoming texts.

AUTHORS

Nathan H. Clemens

Associate Professor, The University of Texas
Department of Special Education
Austin, TX, USA

Katherine E. O'Donnell

Assistant Professor, The University of Utah
Department of Educational Psychology
Salt Lake City, UT, USA

> SRCD involves significant difficulties in understanding text despite adequate skills in reading words accurately.

We identified important strategies such as main idea identification, recognizing text structures, and comprehension monitoring. Over time, Ms. Matthews observed that many of her students, including Jackson, started to understand more of what they read, were better able to recognize when their comprehension broke down, and could apply strategies to "fix up" their comprehension when needed. ⭐

Some students experience difficulties in reading comprehension due to Specific Reading Comprehension Disability (SRCD). SRCD involves significant difficulties in understanding text despite adequate skills in reading words accurately. Although less prevalent than word-level reading disability (i.e., dyslexia), SRCD has been observed across several studies (Fletcher et al., 2019). Writing difficulties tend to co-occur with SRCD. Given the challenges experienced by students with SRCD and their need for explicit and individualized instruction, supports for this population generally align with the red area of the continuum on *The Ladder of Reading & Writing* infographic.

CONSIDERATIONS FOR STUDENTS WITH SRCD

Reading comprehension is the ability to understand and learn from text. It is the singular goal of reading and ultimate objective of all reading instruction. Unfortunately, many students struggle to comprehend what they read, due to various difficulties reading words or unfamiliarity with the language of the text, especially in upper grades as text complexity increases.

Many students of all ages struggle in reading comprehension (with and without formally identified SRCD), despite having strong word-reading skills. In this chapter, we discuss several intervention strategies and considerations appropriate for most students whose reading difficulties are specific to reading comprehension. And although we refer to students with SRCD across the chapter, readers should note that these recommendations could be appropriate for any student with reading comprehension difficulties, not just students formally identified with a learning disability.

> " Many students struggle to comprehend what they read, due to various difficulties reading words or unfamiliarity with the language of the text, especially in upper grades as text complexity increases. "

Attend to Word-Reading Skills

Word-reading skills refer to a student's ability to read words accurately and efficiently (i.e., with little conscious effort), which is the essential first step to connecting printed words to meaningful ideas. We discuss word reading in the context of SRCD because of the tendency for word-reading difficulties to exist even among students who have been referred for reading comprehension difficulties (Brasseur-Hock et al., 2011; Cirino et al., 2013).

As students read increasingly complex and challenging texts, they will encounter longer, unfamiliar words. This can reveal gaps in word-reading skill that were not apparent in easier texts. The implications can be significant because inaccurately reading a word can disrupt the flow of reading, prevent connection to a word's meaning, and impair students' ability to create an accurate mental representation of text. Thus, even when a student is referred for "reading comprehension" difficulties, their word reading skills should not be taken for granted and may still need to be an aspect of instruction.

More Info!

For more information about instructional recommendations to help students read longer, complex words see Chapter 14.

Build Vocabulary Knowledge

Even if words are decoded correctly, unfamiliarity with a word's meaning or use can prevent or disrupt reading comprehension. Unfamiliarity with the meaning of as few as 2 percent to 5 percent of words in a passage is enough to impair reading comprehension (e.g., Schmitt et al., 2011). Below-average vocabulary knowledge is a common characteristic of students with reading comprehension difficulties and SRCD (e.g., Brasseur-Hock et al., 2011; Fletcher et al., 2019). Increasing text complexity and unfamiliar subject matter further increases the possibility of encountering unfamiliar vocabulary necessary for comprehension. Vocabulary knowledge is particularly relevant for emergent bilingual students and students from historically marginalized communities who may have limited exposure to language common in academic texts.

> "Below-average vocabulary knowledge is a common characteristic of students with reading comprehension difficulties and SRCD."

To support students with SRCD, practitioners should focus on vocabulary instruction that most efficiently develops students' knowledge of vocabulary relevant to the texts they are expected to read (i.e., academic or tier 2 vocabulary—words that are infrequent in everyday speech but common in text; see Coxhead, 2000; Gardner & Davies, 2014). Others sources of target vocabulary are the texts students are assigned in their curricula; these resources may include lists of terms important to know for an upcoming unit.

Vocabulary should be taught with an emphasis on efficiency and practicality. Beck et al. (2013) articulated how a sole focus on memorizing dictionary definitions is unlikely to be sufficient and instead recommended teaching brief, student-friendly definitions of words that convey what is important about them. Instruction should focus on helping students connect new word meanings to existing knowledge and experience, use words correctly in speech and writing, and evaluate when words are used correctly in text.

Build Background Knowledge

Readers integrate information in text with their knowledge of the world to make sense of what they read. Like vocabulary knowledge, understanding text often depends on knowledge of the concepts, history, and themes discussed in a text. Although it overlaps highly with vocabulary knowledge, background knowledge also includes one's understanding of the time, location, and context involved in a topic or situation.

Background knowledge is acquired in several ways: through reading, personal experiences, and instruction. Instruction in background knowledge should be considered as needed; it is unnecessary if students appear to have adequate knowledge required for an upcoming text. In these cases, teachers might consider stating or displaying a few statements that help students activate the proper knowledge before reading. Targeted questions or brief knowledge pretests can help teachers identify knowledge gaps relevant to upcoming text or units in a curriculum.

Informational videos, podcasts, or interactive websites can help build students' familiarity with key events, concepts, and important people relevant to an upcoming text or unit. As with other instructional elements, consider brief resources that build relevant knowledge and protect time for actual reading practice.

Learn More!

Vaughn et al. (2022). *Providing reading interventions for students in grades 4–9: Educator's practice guide.* (WWC 2022007). https://ies.ed.gov/ncee/wwc/PracticeGuide/29

Improving adolescent literacy: Effective classroom and intervention practices. IES practice guide. (NCEE 2006–4027). https://ies.ed.gov/ncee/wwc/PracticeGuide/8

Shapiro, E. S., & Clemens, N. H. (2023). *Academic skills problems: Direct assessment and intervention* (5th ed.). Guilford Press.

TEACHING USEFUL READING COMPREHENSION STRATEGIES

Studies indicate that students with reading comprehension difficulties benefit from learning specific strategies or techniques to improve one's understanding of a text (Filderman et al., 2022). It is important, however, to ensure that strategy instruction is not conducted at the expense of instruction in vocabulary and background knowledge that may ultimately be more important. Judicious instruction in practical strategies, combined with language and background knowledge instruction, can represent a balanced approach to reading comprehension instruction. In this chapter, we describe a set of helpful reading comprehension strategies.

Text Structure Identification

Most texts have a general structure. Narrative texts typically involve a sequence of elements such as introducing the characters or setting, the conflict, rising action, the climax of the story, falling action, and a resolution. Expository and informational texts are structured differently and can include description, sequence, compare/contrast, problem/solution, and cause/effect.

Awareness of text structure and the ability to identify text elements are associated with more robust reading comprehension and can help students identify main ideas and erroneous information (Hebert et al., 2016). Text structure knowledge may be particularly useful in informational texts, which are often less familiar to students than a typical narrative text structure. Roehling et al. (2017) provide an excellent description of procedures for teaching expository text structures and discuss instructional sequences, signal words, and graphic organizers helpful in learning different types.

> Judicious instruction in practical strategies, combined with language and background knowledge instruction, can represent a balanced approach to reading comprehension instruction.

Main Idea and Summarization

The ability to summarize a text or identify its most essential details, messages, and conclusions (i.e., main ideas) requires monitoring one's comprehension and filtering important aspects from irrelevant information. Summarizing focuses on students identifying multiple important ideas and relaying them in their own words, whereas main idea identification involves generating a concise statement of what a passage is about.

A meta-analysis by Stevens et al. (2019) indicated that teaching main idea and summarization skills helps improve overall reading comprehension. One example is "Get the Gist" (Klinger et al., 1998), in which students are taught to identify the "who or what" of the text, identify the most important idea about the "who or what," and write the gist statement combining steps one and two. Additional approaches are described by Boudah (2013) and Jitendra and Gajria (2011).

|

Comprehension Monitoring and Questioning Techniques

Proficient readers monitor their comprehension; when it breaks down, they may slow down, back up, and reread previous portions of text to repair their comprehension. Students with comprehension difficulties often fail to recognize when their comprehension degrades, and if they notice, often lack strategies for fixing it (Kinnunen & Vauras, 1995). Some strategies are aimed at improving comprehension monitoring. The Collaborative Strategic Reading Program (Klinger et al., 1998) uses "Click and Clunk" to teach students to recognize when something does not make sense (i.e., a clunk) and apply fix-up strategies such as context clues to help understand a word's meaning or rereading the section.

> Students with comprehension difficulties often fail to recognize when their comprehension degrades, and if they notice, often lack strategies for fixing it.

Questioning techniques can help students monitor their comprehension and read more actively (Joseph et al., 2016). Strategies involve teaching students to ask and answer questions during and after reading (e.g., who, what, where, when, how). Stevens et al. (2020) recommended teaching students to use both specific questions (can be answered from one area of the text) and wide questions (information gleaned from multiple areas) to help students comprehend texts, as well as have students generate questions while reading to focus attention on what is most relevant.

PROVIDING SUPPORTED OPPORTUNITIES TO READ

Above all, students with reading comprehension difficulties need opportunities to read, with support and feedback, to integrate new vocabulary knowledge, connect the information in the text with their background knowledge, and apply strategies to their reading. Although this may seem obvious, one study (Swanson et al., 2016) and our personal experiences have revealed numerous situations in which reading instruction is dominated by teacher-led instruction with minimal (or no) opportunities for students to read. A goal for teachers is to provide opportunities for students to read every day.

Read Aloud or Silently?

For students with reading comprehension difficulties, whether to have them read aloud or silently depends on the student's skills and the text. If a student tends to make word identification errors or a specific text includes several unfamiliar words, having students read aloud may be a better option. Even a small number of word identification errors can significantly disrupt reading comprehension. When students read silently, those errors go unnoticed and prevent opportunities for teachers to provide corrective feedback, prompt decoding strategies, or support mispronunciation correction.

On the other hand, reading silently can be appropriate when teachers are confident in the student's word reading accuracy for the text. Still, students should be reminded to ask for support when unsure of a word's pronunciation. Moreover, even when word-reading errors are unlikely, teachers might experiment with having students read aloud. Reading aloud can prompt more careful text processing or better self-monitoring of comprehension, allowing some readers to detect ideas they may not have noticed reading silently.

Include "Stretch Text"

"Stretch text" refers to passages containing new words, vocabulary terms, syntax, text structures, and background knowledge students may not encounter in text only at their independent reading levels. Stretch texts (Vaughn et al., 2022) are challenging for a reader to understand independently because the subject matter, writing style, or words are unfamiliar. Vaughn et al. recommend having students read stretch texts two or three times out of every five intervention sessions. This is similar to physical fitness training, in which strength and stamina are built through gradually increasing exercise duration or resistance.

> 'Stretch text' refers to passages containing new words, vocabulary terms, syntax, text structures, and background knowledge students may not encounter in text only at their independent reading level.

It is critical that a teacher provides support while students are reading stretch text. Before reading, the teacher can point out unfamiliar terms, or read a section aloud while students follow along, after which students can read the section themselves (Vaughn et al., 2022). Tackling a more challenging text in smaller sections makes it more manageable and allows teachers to support students' self-monitoring and use of other strategies.

Support Comprehension with Checkpoints

Setting checkpoints in a text before reading facilitates several instructional opportunities. Checkpoints can be set at natural transitions in the text (e.g., paragraph or section breaks), but the amount of text read between checkpoints should be spaced based on the readers' skill level and the text—smaller portions should be used for more challenging texts and increased as students are successful. Checkpoints offer opportunities for knowledge and strategy integration. At checkpoints, students can be prompted to reflect on text structure; identify the main idea or summarize portions of text; attend to vocabulary previously taught or new terms or phrases; connect information with background knowledge and experiences; and respond to questions. If comprehension is insufficient, students can be instructed to go back and reread. Ultimately, the goal is for students to be able to read more actively by periodically checking their understanding and employing fix-up strategies when they recognize that their comprehension is insufficient.

Checkpoints also allow teachers to integrate instruction in inference-making. Although strengthening vocabulary and background knowledge will help readers make more inferences as they read, Barnes et al. (1996) showed that students with comprehension difficulties still struggle to make some inferences even when they have requisite background knowledge. At reading checkpoints, teachers can pose questions that help students connect information across the text and their knowledge, infer word meanings from context, and "read between the lines" to make inferences. These questions should go beyond the information stated explicitly in the text and challenge students to make meaningful connections. This integration helps prevent instruction from becoming a set of isolated components and helps students learn to apply new knowledge and skills directly to reading.

 At reading checkpoints, teachers can pose questions that help students connect information across the text and their knowledge, infer word meanings from context, and "read between the lines" to make inferences. ""

Have Students Read All Types of Text

Reading practice should include all types of texts, including narrative (fiction), informational and expository, and "hybrid" texts such as biographies written in a narrative style. However, practice with informational and expository texts should be prioritized. Students with reading comprehension difficulties demonstrate stronger understanding of narrative texts than expository texts (Best et al., 2008), most likely because informational and expository texts are less predictable and involve more unfamiliar vocabulary and concepts. Additionally, texts from students' science and social studies classes are usually informational or expository; therefore, improving students' skills in reading these types of texts is important for facilitating long-term success in school.

Conclusion

Students with Specific Reading Comprehension Disability (SRCD) have significant difficulties in understanding texts. This challenge is compounded as students encounter increasingly complex texts. These students can significantly improve their reading comprehension when they are provided with systematically designed and explicit instruction that includes support to integrate vocabulary, background knowledge, and comprehension strategies. They also benefit from extensive practice opportunities using a variety of text types, especially informational and expository texts.

KEY TAKEAWAYS

Instruction that is beneficial to students with SRCD will:

- Ensure students' word-reading accuracy as texts increase in complexity.

- Develop students' vocabulary and background knowledge.

- Teach strategies for making sense of text.

- Provide extensive opportunities to read with support.

CHAPTER 8

WD WRITTEN EXPRESSION DIFFICULTIES

Our son's writing challenges *were unexpected and increasingly frustrating for us all. Scott was reading before Kindergarten, yet still had trouble writing a sentence at the end of Grade 1. Scott was identified as gifted in Grade 2, yet barely passed the Grade 3 writing exam. His gifted enrichment teacher in Grade 5 told us that he created awesome research projects, but he hated to provide written explanations.*

In Grade 6, Scott was diagnosed with ADHD. In junior high he still wouldn't write and was failing most subjects. What amazed us was that he could spell quite well when he did write but trying to construct sentences and paragraphs to present his thoughts just shut him down. He failed Grade 10. Worried Scott might not graduate, we pushed for reassessment—and he was diagnosed as having dysgraphia in addition to ADHD and being gifted. We moved him to a new school, where a patient literacy specialist coached him over three years. Finally equipped with skills he'd long needed, and with permission to use a keyboard written into his IEP, our son graduated with honors! ⭐

AUTHORS

Jan Hasbrouck

Researcher/Consultant
JH Educational Services, Inc
Seattle, WA, USA

Nancy Young

Educational Consultant
Creator of *The Ladder of Reading & Writing*
Nanoose Bay, British Columbia, Canada

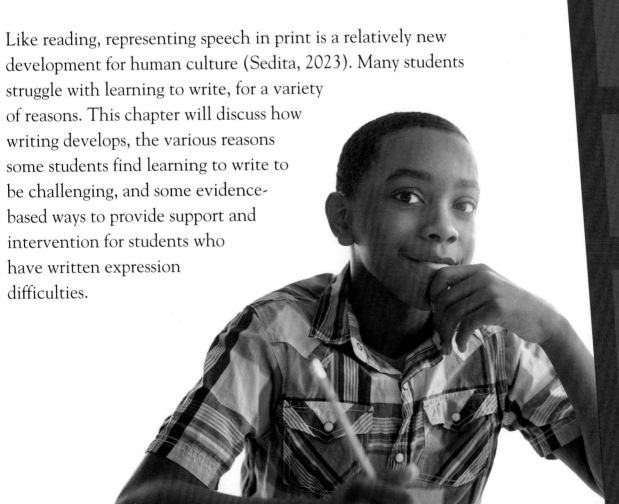

> ❝ Like reading, representing speech in print is a relatively new development for human culture. ❞

The Ladder of Reading & Writing infographic includes "writing" alongside "reading" as an essential literacy skill. Reading and writing are interconnected and mutually supportive (Graham, 2020). Ensuring that all students become fully literate— readers *and* writers—is crucial. Without proficient writing skills, both academic and workplace success can be negatively impacted (Graham, 2019). And while for most children the development of spoken and receptive language is a natural, biologically supported process, communicating thoughts and ideas through written text is not.

Like reading, representing speech in print is a relatively new development for human culture (Sedita, 2023). Many students struggle with learning to write, for a variety of reasons. This chapter will discuss how writing develops, the various reasons some students find learning to write to be challenging, and some evidence-based ways to provide support and intervention for students who have written expression difficulties.

LEARNING TO WRITE

In most environments, children are regularly exposed to a vast multitude of examples of how humans represent speech in symbolic, graphical forms—with letters or other symbols combined to form words. Packages of food sold in markets have labels. A bus ride features signs and posters both inside and outside the bus. Even outdoor parks and playgrounds have signs everywhere. Children may see grownups or older siblings writing words on the family calendar, making a shopping list, composing a report for homework, or signing forms at the doctor's office. Print is all around us! But unlike learning to speak, learning to write does not happen with simple exposure.

Writing is a multifaceted and complex task that requires both cognitive and motor skills (Sedita, 2023). Like reading, learning to write is a developmental process that can be lengthy and improves with practice. Even for those students in the dark green area of the infographic whose writing is advanced, feedback may help improve their writing (Bass, 2020).

Writing can be conceptualized as having two basic components: transcription (e.g., handwriting, keyboarding, and spelling—or the "mechanics" of writing), and generation (e.g., self-regulation, organization, monitoring—or the process of "composition") (Fletcher et al., 2019).

 Students who experience difficulty with mechanical processes may avoid writing, which hinders their writing development.

Transcription (Mechanics)

Transcription refers to the process of forming and combining meaningful symbols to represent oral speech or express ideas. It involves fine motor skills and learned patterns of letter formation as well as phonological skills for combining those patterns to spell (or encode) words. Students who experience difficulty with mechanical processes may avoid writing, which hinders their writing development.

Letter Formation

The ability to correctly form letters and use letters to spell words are the foundational mechanical skills required for writing. Letter formation requires both focused attention and fine motor skills. Providing instruction in handwriting and sufficient time for practice in the early grades goes a long way to prevent later writing composition challenges (Berninger & Wolf, 2009; Graham et al., 2015; Troia et al., 2020; Truckenmiller et al., 2020).

Students who experience difficulty forming letters may have dysgraphia, which will be explored later in this chapter. Some students find cursive writing helps them with letter formation; however, the research is inconclusive as to whether printing or cursive is more beneficial (Schwellnus et al., 2012). Learning to keyboard is an alternative, or an additional skill, that can make the process of writing much easier for many students. For most students, keyboarding should be used along with handwriting, rather than a total replacement.

 The better a student knows a word, the more readily they will recognize it, spell it, define it, and use it appropriately in writing and speech.

Spelling

Learning to correctly spell words has value beyond writing. The correlation between spelling and reading comprehension is strong (Madelaine, 2023). The better a student knows a word, the more readily they will recognize it, spell it, define it, and use it appropriately in writing and speech (Joshi et al., 2008–2009). Learning to spell words is more difficult than learning to read words, especially in a language like English where different letters can represent different sounds at different times and for different reasons. However, most English spellings are phonetically regular, and many words are only slightly irregular (Joshi et al., 2008–2009).

Spelling is not simply memorizing the correct order of letters in individual words. Frequent exposure to words and patterns within words while reading and engaging in other activities, and early exposure to text long before a young child can independently decode, contributes greatly to learning to spell (Pacton et al., 2013; Treiman & Kessler, 2006). For those students for whom reading and spelling mastery does not happen easily, carefully designed and explicitly delivered instruction is important. Integrating spelling (encoding) instruction with the process of learning to read words (decoding) helps students become better spellers, writers, and readers (Graham et al., 2015). Understanding how the English writing system works (e.g., morphology, syntax, and semantics) can also assist students in spelling words accurately (Berninger et al., 2000).

> Integrating spelling (encoding) instruction with the process of learning to read words (decoding) helps students become better spellers, writers, and readers.

Generation (Composition)

The second major component of writing involves generation, or the process of creating written text, sometimes referred to as composition. Different from transcription, which is specific to writing, this element overlaps with other areas of language and thought development. Composition involves critical thinking (generating ideas, drafting, and revising), syntax (grammar and syntactic awareness, sentence elaboration, punctuation), text structure (genres, organization of paragraphs, transitions), and writing craft (word choice, awareness of purpose and audience) (Sedita, 2023).

The ability to compose text is constrained by many factors including fluency in transcription skills, background knowledge, and vocabulary, as well as functional skills like attention, self-control, perseverance, and working memory (Berninger & Wolf, 2009). Students with written expression difficulties face significant challenges with generation, even if their transcription skills are adequately developed (Fletcher et al., 2019).

ASSESSING WRITING

There are three general ways that writing is assessed. Teachers often rely on qualitative assessment of writing, scoring on-demand writing or a more developed composition using a designated rubric for the type and purpose of the writing. A rubric for general writing might include legibility, conventions, ideas, organization, and expression with descriptors provided on a scoring scale, perhaps ranging from 0 to 4.

The curriculum-based measures (CBM) of correct word sequences (CWS) and total words written (TWW) are another way to assess students' writing abilities. These measures have been validated as a more quantitative way to assess students' writing. Students are given a writing prompt and one minute to think about what they will write. They then write for three minutes. Standardized scoring procedures have been developed along with norms for total CWS and TWW for grades K–8 (Hosp et al., 2016).

Finally, weekly tests have long been used to assess spelling. However, according to some studies, presenting a random list of words for students to memorize is not an effective way to organize spelling instruction or assessment (Madelaine, 2022). Scoring a word as fully correct or incorrect misses an opportunity to evaluate and provide feedback on a student's understanding of the underlying language structures (Joshi et al., 2008–2009). CBM measures of correct letter sequences (CLS) is one alternative for scoring that can support this kind of analysis (Hosp et al., 2016).

WD WRITTEN EXPRESSION DIFFICULTIES

SPECIFIC CHALLENGES

Given its complexity, it is understandable that many students find writing to be challenging. For some, skill mastery is especially difficult, and support is essential whether the challenge is predominantly transcription or generation—or both. Students with learning disabilities in reading typically have some form of written expression difficulty, as do students with attention deficit/hyperactivity disorder (ADHD) and developmental language disorder (DLD). Researchers are still determining whether difficulties with written language occur in the absence of other learning disabilities, language challenges, or ADHD (Fletcher et al., 2019).

Dysgraphia

Like dyslexia, dysgraphia is widely considered to be a neurological disorder, meaning that a child is born with brain anomalies that make learning to write and spell difficult. Dysgraphia has been defined as an unusual difficulty with handwriting and/or spelling (Berninger & Wolf, 2009). Students with dysgraphia typically have trouble forming letters legibly and fluently, and the letters they write are often inappropriately sized and spaced. As previously discussed, letter formation is an essential part of transcription, so students with dysgraphia encounter a significant roadblock when learning to write. These difficulties with handwriting in turn affect the accuracy of spelling and impede the complex cognitive processes involved in planning, organizing, transcribing, and revising text. Due to challenges with transcription, these students often also struggle with generation/composition.

 Students with learning disabilities in reading typically have some form of written expression difficulty, as do students with attention deficit/hyperactivity disorder (ADHD) and developmental language disorder (DLD). ""

Identifying Dysgraphia

It is possible to make an informal determination of dysgraphia by its common characteristics. Parents with no specialized training and classroom teachers may notice when an activity that is easy and even joyful for their peers is hard and frustrating for a student because of difficulties forming letters. Just copying or tracing letters can be a challenge for students with dysgraphia.

A more formal determination or diagnosis of dysgraphia is commonly made by a school psychologist or diagnostician, often in collaboration with an occupational therapist (OT). Fine motor difficulties can exacerbate the challenges of writing caused by dysgraphia; an OT can assess a student's ability to utilize the small muscles in their hands and wrists. An assessment of dysgraphia would likely include having the student copy words or sentences, then write words from dictation. For older students, an assessment may include their ability to put thoughts into words (generation/composition).

Some students with dyslexia and dysgraphia also have neurological challenges like ADHD or DLD. Many students with dysgraphia also have anxiety (Hendren et al., 2018). Co-occurring issues can significantly add to a student's challenges when climbing the Ladder.

SUPPORTING STUDENTS WITH WD

Although difficulties with writing can be persistent when not addressed in the early grades, research has identified effective ways to support students' writing needs. The following overview provides a snapshot of best practices and interventions to support writing skill development.

Evidence-Based Best Practices

Evidence-based approaches for *general* writing support should include:

- differentiated instruction
- engagement (including choice)
- time to practice

Let's look at each of these practices and how they support students with written expression difficulties.

Differentiated Instruction

Students' writing skills progress at different rates, so writing instruction must be differentiated (Graham, 2019). Students should be grouped for instruction to address their specific writing challenges and identified needs (Berninger & Wolf, 2009). Work with students to set writing goals that are attainable, but slightly beyond what they are already capable of doing. For elementary students, adding more detail and/or new ideas to a composition is a reasonable suggestion. Brainstorming new content may involve visualizing writing through illustrations or completing a graphic organizer.

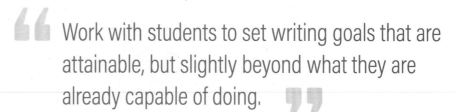

> " Work with students to set writing goals that are attainable, but slightly beyond what they are already capable of doing. "

Providing instruction in specific writing strategies related to planning, drafting, evaluating, and revising writing equips students with greater confidence and more tools to problem-solve throughout the writing process (Graham & Harris, 2013). Though often thought of as a linear step-by-step process of planning, drafting, revising, editing, and publishing, writing is in fact iterative and recursive. Effective writers revisit their writing repeatedly. Thus, differentiated instruction should address foundational writing skills and support the development of the writing process as needed.

A common writing strategy involves the use of model or "mentor" texts. Examining model texts closely helps students identify the key features of a particular text type or genre and provides an example all students can reference throughout the writing process. Explicit instruction will involve teacher modeling, explanation, scaffolding, and purposeful practice that prepares students to apply strategies to their own writing.

 Writing for a specific purpose, such as a real audience, is one way to engage writers.

Engagement

Central to these approaches is the need for explicit instruction, yet evidence-based approaches allow for "novelty" (Berninger & Wolf, 2009, p. 94). Effective instruction will include ways to make the learning intellectually engaging and fun (Harris et al., 2008; Saddler, 2012). For example, writing for a specific purpose, such as a real audience, is one way to engage writers. Writing for the sake of writing can be contrived and potentially unmotivating. Students can write to explain, persuade, or even entertain a particular audience.

It may also help to provide some choice writing topics, so students can write about topics that interest them. Writers encounter difficulties when they lack content knowledge about a particular topic. This is one reason that allowing students to choose their own topic can be more engaging for students. However, knowledge-building for the purpose of writing can be accomplished through brainstorming activities, gathering of sources, inquiry-based explorations, and reading about the topic. It is important to create a supportive environment for writing. Writing is a challenge for most students, and especially for those with written expression difficulties. Make sure students have sufficient and continuous guidance and on-going positive and specific feedback to feel supported in their learning.

Time to Practice

Graham (2019) emphasizes repeatedly that time must be provided for students to practice writing in the school setting. Students spend very little time writing in school and, when they do write, it is often shorter than one paragraph (Applebee & Langer, 2011; Kiuhara et al., 2009). For students who struggle, even more time is needed (Berninger & Wolf, 2009). All students should write frequently for a variety of purposes and for extended periods of time.

Interventions for Specific Needs

Students with written expression difficulties benefit from differentiated and explicit instruction to build general writing skills. However, they may also require interventions that address specific needs. Here are some suggestions for interventions that address common challenges for these students.

Handwriting

Handwriting instruction benefits all students, and especially those who have transcription challenges (Graham, Harris, & Adkins, 2018; Truckenmiller & Chandler, 2023). Berninger and Wolf (2009).

- Build fine motor skills. This can start in early childhood, even before preschool. It can be accomplished by tracing shapes and following maze-like paths drawn on paper or a whiteboard. Have the student move their pen or pencil from top to bottom and left to right.

- Teach students the tripod pencil grip. Be sure to determine each student's hand preference, accessing support from an occupational therapist (OT) if needed. Ways to teach this include having the student practice writing with small pieces of chalk or crayons that requires them to grip with their fingers instead of their fist or engaging in tasks that require the use of smaller hand muscles. It may also help some students to use a plastic pencil grip slipped on the pen or pencil.

- Teach correct letter formation. Initially, use general strokes involving gross motor movements with accompanying self-talk. Having students begin with drawing shapes can provide early practice in forming letters. The actions involved in drawing (or tracing) circles, squares, and vertical or horizontal lines can support later printing of letters and words.

- Teach lowercase letters first and provide a letter formation chart.

- Provide lined paper for practice that transitions from wide-to-narrow spacing.

Learning and practicing these foundational transcription skills so that handwriting is fluent and effortless removes barriers to the development of the more challenging skills involved in composition.

> **Effective Handwriting Instruction**
>
> - Build fine motor skills.
>
> - Teach the tripod pencil grip.
>
> - Teach correct letter formation.
>
> - Teach lowercase letters first.
>
> - Provide paper that transitions from wide-to-narrow spacing.

Technology

Explicit instruction on keyboarding skills may benefit students with written expression difficulties. There are several computer programs that can be used to teach keyboarding. Keyboarding instruction can start as early as 1st grade; by the end of 2nd or 3rd grade, students should be able to type as fast as they can write by hand (Graham et al., 2018). Beyond learning to keyboard, there are many other ways that technology can support writing. Multiple programs offer voice recognition that can be used for dictation, and settings in software programs that can provide text suggestions, check grammar and spelling, and autocorrect misspelled words. Using these features could provide differentiated support for writing and would be especially beneficial for students with writing difficulties.

More Info!

For more information about technology, see Chapter 19.

Self-Regulated Strategy Development (SRSD)

Self-Regulated Strategy Development (SRSD) is both an instructional method for teachers and a set of strategies that helps develop student ownership of their writing, builds confidence, and helps them to take responsibility for their own learning. SRSD is the most thoroughly researched and effective practice for students with writing difficulties (Fletcher et al., 2019). Teachers use the SRSD process to teach strategies systematically and explicitly for varying types and genres of writing while developing executive functioning skills that are essential to successful writing, such as goal-setting, problem-solving, planning, and self-regulation.

Teachers Use Six Stages* to Teach Writing Strategies for Different Genres

1. Develop background knowledge.

2. Discuss it.

3. Model it.

4. Memorize it.

5. Support it.

6. Independent performance.

* Full descriptions of these stages can be found at the SRSD website: https://srsdonline.org/each-step-of-srsd/.

Teachers using SRSD differentiate their pacing and task sequence based on individual need and current skill development. For free SRSD teaching resources see https://www.thinksrsd.com/free-resources-to-share/.

Learn More!

Berninger, V. W., & Wolf, B. J. (2016). *Teaching students with dyslexia, dysgraphia, OWL LD, and dysscalculia* (2nd. ed.). Brookes.

Graham, S., Bollinger, A., Booth Olson, C., D'Aoust, C., MacArthur, C., McCutchen, D., & Olinghouse, N. (2018). *Teaching elementary school students to be effective writers: Educator's practice guide* (NCEE 2012–4058). What Works Clearinghouse, National Center for Education Evaluation and Regional Assistance, Institute of Education Sciences, U.S. Department of Education.

Saddler, B. (2009). Sentence Combining. *Perspectives on Language and Literacy. Preventing School Failure, 5*(3), 27.

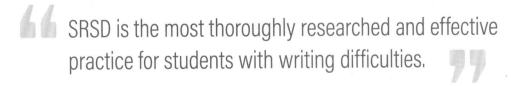

> SRSD is the most thoroughly researched and effective practice for students with writing difficulties.

Sentence Combining

Sentence combining is another type of intervention for students with written expression difficulties. Although many adults associate text generation with the composition of paragraphs, a foundational component of skilled writing is sentence generation (Saddler & Graham, 2005). Organizing words to create a sentence can pose a hurdle to students with writing disabilities (Hebert et al., 2018). Sentence combining is an evidence-based approach to sentence development that has been found to meet a wide range of needs (Hebert et al., 2018; Saddler & Asaro-Saddler, 2009).

Sentence combining instruction usually begins with discussion, often using sentences taken from books or student work for modeling and practice. Have students read aloud two simple sentences such as "I have a big dog. Molly has a little dog." Discuss ways to combine the sentences such as "I have a big dog, but Molly has a little dog." Then have students write the combined sentence. Teach students the acronym FANBOYS for a list of words commonly used to combine sentences (*for*, *and*, *nor*, *but*, *or*, *yet*, and *so*). Practice together until students are ready to work in pairs or small groups to combine sentences.

During the process of teaching sentence combining, grammatical concepts can be taught in context. What struggling writers and their teachers may find especially appealing about sentence combining is that instruction is provided in a discovery-oriented environment that "allows for the possibility of more than one 'right' answer" (Saddler, 2012, p. 14). Students are encouraged to think of the process of transforming and manipulating words to improve sentences as experimentation; solving word puzzles using a logical approach can be intellectually stimulating.

> Organizing words to create a sentence can pose a hurdle to students with writing disabilities.

As emphasized throughout this book, instruction and intervention must be differentiated to address each student's specific needs. No one best practice or intervention will work with every student in every situation. However, the strategies presented here make clear that there are effective ways to address the challenges faced by students with written expression difficulties; these strategies deepen students' confidence by expanding their tool sets and increasing engagement.

Conclusion

The ability to write proficiently impacts students' success during their school years and beyond. Although students are likely exposed to text daily at home and school, creating text independently involves a variety of different skills that are difficult for some students to master.

Writing encompasses both transcription skills (the mechanics of letter formation and spelling) and generation skills (composing sentences and paragraphs to express ideas in well-organized texts). Students may struggle with transcription or generation—or both.

Research over many decades has supported effective methods of teaching writing, including Self-Regulated Strategy Development (SRSD) and sentence combining. For students with written expression difficulties, these methods support skill mastery delivered in flexible ways according to student need as well as address the link between self-regulation and skill development.

KEY TAKEAWAYS

- Learning to write requires the development of both transcription and generation skills.

- Students with a written expression difficulty may be challenged by transcription or generation tasks—or both.

- Self-Regulated Strategy Development (SRSD) and sentence combining activities are two effective approaches to support skill building for students with written expression difficulties.

- Evidence-based best practices include differentiated instruction, increased engagement (including choice), and abundant time to practice.

DLD DEVELOPMENTAL LANGUAGE DISORDER

We were asked to consult *on a perplexing case at a local elementary school. David, a 4th grader, had made slow but steady progress learning to read words but didn't seem to understand what he read. David had no other academic difficulties but was noted to be a bit inattentive in the classroom and shy around his peers.*

Upon observing David read aloud it was clear he was now a fluent reader of grade-level texts. When David finished, his teacher asked him to retell the story. His retell was short, using simple sentences and omitting key details. The sequence was incorrect and left out important information. We asked David a few questions about his experiences in school. He said he liked school, but it was hard to keep up sometimes. We requested language testing, and, as expected, David had low scores in line with a developmental language disorder or DLD. Unfortunately, it appeared that this student had slipped through the cracks, and no one had considered DLD earlier.

AUTHORS

Maura Curran

Clinical Speech-Language
Pathologist
Boston, MA, USA

Tiffany Hogan

Professor, MGH Institute
of Health Professions
Boston, MA, USA

> DLD is the result of a neurobiological, brain-based difference that makes learning language from the environment difficult.

Communicating through spoken language is something most of us do every day. However, for students with developmental language disorder (DLD), producing and/or understanding language may prove difficult, without any clear cause (Bishop et al., 2016). DLD is the result of a neurobiological, brain-based difference that makes learning language from the environment difficult. This difficulty is associated with challenges in education, communication, and other key life areas. DLD is a learning disability that occurs in approximately 7 percent of students (Tomblin et al., 1997), or 1–2 students in every classroom. This chapter presents an overview of the challenges of DLD and summarizes evidence-based supports that can assist students with DLD in learning new language and literacy skills, accessing the curriculum, and meeting their potential.

THE CHALLENGES OF DLD

Although it is difficult to diagnose DLD accurately in children under 5 years of age, skilled professionals such as Speech/Language Pathologists (SLPs) can make a reliable diagnosis by age 5 (Bishop et al., 2016). Students with DLD are highly likely to continue to exhibit difficulties with language throughout their school years. They do acquire new language skills, and make ongoing progress, but they are unlikely to achieve "typical" language skills (Rice & Hoffman, 2015).

It is important to note that DLD is not a problem with making the sounds in words when speaking; it is not a speech problem. It is not uncommon for a person with DLD to have clear speech like their typical development (TD) peers yet struggle to produce grammatically correct sentences, tell complete stories, or find the right words to describe their experiences.

Students with DLD have difficulty comprehending texts, primarily because of their trouble understanding the language in written texts. Although there is a range of difficulty, approximately 50 percent of students with DLD will fall into the red and orange areas of the continuum in *The Ladder of Reading & Writing* infographic. This means they will require code-based, explicit instruction as part of a comprehensive analytical approach to learning language structure. About 10–15 percent may require instruction that is especially intensive and provides a great deal of repetition.

Identifying DLD

Preschool children with DLD speak with peers and adults, but they often use shorter sentences with more restricted vocabulary. Their vocabulary, grammar, and narrative skills are weak when compared to TD children the same age (Leonard, 2014). For example, a 4-year-old with DLD that we worked with once asked "Miss Maura, you happy I four?" meaning "Miss Maura, are you happy I'm four?"

Although some students with DLD may appear to understand language well, others have difficulties comprehending language in the classroom. They may not follow verbal directions or may respond inaccurately to a teacher's questions—even when paying attention and trying their best. For example, we asked one preschooler "Why did the kite crash?" and he confidently responded, "At the library!"

As they move through their school years, students with DLD improve their communication skills, but continue to exhibit difficulties as compared to their TD peers. Students with DLD struggle to learn new academic vocabulary and may have smaller vocabularies in general. They may use general words (e.g., "thing" or "stuff") instead of more specific terms (Rice & Hoffman, 2015). They acquire grammatical skills later than peers and struggle with complex sentences (Novogrodsky & Friedmann, 2006). Their narratives may be immature, and they may struggle to answer questions about narratives they have read or heard. Lengthy, complex verbal information can be challenging, even for those students who understand casual conversation.

Learn More!

Adolf, S. M., & Hogan, T. P. (2019). If we don't look, we won't see: Measuring language development to inform literacy instruction. *Policy Insights from the Behavioral and Brain Sciences, 6*(2), 210–217.

McGregor, K. K., Van Horne, A. O., Curran, M., Cook, S. W., & Cole, R. (2021). The challenge of rich vocabulary instruction for children with developmental language disorder. *Language, Speech, and Hearing Services in Schools, 52*(2), 467–484.

Tighe, J. (2022). *Developmental language disorder: A guide for parents and families.* https://radld.org/wp-content/uploads/2022/11/DLD-A-guide-for-parents-and-families-2.pdf.

> **Students with DLD struggle to learn new academic vocabulary and may have smaller vocabularies in general.**

DLD DEVELOPMENTAL LANGUAGE DISORDER

DLD IMPACT ON LEARNING TO READ

There is considerable comorbidity between DLD and dyslexia. That is, students with DLD are far more likely than TD peers to have dyslexia, though research is unclear exactly how much that risk is increased (Catts et al., 2005; Alonzo et al., 2020; Snowling et al., 2020). Students with dyslexia and DLD exhibit traits of both conditions and require accommodations and interventions targeted at oral language development as well as reading and writing skills (McGregor, 2020).

Decoding Skills

Students who have DLD but not dyslexia appear to acquire early foundational reading and writing skills well, especially decoding skills. During the early grades, instruction and progress monitoring are highly focused on decoding; however, students are not expected to comprehend complex language in text. We have spoken with first grade teachers who confidently identify students with DLD as "good readers" in first grade based on assessment data.

Reading Comprehension

As students with DLD move into mid and late elementary school, they often begin to struggle with reading comprehension. At this point, the increasingly complex vocabulary, sentence structure, and content students are expected to understand and generate, for both reading and writing, taxes the language skills of students with DLD. Students had these difficulties in oral language all along, but they were not identified because early monitoring and testing focused primarily on decoding.

As students with DLD move into mid and late elementary school, they often begin to struggle with reading comprehension.

The language and literacy needs of students with DLD continue in middle through high school. Adolescents are less likely to exhibit grammatical errors when speaking, and difficulties may appear more subtle outside of an academic context. However, these students experience difficulty with the abstract vocabulary, complex sentences, and varied types of discourse required in the upper grades, along with the language demands in content-area courses (e.g., Math, Science). (Nippold et al., 2008; Joffe et al., 2019).

Lack of Awareness of DLD

The general public has little awareness of DLD. Parents and teachers may be unaware that a student is struggling before formal testing is completed (Hendricks et al., 2019). Students may be perceived as lazy, inattentive, unmotivated, or misbehaving.

Although students with DLD are at a very high risk for literacy difficulties, this population is under-identified. In the US only about one-third of students with DLD are identified for IEP-based services (Hendricks et al., 2019; Wittke & Spaulding, 2018). Teachers are rarely provided sufficient professional education around DLD, so it can be difficult for them to recognize this disorder. Students with DLD—even those who are strong decoders—exhibit early-emerging difficulties in language comprehension; however, they are frequently not identified until later in elementary school. We can identify and support these students better if we improve general awareness and understanding of DLD, as well as the supports these students require.

> ### Check Your Understanding
>
> **Check all that apply. Problems identifying students with DLD include:**
>
> ___ early assessments focus on decoding
>
> ___ difficulties may be limited to academic contexts
>
> ___ students may be mistaken as disruptive or disengaged
>
> ___ simplified vocabulary may be assumed normal
>
> ___ lack of educator and public awareness

DLD DEVELOPMENTAL LANGUAGE DISORDER

SUPPORTING STUDENTS WITH DLD

Language is the backbone of school interactions and learning—talking with peers, exploring new concepts, understanding instructions for an assignment, and conveying one's needs. When a student with DLD cannot communicate effectively, they may act out in other ways that are disruptive, or they may shut down and not participate. Students with DLD need support in schools from caring adults to ensure that they understand the language around them. This includes their teachers, librarians, and administrators working together to ensure continuity of services across the school day (Chow, 2018).

Educators and others should be aware that students with DLD may appear disruptive or inattentive. These behaviors may indicate that a student is struggling to understand what they hear and/or to express themselves in school. The social and emotional impact of unmet language needs for students with DLD can be devastating. For example, middle schoolers with DLD experience more anxiety in social situations, fewer friends, greater risk of victimization (especially females), and depression compared to their TD peers (Brownlie et al., 2007). They may also internalize the feeling that they are not able to learn (Donolato et al., 2022)

 When a student with DLD cannot communicate effectively, they may act out in other ways that are disruptive, or they may shut down and not participate. 〞

Educators should also remember that screening and progress monitoring tools commonly used for reading in the early grades do not identify students with DLD (Adolf & Hogan, 2019). Screening tools specifically designed for oral language in the younger grades do exist and can be used to identify language needs (Hogan et al., 2022). (See Recommended Resources on page 144.)

Classroom Language Supports

Educators and others can provide ongoing support to students with DLD by ensuring that these students receive consistent, high-quality language input. This may require consulting with a Speech/Language Pathologist (SLP). Teachers have a great deal of impact here as students' language growth is associated with teachers' language usage (Dickinson, 2011). Many teachers already adjust their language based on individual student's needs, but being deliberate about providing high-quality language input to students struggling with oral language could aid in this differentiation.

Classroom Language Supports

Below are examples of ways teachers can support language development in their classrooms:

- **Teacher Directions:** Make clear, explicit statements and rephrase with written supports. For example, instead of saying, "It's time to go home now," say, "School is over. Please line up at the door," while pointing to a visual schedule that shows the end of the day.

- **Peer Communication:** Teach students conversational rules and sentence starters. Create an anchor chart displaying words to start a peer conversation: "What do you like to do?" or "I would like to share … "

- **Written Language Tasks:** As students with DLD matriculate to middle and high school, they still need support, especially when instructions and information are conveyed in writing. Break down larger chunks of information in text by adding bullet points, highlighting key words or dates, or incorporating graphic organizers whenever possible.

More Info!

For more information, see https://dldandme.org/supporting-a-child-with-dld-in-the-classroom.

Intervention Teams

Students with DLD often receive support from SLPs. While these direct services are key to successful intervention, students cannot acquire new skills from the SLP's intervention alone. They benefit from coordinated support across settings. The SLP should include the entire team of students' teachers and their families and caregivers. For example, when students with DLD hear and practice new vocabulary words across settings, they have more opportunities to internalize these words (McGregor et al., 2021).

Recommended Resources

There are a growing number of resources for educators, SLPs, and others supporting students with DLD. Here are a few recommended key resources:

- **RADLD (Raising Awareness of Developmental Language Disorder):** international organization to create awareness about DLD. Full of informational international resources and videos about DLD

- **DLD and Me:** United States-based group focused on increasing awareness of DLD and providing resources for parents, professionals, and others

- **Engage DLD:** connects people with DLD, their families, and those who support them to academic research as findings become available

- **The DLD Project:** Australian-based resources for DLD

- **Free e-book about DLD:** written by US RADLD ambassador and SLP, https://bcpractice.com/wp-content/uploads/2022/10/DLD-A-guide-for-parents-and-families.pdf

- **Language Screeners Resource:** an open-source site providing information on language screeners for students with DLD, https://osf.io/cajp5

Conclusion

Students with DLD have trouble understanding and using language without any clear cause. These language difficulties are associated with challenges around education, communication, and other key life areas. As a community of educators, other professionals, and caregivers, we must increase awareness about these students' needs and the best strategies to support them. Currently, these students are under-identified and insufficiently supported. Targeted assessments and appropriate language comprehension interventions are needed, as well as support for reading and writing challenges. Increased awareness and collaborative efforts among educators will help to create supportive learning environments for students with DLD to achieve their full potential.

KEY TAKEAWAYS

- Students with DLD have a brain-based difficulty that requires support for understanding oral and written language, including teacher directions and peer communication.

- Over half of students with DLD have significant difficulty learning to read words and some may also have dyslexia.

- There is a need to raise awareness of DLD among educators and abroad. It is a learning disability affecting 7–10 percent of population or 1–2 students per classroom.

- Educators and families can support students with DLD by working to identify them and address challenges with evidence-based based instruction and support.

ADHD ATTENTION DEFICIT/ HYPERACTIVITY DISORDER

The first day of Kindergarten *was a joyful milestone. Our daughter, Kate, couldn't wait to join her big brother at school. Sadly, that joy was short-lived. Her teacher called home later that day; Kate was sobbing, begging to go home. From then on, everything about school was a struggle. Kate needed constant encouragement to stay engaged and finish assignments, and homework was exhausting.*

We decided to have her tested and were shocked by a diagnosis of ADHD. Aren't kids with ADHD hyperactive and defiant? Kate is sweet and eager to please. We quickly found there is more to ADHD than the rambunctious stereotype.

As we learned more about ADHD, we helped Kate learn how to steer her "race car brain." She's in high school now and still uses the imagery of an empty tank and worn-out brakes at the end of a long day. Kate is very bright, but without proper support, she becomes overwhelmed. When she was young, we advocated for extra time, quiet workspaces, checklists, and patience. Kate now advocates for those things herself. Coping with ADHD is challenging, but we both know she can meet it with the right tools. ⭐

AUTHOR **Carolyn A. Denton**
Educational Consultant
Port Townsend, WA, USA

> " Although students with ADHD can be in any of the colored areas of the infographic, many will need support to learn to read. "

Learning to read and write can be especially difficult for students with attention deficit/hyperactivity disorder (ADHD). Attentional challenges are represented in the blue arrow on *The Ladder of Reading & Writing* infographic as one of the "within-student factors." Although students with ADHD can be in any of the colored areas of the infographic, many will need support to learn to read—and even those who learn to read without support are likely to require support for writing due to their unique challenges. This chapter provides an overview of the research related to ADHD and learning to read and write, along with suggestions for teaching strategies that may make instruction more effective for these students.

WHAT IS ADHD?

The terminology used to describe ADHD can be confusing. Currently, clinicians use the term ADHD to describe the condition with three subtypes. Depending on symptoms, a student may be identified as having ADHD-primarily inattentive type, ADHD-primarily hyperactive/impulsive type, or ADHD-combined type (displaying both inattentive and hyperactive/impulsive symptoms). The inattentive and combined types are the most common, and they are the conditions most often associated with difficulties in reading and writing.

It is important that educators, parents, and caregivers understand ADHD is a real, neurologically based condition. Russell Barkley, a widely acknowledged expert in ADHD, describes it as "a developmental disorder of self-control" (Barkley, 2020, p. 19). Barkley describes the evidence as "unquestionable" that ADHD is related to either a delay in brain development or differences in brain functioning. These differences are generally the result of genetic influences, although it is possible for ADHD to result from injuries during pregnancy, birth, or early childhood. ADHD is not caused by bad parenting, although there are evidence-based parenting practices that can improve symptoms and functioning of children with ADHD.

Subtypes of ADHD

- ADHD-primarily inattentive

- ADHD-primarily hyperactive/impulsive

- ADHD-combined

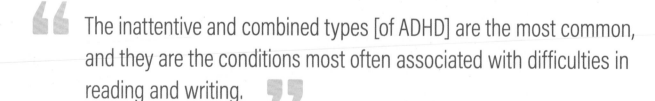

" The inattentive and combined types [of ADHD] are the most common, and they are the conditions most often associated with difficulties in reading and writing. "

SYMPTOMS OF ADHD

People with ADHD struggle with self-control. Most people are aware of the difficulties students with ADHD may have controlling their attention and/or their physical activity, but the characteristics go beyond inattention and hyperactivity. People with ADHD have significant differences in the size and function of brain areas that affect inhibition, planning, problem-solving, and self-regulation. As a result, students with ADHD may particularly struggle with self-monitoring, recalling and applying reading strategies, and following instructions and rules. They may be unable to sustain attention, especially when tasks are uninteresting to them. These difficulties directly result from neurological differences.

 It is estimated that from 50 percent to 80 percent of students with ADHD have clinically significant learning difficulties and/or low achievement.

The symptoms of ADHD typically result in both academic and social difficulties. Because of their impairments, it is harder for students with ADHD to engage in many social and academic processes than it is for other students. It is estimated that from 50 percent to 80 percent of students with ADHD have clinically significant learning difficulties and/or low achievement (DuPaul & Stoner, 2014). As a result of their academic struggles, students with ADHD are more likely to be retained in a grade and to drop out of school. Like other students with academic difficulties, those with ADHD may struggle with word reading, reading fluency, reading comprehension, and/or writing. Many students with ADHD begin Kindergarten performing significantly below average in early literacy skills.

Decoding and Text Reading Fluency

As students with ADHD progress through the grades, they may struggle with decoding unknown words and with applying strategies for breaking multisyllabic words into smaller, pronounceable word parts. Students with ADHD are also frequently impaired in text reading fluency. The struggle that students with ADHD have with reading text as fluently as other students may be result of poor decoding skills or it may be more directly a result of their neurological disorder specifically: Poor self-monitoring skills, challenges with recalling information which makes reading slower, and struggles with sustaining attention to a specific task.

 Reading for understanding requires sustained and flexible attention. Students with ADHD tend to have difficulties controlling their thoughts and attention, making these processes very challenging.

Comprehension

Reading comprehension places large demands on the kinds of processes that are particularly difficult for students with ADHD. Reading for understanding requires sustained and flexible attention. Students with ADHD tend to have difficulties controlling their thoughts and attention, making these processes very challenging. When the text does not make sense, proficient readers apply strategies to repair their understanding; students with ADHD may struggle with planning and strategic thinking, so they may not reread or apply strategies to interpret the text. As students progress through the grades, they are expected to read longer texts independently, requiring sustained attention that is often impaired in students with ADHD.

ADHD and reading or writing disabilities affect different regions of the brain, but they frequently co-occur. About 25 percent to 30 percent of students with ADHD also have serious reading disabilities, including dyslexia (DuPaul & Stoner, 2014). Students with both ADHD and reading disabilities face more severe reading challenges than those with reading disabilities alone, and they have more severe attention difficulties than students who have only ADHD.

Writing

About 55 percent of students with ADHD are also diagnosed with dysgraphia, which further exacerbates the difficulty of certain academic tasks (Mayes et al., 2019). Like reading, writing is a cognitively demanding and highly complex process that may prove problematic for students with ADHD. The demands of attention, focus, and self-regulation that these students face makes writing an enormous challenge, whether at the letter formation, word, sentence, or text levels. They may write slowly, use an uncomfortable or dysfunctional grip, or have difficulty with spacing letters accurately on the paper. One study found that 92 percent of students with ADHD had difficulties with handwriting (Mayes et al., 2019). Even those students with ADHD who are advanced readers, in the dark green areas of the colored continuum on *The Ladder of Reading & Writing* infographic, may require support to develop their writing skills.

Learn More!

Barkley, R. (2018). *Managing ADHD in school: The best evidence-based methods for teachers.* PESI.

Barkley, R. A. (2020). *Taking charge of ADHD: The complete, authoritative guide for parents* (4th ed). Guilford Press.

ADHD: Making a difference for children and youth in the schools. (Winter 2015). *Perspectives on Language and Literacy, 41*(1). https://app.box.com/s/xozzhvom3273gi57qutv0db22gcoc6wq

ADHD ATTENTION DEFICIT/HYPERACTIVITY DISORDER

ADDRESSING ADHD CHALLENGES

ADHD is not curable but appropriate interventions may improve individual functioning and decrease symptoms, though the effects may not endure if the treatments are stopped. The goals of ADHD interventions are to support students' ability to function successfully academically and help with their social-emotional regulation. There are two evidence-based approaches to the treatment of students with ADHD—medication and behavioral interventions. The American Academy of Child and Adolescent Psychiatry (Pliszka, 2007) recommends combining these approaches.

Medication Intervention

There is much controversy surrounding ADHD medications, despite strong evidence of the effectiveness of appropriately prescribed and monitored medications to reduce ADHD symptoms and improve functioning in persons who have a confirmed diagnosis. A discussion of the benefits and risks of medication treatments for ADHD is beyond the scope of this chapter, but I recommend the book *Taking Charge of ADHD* by Russell Barkley (2020) for an excellent discussion of this topic, written for parents/caregivers and educators. Barkley also includes a list of common myths regarding ADHD medications and provides questions caregivers should ask doctors when considering ADHD medications for their children.

 Since ADHD symptoms are typically most apparent in school settings, regular communication between home and school is critical.

When medications are prescribed, it is important that their effects are carefully monitored by physicians, parents and caregivers, and teachers. Observations of their children in various settings by parents and caregivers is especially important to determine whether the medications appear to benefit the children and to identify any unwanted side effects. Since ADHD symptoms are typically most apparent in school settings, regular communication between home and school is critical to determine whether a child's classroom functioning is improving with the medication and to discuss any observed, problematic side effects. Doctors can adjust the dosage of medications, try different types of medications, or, in some cases, remove medications completely, based on information from home and school.

Behavioral Interventions

Behavioral interventions are purposeful changes, approaches, or strategies implemented to improve students' behavioral and academic outcomes. Multiple, evidence-based interventions have been devised.

Effective Behavioral Interventions

- modifications to the classroom environment, such as increasing structure and actively teaching expectations for classroom routines

- modifications to instructional approaches and academic tasks, such as teaching in small groups and increasing hands-on activities

- clearly delineated consequences for both appropriate and inappropriate behaviors

- home-school communication and collaboration

- teaching self-management strategies such as breaking tasks into smaller steps and using checklists to monitor progress

- allowing movement when appropriate (e.g., squeezing a rubber ball, incorporating movements into academic responses), providing frequent exercise breaks, and ensuring students have access to recess

The most effective behavioral interventions have clear goals individually tailored to students' needs to address problematic behaviors and increase behaviors that support academic and social progress, such as organizational skills, work completion, and positive social interactions. The effects of interventions must be monitored closely, and the interventions should be changed if they do not result in positive effects on a student's ability to function in the classroom.

More Info!

For more information about ADHD interventions, see *Taking Charge of ADHD* by Russell Barkley (2020).

Reading Interventions

The impact of reading interventions depends on the nature of students' difficulties. Some students with ADHD have the required knowledge and skills to read adequately but are unable to use (and demonstrate) what they know because of problems with sustained attention and self-regulation. Other students with ADHD have additional, more serious reading difficulties and disabilities that require systematic and ongoing reading intervention. Simply improving students' ADHD symptoms will not likely increase their reading proficiency, especially if the students are performing at substantially below-grade-level expectations.

Appropriate interventions for students with ADHD should follow the same guidelines for effective, data-informed instruction outlined in Chapters 3 and 4. If a diagnostic skills assessment indicates that the student is struggling with decoding single syllable words for example, lessons should be systematically designed to address this skill deficit and explicit instruction provided, with sufficient repetition and high levels of interaction and engagement. Support for the student's specific challenges with attention and recall should be incorporated into those lessons. See the next section for specific instructional adaptations for students with ADHD.

There is some evidence that treatment with ADHD medications can positively impact *word reading* performance of students with ADHD and reading difficulties, although this may not be true for students with severe reading difficulties (Tamm et al., 2017). Denton et al. (2020) found positive effects of ADHD medications on *reading comprehension* in students with ADHD and serious reading difficulties, but further research is needed. Findings have been mixed regarding the effects of ADHD medications on reading fluency in students with ADHD.

Check Your Understanding

Match each intervention to the correct description.

a. Medication intervention

b. Behavioral intervention

c. Reading intervention

___ will vary according to the nature of a student's difficulties.

___ must be monitored for effectiveness and side effects.

___ includes environmental modifications and teaching strategies for self-regulation.

INSTRUCTIONAL ADAPTATIONS

The principles of effective instruction discussed in Chapter 3 generally apply for students with ADHD, including those with additional reading and/or writing difficulties or disabilities. There are also instructional adaptations that teachers can make to promote the success of these students. Like other students with learning difficulties, students with ADHD who have co-occurring literacy challenges benefit from intervention that is systematic, explicit, and differentiated based on their individual needs. The suggestions on the following page apply specifically to students with ADHD.

> " Like other students with learning difficulties, students with ADHD who have co-occurring literacy challenges benefit from intervention that is systematic, explicit, and differentiated based on their individual needs. "

Instructional Adaptations for Students with ADHD

- Provide intervention in small groups. The smaller the group, the better the teacher can monitor students' responses, correct their errors, and prompt students to actively attend and participate.

- Seat the student with ADHD close to the teacher. Consider arranging the seating in the small group so that the teacher and the student with ADHD can be seated side-by-side.

- Teach all students in the group the behavioral expectations and routines. Have no more than four simple rules and illustrate them on a poster or anchor chart. (See example below.) Refer to the poster when a rule is not followed and provide positive reinforcement when a rule is followed. Remind students of the rules at the beginning of each lesson.

- Keep the instruction energetic and the pacing brisk. Prepare for each lesson and organize the materials beforehand.

- Include a variety of instructional activities to promote active engagement and frequent response. Many reading programs include oral responses. Supplement this format with written responses on individual whiteboards or manipulation of letter tiles or magnetic letters.

- Give clear directions for one activity at a time. Have students repeat the directions. Avoid multistep directions. Use familiar routines rather than new directions for every activity.

- Reduce "teacher talk" in intervention lessons. This helps students pay attention and provides more time for students to respond.

- Avoid "round robin" reading where students "follow along" while other students read. Students with ADHD will likely find this difficult or impossible. Instead, divide the group into pairs and have partners take turns reading while the teacher monitors, then discuss the text after reading.

- Avoid having students with writing challenges engage in peer editing, which can be frustrating for both students and humiliating for the student who is struggling.

- When teaching reading or writing strategies, avoid introducing too many strategies at once. Students with ADHD benefit from using only a few strategies, carefully selected to focus students' attention on important components of the text and support their need to self-monitor for repairing errors and misunderstandings.

- Consider using peer tutoring routines and computer activities to provide independent practice on skills students have already learned.

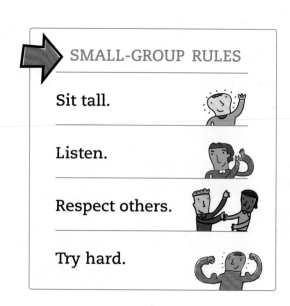

SMALL-GROUP RULES

Sit tall.

Listen.

Respect others.

Try hard.

Conclusion

ADHD is a neurologically based condition that results in differences in brain functioning. Students with ADHD have difficulties regulating their emotions, thoughts, and actions. This makes it more challenging for many of these students to complete tasks, learn skills, and master academic content than for students without ADHD.

It is important that educators and families provide appropriate intervention for students with ADHD as early as possible. ADHD intervention may be particularly critical during the early elementary school years since students who do not learn to read and write adequately during this time are likely to have difficulties throughout their school careers. Students with both ADHD and reading and/ or writing difficulties likely need both literacy interventions and behavioral interventions. Many also benefit from well-monitored ADHD medications. It is important that educators and caregivers understand the basic principles of intervention for students with ADHD, so they can act to prevent serious social-emotional and academic consequences.

KEY TAKEAWAYS

- Learning to read can be challenging for many students with ADHD, and writing is a challenge for most.

- Many students with ADHD have co-occurring reading disabilities that require instruction that is systematically designed to be comprehensive, analytical, explicit, and differentiated to address individual needs.

- For many students with ADHD, mastering writing is particularly difficult; even advanced readers who have ADHD may need support in writing.

- Along with strategies to support the learning of students with ADHD, well-monitored medication may be beneficial.

More Info!

For more information on instructional adaptations for students with ADHD, see *Managing ADHD in School* by Russell Barkley (2018).

ID INTELLECTUAL DISABILITY

Maci is an outgoing six-year-old, *always eager to be a part of the group. When Maci was a baby and toddler, her parents noticed delays in her development such as learning how to walk and difficulty communicating. When she turned three, Maci continued to struggle with communication skills and her ability to read social cues with other kids. After addressing their concerns with their pediatrician, Maci was formally assessed. Results on the IQ test indicated her intellectual functioning was low (I.Q. 59); she also scored low on an adaptive behavior assessment. Maci was identified as having an intellectual disability.*

After her diagnosis, Maci began receiving early intervention services in preschool and was served through an IEP in elementary school. Since beginning Kindergarten, Maci has enjoyed small-group reading instruction, particularly during read-alouds. Maci is also receiving instruction on letter-sounds and beginning decoding.

AUTHORS

Jennifer Stewart

Postdoctoral Research Fellow
University of Virginia, School of
Education & Human Development
Charlottesville, VA, USA

Carlin Conner

Senior Research Scientist
University of Virginia, School of
Education & Human Development
Charlottesville, VA, USA

Stephanie Al Otaiba

Professor and Patsy Ray Caldwell
Centennial Chair
Southern Methodist University
Dallas, TX, USA

> **[There are] strategies for students with ID that teachers can use with any systematic literacy program.**

Maci requires frequent redirection and positive reinforcement to stay focused during instruction. Her teacher demonstrated strategies being used at school to Maci's parents, so their reading practice at home aligns with what the school is doing. ⭐

This chapter provides an overview of evidence-based practices for literacy instruction intended to meet the needs of students with intellectual disability (ID). We describe strategies for students with ID that teachers can use with any systematic literacy program. Our intent is to provide teachers with useful information to support students with ID across a range of settings, from special education to full inclusion that still provides multitiered systems of support for students who require intensive intervention.

ID INTELLECTUAL DISABILITY

IMPACT ON READING AND WRITING

ID is a developmental disability characterized by significant limitations across three criteria (Schalock et al., 2021): (a) an IQ test (typically with a score of 70 or below), (b) an adaptive behavior assessment of conceptual skills (e.g., language and literacy), social skills, and practical skills (e.g., daily living, schedule, and routines), and (c) originates during the developmental period (with onset before the age of 22).

> ### Criteria for ID Diagnosis
>
> - IQ test score of 70 or below
>
> - Adaptive behavior assessment of conceptual, social, and practical skills
>
> - Originates during developmental period (onset before age 22)

Literacy Expectations

Roughly four out of five students with ID do not meet minimal levels of literacy (Katims, 2001). Students with ID will generally be in the red area of the continuum in *The Ladder of Reading & Writing* infographic.

 Roughly four out of five students with ID do not meet minimal levels of literacy.

While research on effective literacy instruction, including both decoding and language comprehension instruction, for students with ID has been historically limited, there is growing evidence to support the benefit of providing explicit instruction for this population (Ahlgrim-Delzell et al., 2016; Allor et al., 2014; Conner et al., 2022; Lemons et al., 2017). If appropriate instruction is provided, "children and adolescents with ID can obtain higher levels of reading achievement than previously anticipated" (Lemons et al., 2016, p. 19).

Instructional Goals

According to Browder et al. (2009), literacy instruction for students with ID should be based on two goals: accessing text and enabling as much independence as possible. The attainment of those goals may take much more time for students with ID than for other students, but even what seems a small step to a typical reader can positively impact the life of a student with ID.

> Literacy Goals for Students with ID
>
> • Support access to text.
>
> • Foster independence.

INSTRUCTIONAL NEEDS OF STUDENTS WITH ID

Students with ID may demonstrate both strengths and difficulties in reading tasks such as word recognition, comprehension, phonemic awareness, and vocabulary. Due to their unique patterns of strengths and areas of challenge, including memory deficits and additional language and behavioral support needs, students with ID often have difficulty accessing general reading instruction. Teacher knowledge of what to teach and how to teach is essential for students with ID to make progress (Lemons et al., 2016).

" Teacher knowledge of what to teach and how to teach is essential for students with ID to make progress. "

Teacher Awareness

Reading instruction for students with ID has shifted over the past twenty years from an exclusive focus on sight word, high-frequency, and irregular word recognition to more comprehensive, multicomponent instruction that includes decoding words and developing language comprehension skills (Afacan et al., 2019; Allor et al., 2022; Browder, 2008). Teachers may not be aware that students with ID can progress beyond simply memorizing high-frequency words if they are provided with appropriate explicit instruction and more time to master decoding and spelling skills as compared to their peers without disability (Joseph & Konrad, 2009; Lemons et al., 2015; Lemons et al., 2017). While there have been developments in systematically designed programming intended for students with more intensive needs, these curricula are not always available to teachers.

Oral Language

Many reading curricula are written with the assumption that students accessing them have developed proficient oral language abilities. Expressive oral language, such as producing initial phonemes, can be difficult for students with developmental disabilities, particularly those who have intensive communication needs or use augmentative communication device(s) to interact with their environment. Adjusting reading and writing instruction to integrate each student's method of communication, verbal or nonverbal, is essential for their participation. Students with ID can develop oral language skills with explicit and systematic instruction, just as they can develop decoding skills.

Visual Schedules

In addition to communication supports, behavioral supports, such as visual schedules, may be beneficial to support learning sequences within reading and writing tasks and to facilitate transitions between activities during instruction (such as between a decoding task to reading a decodable book or writing a sentence).

Learn More!

Lemons, C. J., Allor, J. H., Al Otaiba, S., & LeJeune, L. M. (2016). 10 research-based tips for enhancing literacy instruction for students with intellectual disability. *Teaching Exceptional Children, 49*(1), 18–30.

Foorman, B., Coyne, M., Denton, C., Dimino, J., Hayes, L., Justice, L., Lewis, W., & Wagner, R. (2016). *Foundational skills to support reading for understanding in kindergarten through 3rd grade: Educator's practice guide* (NCEE 2006–4008). https://ies.ed.gov/ncee/wwc/PracticeGuide/21.

Kosanovich, M., & Foorman, B. (2016). *Professional learning communities facilitator's guide for the What Works Clearinghouse practice guide: Foundational skills to support reading for understanding in kindergarten through 3rd grade* (REL 2016–227). https://ies.ed.gov/ncee/rel/regions/southeast/pdf/REL_2016227.pdf.

TEACHING STUDENTS WITH ID

The instructional requirements of students with ID align with the needs of other students in the red area of the continuum in the Ladder infographic, but they often require additional intensity to acquire foundational reading and writing skills. Appropriate instruction will include small sequential steps that progress from simple to more complex, and include more explicit modeling, more frequent exposure, ongoing cumulative review and practice (connecting prior knowledge and prerequisite skills), and immediate corrective feedback (Gadd et al., 2021; Lemons et al., 2017; Lemons et al., 2015).

Characteristics of Appropriate Instruction

When provided with appropriate, systematic, and intensive instruction that includes prompting and feedback, frequent opportunities to respond, modeling and guided practice, and opportunities to generalize information to familiar settings, students with ID can develop literacy skills, including writing and the ability to decode words (Browder et al., 2009; Conner et al., 2022; Joseph & Konrad, 2009).

> There is evidence that high-quality reading and writing instruction and intervention for students with exceptionalities, including dyslexia, is also effective when delivered to students with ID.

There is evidence that high-quality reading and writing instruction and intervention for students with exceptionalities, including dyslexia, is also effective when delivered to students with ID (Allor et al., 2009, 2018; Browder et al., 2008, 2009; Gadd et al., 2021). Progress monitoring is key to making adaptations that address individualized needs during instruction. By utilizing a comprehensive approach that emphasizes phonemic awareness, phonics, fluency, vocabulary, and comprehension, students may experience immediate literacy benefits, such as learning to read their names, as well as long-term benefits, such as being able to decode words and comprehend text, all of which increase their opportunities for independence (Browder et al., 2006; Lemons et al., 2016).

Appropriate Instruction for Students with ID will:

- focus on small, sequential steps

- progress from simple concepts to more complex

- include more explicit modeling, exposure, and cumulative review

- provide opportunities for frequent response and immediate corrective feedback

- emphasize phonemic awareness, phonics, fluency, vocabulary, and comprehension

Teacher Modeling and Feedback

Students with ID require more code-based, explicit, and intensive instruction than their peers without ID. Lesson delivery should include teacher modeling (my turn/your turn) to show or demonstrate each task as necessary, providing immediate corrective feedback and assessment of understanding.

Student/teacher interaction during corrective feedback, including praise, is important. The instruction provided in the following example demonstrates how this might be done.

Teacher: *Let's look at this word together.* **(points to the word)** *I can sound out this word.* **(slowly points to letters)** */mmm/ /a/aa/ /p/,* **map***, this word is* **map***. Now you try!*

Maci: */mmm/ /aaa/ /p/* **map***.*

Teacher: *Good job sounding out* **map***! Now, you try the next one.*

Maci: (Interrupting) **Map. Map. Map. Maps are cool**.

Teacher: *OK Maci, we'll read and sound out the word one time. Try again.*

Maci: */mmm/ /aaa/ /p/,* **map***.*

Teacher: *Thank you, Maci. Great job.*

The student follows along and sounds out the word without interrupting.

Teacher: **(Turns to Maci)** *Thank you for following along without interrupting. That was great reading and listening!* **(Teacher marks a check on Maci's reward tracker)** *Good, let's do another. Ready? You try. Points to* **milk***.*

Maci: (Turns to teacher, starts to look upset) */m/ /m/ /mom/.*

Teacher: *Let's try again. I will read the sounds first. Ready? Listen to me. /mmm/ /i/ /lll/ /k/,* **milk***. Now, let's try it together. Ready?*

Maci: (Takes a deep breath) OK. Ready.

Teacher: *Let's say the sounds together.*

(Teacher points to the first letter to indicate that it is time to read together.)

Teacher and Maci: */mmm/ /i/ /lll/ /k/,* **milk***.*

Teacher: *Good! We read the word together. Now, you try. Read the sounds and say the word.*

Maci: */mmm/ /i/ /lll/ /k/,* **milk***.*

Teacher: *Great job! You read the word* **milk***.*

(**Note:** This interactive process could be extended to include spelling of each word.)

Strategies to Focus Attention

While providing explicit instruction to students with ID, teachers might consider the need for additional adaptations, including strategies to help a student focus. Examples of appropriate adaptations include:

- touching next to the item to focus attention

- supplementing instruction with a visual cue (e.g., visual schedule for each stage of the instructional routine, graphic organizer, story map)

- providing sufficient think time (i.e., 5–7 seconds between cue and signal)

- immediate presentation of the next practice item after reinforcement

Students with ID benefit from separating tasks into sequential steps with explicit modeling and corrective feedback for each step. This also helps teachers match the instructional pacing of content delivery to each student's needs, which supports student attention and success. Visual demonstrations as well as kinesthetic, hands-on experiences with immediate feedback are beneficial.

ADDITIONAL SUPPORTS

Most core literacy programs will need to be adapted meet the instructional needs of students with ID. Although programs have been developed specifically for students with ID, special education teachers can use a general core literacy curriculum as the foundation for instruction with adaptations to meet the instructional needs of these students.

> " Adaptations for students with ID should be based on data that identify students' current reading strengths and needs. "

Data-Informed Adaptations

Adaptations for students with ID should be based on data that identify students' current reading strengths and needs. Formal and informal progress monitoring should happen frequently. Results are used to guide individualization and to assess whether students have mastered sub-component skills for decoding and spelling, identifying the main idea within comprehension, and written expression. Lemons et al. (2014) provide guidance for data-based individualization (DBI) that maintains focus on foundational reading skills, including phonemic awareness, phonics, spelling, fluency, vocabulary, comprehension, and written expression. For students with more intensive learning needs, including those with ID, weekly progress monitoring is important to determine skill mastery and support instructional planning for next steps.

More Info!

See Chapter 4 for more information about collecting and using data.

Planning considerations include:

- measurable, meaningful goals for instruction that connect previously learned skills to next steps

- built-in opportunities to transfer across skills (e.g., decoding and spelling) and genres (e.g., decodable books to content area texts in social studies or science)

- incorporating a student's interests into reading instruction to activate background knowledge and support engagement

- systematic cumulative review and practice

- frequent opportunities to generalize skills across content areas and learning environments

Supporting Student Access to Text

Providing access to a variety of texts and different access points to printed text is important to build literacy skills within this population. From adapting text to using technology supports, these accommodations increase opportunities for students with ID to access printed work. Browder and colleagues (2009) outlined some additional ways to increase access to text for students with ID: (a) adapted books, (b) time for literacy, (c) opportunities to share text with others, and (d) the use of technology.

> " Adapted books help to make age-appropriate reading material accessible to students with ID and those that support them. "

Adapted books, simply put, are any book that has been modified in the text and/or the format to fit the needs of an individual student. Adapted books help to make age-appropriate reading material accessible to students with ID and those that support them. One of the benefits of adapted books is the ability for them to be designed to best fit the instructional needs of a specific student. This may be done by adjusting the difficulty of the text (e.g., using an abridged version of the text, limiting the number of words on the page, adjusting the size of the text) or the format of the text (e.g., adding pictures to support engagement, increase vocabulary or reading comprehension, and/or connect to students' background knowledge).

Check Your Understanding

Check all that apply. Students with ID:

___ require code-based, explicit, and intensive instruction

___ can develop foundational or basic literacy skills with appropriate instruction

___ benefit from strategies to focus attention and exposure to varied text types

___ should have measurable literacy skill goals on an individualized education plan (IEP)

Additionally, adaptive texts are designed to be reproducible to share with other teachers, related service providers, parents, and caregivers. Additional instruction may be needed to support students' initial use of adapted text, but that is time well spent as this form of print individualizes access and motivation. The use of technology (e.g., audiobooks, text readers) is another way to provide immediate engagement with literature when students with ID are still developing the skills necessary to access age-appropriate reading material.

> " Additional instruction may be needed to support students' initial use of adapted text, but that is time well spent. "

More Info!

For more information about using technology, see Chapter 19.

Conclusion

Students with ID are typically represented within the 10–15 percent of students in the red area of the continuum on *The Ladder of Reading and Writing* infographic. When considering comprehensive instructional practices and interventions for these students, teachers need to be aware that these students may require intensive support with increased cumulative review and practice. Certain modifications and accommodations have been found to support reading development for students with ID, including immediate corrective feedback, positive behavior reinforcement, and increased deliberate practice, guided by frequent formal and informal progress monitoring to guide ongoing individualization of instruction.

KEY TAKEAWAYS

- Students with ID require more code-based, systematic, explicit, and intensive instruction than their peers without ID.

- Both formal and informal assessment data can be used to identify students' current strengths and instructional needs to plan and monitor next steps.

- Appropriate instruction for students with ID is systematic with small sequential steps that progress from simple to more complex, with frequent practice, response opportunities, and immediate corrective feedback.

- Research indicates that when provided with appropriate instruction, students with ID may attain greater levels of reading and writing skill mastery.

D/HH DEAF OR HARD OF HEARING

Alana was born *with a moderate bilateral sensorineural hearing loss. She wears hearing aids. In addition to Alana's hearing loss, she has been diagnosed with ADHD, dyslexia, and other language-based learning differences. She is currently enrolled in third grade at a school for students with dyslexia and other language-based learning disabilities. These students are served by a team of specialists in small, self-contained classes.*

Alana's teaching team utilizes remote microphone technology in her classroom as they understand the importance of Alana hearing all sounds of speech and how crucial this is for developing her deep reading brain. Alana loves to read, swim, roller skate, and play softball. She's a bright light to everyone she meets and has a winsome smile. ⭐

Literacy is the destination for all children who are deaf/hard of hearing (d/hh). Whether the language of the family is a spoken language (e.g., English, Spanish, Mandarin) or a signed language (e.g., American Sign Language, British Sign Language, Nigerian Sign Language) or a combination of the two, language is the means to literacy. The depth and breadth of the language(s) in which a child is engaged are key.

AUTHOR **Erica W. Jones**

Program Director/Teacher
Atlanta Speech School
Atlanta, GA, USA

> " Early access to a full and complete language prepares students who are d/hh for learning to read and write alongside their peers with hearing. "

It is the habits of the adults that surround a child that lead the child to develop language commensurate with their hearing peers. Early access to a full and complete language prepares students who are d/hh for learning to read and write alongside their peers with hearing.

Much like a student who is not d/hh, the variability of needs among students who are d/hh is vast. A student who is d/hh may also have an autism-spectrum diagnosis, learning disability, or be formally identified as gifted. Where these students will be on the continuum of *The Ladder of Reading & Writing* infographic will vary, but when specific, early efforts by caregivers become habits, combined with the efforts of informed educators, the sky is the limit for students who are d/hh.

RESOURCES FOR FAMILIES

In 1999, a universal newborn hearing screening program was established in the United States. This program ensures that all children are screened for hearing loss prior to discharge from the hospital where they were born (AAP, 1999). However, proactive support of language acquisition can begin well before a baby is born.

> " Proactive support of language acquisition can begin well before a baby is born. "

More recent initiatives include *Talk With Me Baby* (Rollins Center, n.d.) underway at Grady Memorial Hospital in Atlanta, Georgia, to help parents learn about the importance of language from before a baby is born throughout childhood. *Talk With Me Baby* focuses on training maternal and infant health staff how to coach new and expectant parents on the importance of talking with their child. Every expecting parent learns about *Language Nutrition*, or the importance of regular, rich interactions to foster language development (Zauche, 2016). This program teaches that words are as crucial to a baby's brain as food is to their body. Parents learn the extreme power of language and are emboldened to talk with their baby from as early as the third trimester, based on scientific evidence that indicates babies hear in utero (Ilari, 2002). Not only is this exposure to language important, but the depth and breadth of the language to which a child is exposed are paramount (McCreery & Walker, 2022).

> " Words are as crucial to a baby's brain as food is to their body. "

More Info!

For more information on the *Talk With Me Baby* program at Grady Memorial Hospital, visit https://learn.coxcampus.org/courses/talk-with-babies-make-a-difference/.

When these two programs, *Talk With Me Baby* and universal newborn hearing screening, are utilized in conjunction, they encourage parents to take action. When parents realize the importance of language and then learn through a hearing screening that their baby does not have access (complete or partial) to their powerful, loving words due to a hearing loss, they are motivated to seek solutions, urgently.

> " When parents realize the importance of language… they are motivated to seek solutions, urgently. "

Learn More!

Zauche, L. H., et al. (2017) The power of language nutrition for children's brain development, health, and future academic achievement. *Journal of Pediatric Health Care, 31*(4), 493–503.

Rollins Center for Language & Literacy at The Atlanta Speech School. (2023). *Talk With Me Baby: TWMB @ Birthing Centers.* Cox Campus. https://learn.coxcampus. org/courses/talk-with-babies-make-a-difference/.

Scora, K., & Smith, D. (2021). The benefit and the "And" for considerations of language modality for deaf and hard-of-hearing children. *Perspectives of the ASHA Special Interest Groups, 6*, 397–401.

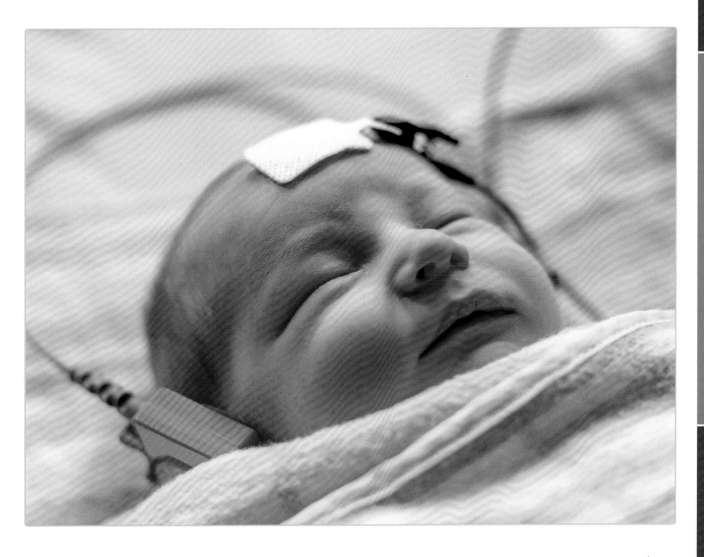

D/HH DEAF OR HARD OF HEARING

RESPONDING TO HEARING LOSS

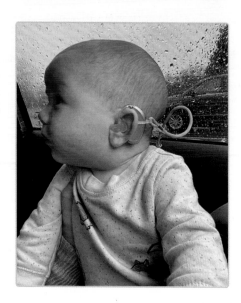

Over 90 percent of children born with hearing loss are born to hearing parents (Vaccari, 2006). Parents who understand the importance of Language Nutrition are more prepared to act decisively if their newborn baby is found to have hearing loss. Children who enter the world with hearing loss have already missed opportunities to hear their parents' loving communication during the third trimester of pregnancy. With each succeeding day, the newborn child without access to spoken words is missing additional language opportunities.

Therefore, within their child's first few days of life, the parents of these newborns are faced with a decision: to embrace hearing technology (e.g., hearing aid(s) and/or cochlear implant(s)) or immediately adopt a visual language, like American Sign Language (ASL). Some may choose to do both. Not one of these choices is wrong, but a choice must be made—and made quickly.

 Over 90 percent of children born with hearing loss are born to hearing parents.

Assistive Hearing Technology

Many parents who are hearing choose hearing technology that is specifically designed to support a child in the development of listening and spoken language. They want to maximize every opportunity for their child to hear as they do. Hearing aids and cochlear implants do not "fix" deafness in the same way that glasses or contact lenses can often correct vision. Hearing technology makes sounds, including the sounds of speech, more available to the child. However, the result is not crystal-clear hearing in all surroundings; noise and distance may create omissions and distortions. Remote microphone technology, where the parent or other individual speaking wears a microphone that sends their spoken signal directly to the hearing technology, can be beneficial in these settings.

Visual Language

About 10 percent of children who are born with hearing loss are born to parents who are deaf/hard of hearing (Vaccari, 2006). Some of these parents may choose the route of a shared visual language, like ASL. Although ASL is a full and complete language, the provision of literacy instruction for children for whom a visual language is the primary mode of communication entails specific features and methods and is beyond the scope of this chapter.

> " Parents who are d/hh may choose the route of a shared visual language. "

LANGUAGE RICH EXPERIENCES

Supporting language development, which is essential for all students to learn to read and write, begins with parents and caregivers who make it a habit to converse with their child. This is especially true for children who are d/hh. Talking *with* rather than *to* a child allows for a great number of conversational turns between adult and child. The number of conversational turns is as critical as the number of words, phrases, and sentences to which the child is exposed (Zauche, 2017).

> ### Language Development Habits
>
> - Engage in lots of conversations.
>
> - Make all speech sounds accessible all waking hours.
>
> - Support listening by adjusting the environment whenever possible.
>
> - Utilize remote microphone technology.
>
> - Expose children to lots and lots of experiences.

Another critical habit for parents, caregivers, and educators to establish is guaranteeing that each child has access to language. Whether the family desires for the child to use a spoken language or a visual language, the child must engage fully with that language. For a family seeking a spoken language outcome, the child must be fitted with well-programmed hearing technology. That technology must be in working order and worn every waking moment of the day ("Eyes open, hearing technology on!" is the mantra!) to ensure access to the language-rich environment created by the important adults in their lives (McCreery & Walker, 2022).

 Supporting language development, which is essential for all students to learn to read and write, begins with parents and caregivers who make it a habit to converse with their child.

Maximizing Language Growth

An acoustically-sound environment (making every effort to decrease background noise and increase access to the speaker's voice) is essential for a child whose family is looking to technology to maximize access to their spoken language. Life is noisy and individuals with hearing loss put forth great effort to pick out the intended message (e.g., dishwasher running, multiple people talking, TV on, traveling on an airplane, playing at daycare). In these instances, remote microphone technology can make the speaker's voice more audible than the background noise. Remote microphone technology is an invaluable tool for listening, spoken language, and literacy outcomes (Schafer et al., 2020).

Children build knowledge of their world through language-rich experiences, including books and complex conversations. Without these experiences, reading and writing will pose a challenge. Children who are d/hh can participate in the same experiences as their peers with hearing (e.g., visiting an ice cream parlor, going to the library, fishing with Grandpa), but they don't have full access to the language that surrounds the experience without adult intentionality. For example, while visiting a zoo a child who is d/hh can benefit from having an adult who ensures that the child is wearing their functioning, properly programmed, hearing technology—and finding a zookeeper willing to wear the remote microphone as they share fascinating facts about ape play—is hugely valuable.

Check Your Understanding

Match each intervention to the correct description.

a. Early detection of hearing loss

b. Language nutrition

c. Remote microphone technology

d. Conversing *with* rather than *to*

___ reduces the negative interference of distance and noise when worn appropriately.

___ allows for critical conversational turns between the adult and d/hh child.

___ recognizes that words are as crucial to a baby's brain as food is to their body.

___ is supported by a 1999 federal initiative to promote universal infant screening.

D/HH DEAF OR HARD OF HEARING

CLASSROOM SUPPORT

Students who are d/hh come to the classroom with an extensive background of experiences constructed by the cumulative auditory/ visual experiences they have gained through the use of personal hearing technology and/or their exposure to a visual language. Ideally, adults have set the stage with great habits (see Language Rich Experiences). This prepares students who are d/hh for the same reading and writing instruction as their peers with hearing. Some students who are d/hh may initially need extra emphasis on phonological awareness or phonemic awareness depending on the auditory experiences of the child, but the other components of instruction will be taught based on need as appropriate for all students climbing the Ladder. (See Chapter 3).

It is important that the classroom environment in which a student who is d/hh is taught offers the same "ecosystem" as that which has been offered outside the classroom—that is, complete access to robust and bountiful language. Students who are d/hh are reliant on educators to ensure that they can access the voices of teachers and peers. This involves physical modifications to the classroom including carpeted floors, curtains on windows, closed classroom doors and windows, background music off, and acoustic paneling.

 It is important that the classroom environment in which a student who is d/hh is taught offers the same "ecosystem" as that which has been offered outside the classroom—that is, complete access to robust and bountiful language.

Continued exposure to a clear speech signal is ensured when a teacher uses remote microphone technology, enabling their spoken signals to go directly to the hearing technology of the student who is d/hh which avoids the negative effects of distance and noise. Using microphone technology will make a vital difference to the student who is d/hh. Educators should be aware that if a student wears hearing technology, the technology must be in working order and worn every moment of the school day.

Interventions for Students Without Early Support

The importance of early exposure to robust language experiences has been discussed. Unfortunately, there are families who, for one reason or another, remain unaware or lack the support they need. Perhaps …

- The infant did not pass their newborn hearing screening, but families were not informed of the importance of early access to language, nor advised to see an audiologist who could evaluate, diagnose, treat, and monitor the hearing loss. A child in this scenario will often be enrolled in speech/language therapy at three years old because they aren't using words or have unintelligible articulation.

- The child was diagnosed with hearing loss (whether mild, moderate, severe, or profound), but families were not advised of the benefits of hearing technology or its appropriate use. Because the child did not have access through hearing technology some speech sounds did not reach the brain with fidelity and are therefore not known or used by the child.

- The child's family was not professionally advised about the importance of Language Nutrition. As a result, parents and caregivers use single signs or words rather than full sentences (signed or spoken) with the child.

These limitations of language over time incur devastating results that require intensive intervention and sometimes candid conversations with families that include:

- Preparing the family/caregivers to build new language habits at home: The length of time the child was without complete access to full language will not be made up in the classroom alone. New Language Nutrition habits must be formed at home.

- Encouraging the family to enroll in Auditory-Verbal Therapy: This therapy focuses on building caregivers' skills to maximize the language input a child hears through their day and promote acquisition of spoken language.

Educators should anticipate that the lack of early access to a full and complete language may affect some students' ability and/or readiness to map sounds onto letters. Expanded support will be beneficial, including preteaching key vocabulary and concepts before students participate in whole-group or small-group conversations.

More Info!

For more information to locate a Certified Auditory-Verbal Therapist, visit https://www.agbell.org/Families/Find-a-Professional-Near-You.

Conclusion

A child who is d/hh is set up for success when their family provides immediate and complete access to language early and often. Teachers can build on this foundation by continuing an atmosphere of fully accessible language. Some students who are d/hh may initially need extra emphasis on phonological awareness or phonemic awareness depending on the auditory experiences of the child, but the other components of instruction will be taught based on need as appropriate for all students climbing the Ladder. With key components in place, a student who is d/hh can achieve everything their hearing peers can achieve and more.

KEY TAKEAWAYS

- Every child needs to hear (and/or see) a full and complete language. Language Nutrition is a term used to emphasize that spoken language is as crucial to a baby's brain as food is to the body.

- The early experiences of a child who is d/hh impact how quickly and easily they climb the Ladder to master reading and writing.

- If a child wears hearing technology, the technology must be in working order and worn all waking hours of the day. Remote microphone technology can reduce the negative effects of distance and noise in environments that are not acoustically sound.

- Support students who are d/hh by ensuring full access to language in the classroom environment. Some students may initially need extra emphasis on phonological awareness or phonemic awareness depending on the auditory experiences of the child, but the other components of instruction will be taught based on need as for all students climbing the Ladder.

AIR ADVANCED IN READING

It was my first year of teaching. *The need to build foundational skills in Kindergarten had been drilled into me during my university courses. I had my lessons all prepared. My students were going to know their letters! They were going to learn the sound-symbol correspondences. I had decodable books that aligned to my sequence of phonics instruction.*

And then five-year old Roshni walked into my classroom, with a thick book in her hand. Roshni was not only reading books that many eight-year-olds would find difficult, but her vocabulary astounded me. She radiated an eagerness to learn!

I was totally unprepared to teach a student who was already reading at five. My preservice courses had not once touched on the literacy needs of advanced students. As I sought out professional development to support Roshni and students like her, I was so grateful that my principal encouraged my learning journey. Together, we worked to bring the research about the learning needs of advanced readers to the rest of the team at our school. ⭐

AUTHOR Nancy Young
Educational Consultant
Creator of *The Ladder of Reading & Writing*
Nanoose Bay, British Columbia, Canada

> **Students who are advanced in reading (AIR) require programming appropriate for their learning needs or their progress may be delayed.**

Represented in the dark green area of *The Ladder of Reading & Writing* continuum are students with advanced literacy skills. These students require programming appropriate for their learning needs or their progress may be delayed. This chapter presents ways to support students who demonstrate advanced reading abilities in the early grades, recognizing that their literacy programming and materials must be differentiated to provide continued growth and challenge.

The information and recommendations in this chapter combine research from two areas, research related to learning to read and research on the learning needs of academically advanced (gifted) students.

IDENTIFYING STUDENTS WHO ARE ADVANCED IN READING

On day one of Kindergarten, some students are already able to read. Some of these students may be reading two, three, or even more years ahead of what is typical for their age (Gross, 1999; Henderson et al., 1993; Papadopoulos et al., 2020). However young they are, whether two or four years ahead, and by whatever means they have mastered skills before formal schooling, their literacy programming should reflect their advanced skills and support their continued growth. Unfortunately, appropriate programming is rarely provided for students whose reading skills are advanced as compared to what is typical for their age (Reis & Fogarty, 2020; VanTassel-Baska, 2023).

While recognizing that a variety of factors can impact reading skills in the early years of school, the term "advanced in reading" (AIR) is used throughout this chapter.

The descriptor "AIR" in this chapter *primarily* applies to:

- students who begin school already reading having learned implicitly without formal instruction, and who demonstrate advanced abilities well ahead of what is age typical (Papadopoulos et al., 2020)

The descriptor "AIR" in this chapter *may* also apply to:

- students who demonstrate strengths in literacy once in a school setting, despite limited early exposure to literacy (Peters, 2022)

- students who begin school reading, having been taught to read by a parent/caregiver or in an academically focused preschool program (Shanahan, 2015)

Using various methods, including teacher and caregiver observations, some students who are AIR will have been formally identified as gifted before or during Kindergarten (National Association for Gifted Children, 2008). Others may be formally identified as gifted in the years ahead. Some students who are AIR may demonstrate reading abilities ahead of what is typical, yet formal identification as gifted will not be pursued. Students who are AIR may be from any background or culture (Flowers, 2016; Davis & Douglas, 2021). All students who are AIR, whether identified as gifted or not, require programming based on their current skills and individual needs beginning in Kindergarten and throughout their school years (Dixson et al., 2020; Peters, 2022).

> **All students who are AIR, whether identified as gifted or not, require programming based on their current skills and individual needs.**

There is a scarcity of research under the "science of reading" umbrella on young children who demonstrate advanced reading abilities despite having received no formal instruction (Papadopoulos et al., 2020). Given that most studies on the academic needs of students who demonstrate advanced reading abilities have been carried out by those studying giftedness, this chapter will bridge between these two fields of research. Writing will be specifically addressed later in the chapter.

GENERAL PROGRAMMING FOR ACADEMICALLY ADVANCED STUDENTS

To support AIR students, it is first necessary to dispel the myth that advanced learners will "do fine on their own" (Assouline et al., 2015; National Association for Gifted Children, n.d.). Research suggests certain programming essentials are critical for advanced learners to continue to progress in their acquisition of skills and knowledge.

Advanced academics programming essentials include:

- instruction based on skill mastery, not age or grade

- adjustments in pacing to allow for rapid skill mastery

- recognition of the role of implicit learning and intrinsic motivation to learn

- in-depth study of complex topics and issues requiring critical thinking and problem-solving

- guided inquiry learning, enabling choice and considering interests where possible

- brief instruction of skills and strategies, provided only as needed

- grouping with peers of similar ability as well as time to work independently

- daily challenges with higher-level of rigor than typical

(Hockett & Doubet, 2020; Rimm et al., 2018; Rogers, 2007; VanTassel-Baska, 2023)

On *The Ladder of Reading & Writing* infographic, two general programming approaches for students who are AIR are listed to the right of the dark green area of the continuum: 1) Extended learning and 2) Acceleration.

Extended Learning

For students who are academically advanced, programming designed for extended learning increases and extends learning in deeper and broader ways than typical. Programming for extended learning is systematically developed and based on frameworks that are progressively more difficult. This enables the development of higher-level thinking and critical analysis while students are engaged in increasingly enriching and complex tasks (Hughes et al., 2014; Reis & Boeve, 2009; Renzulli et al., 2020; VanTassel-Baska, 2023).

Providing students with appropriate extended learning requires grouping of students with similarly advanced students. Such grouping may occur within a class or grade, but cross-grade grouping (enabling programming based on skill not age) is an especially effective way to support learners with advanced abilities (Kulik & Kulik, 1992; Peters, 2022; Rogers, 2007). Extended learning also provides students the opportunity to work independently, including self-directed study (Rogers, 2007).

 Cross-grade grouping . . . is an especially effective way to support learners with advanced abilities.

Academic Acceleration

Academic acceleration recognizes a student's ability to receive instruction or move forward at a faster pace than is typical for their age (Steenbergen-Hu et al., 2016).

Academic acceleration options:

- **Early entrance**—beginning Kindergarten prior to five years of age

- **Grade skipping**—by-passing one or more grades

- **Subject-specific acceleration**—enabling students to participate in lessons with older students

- **Compacting the curriculum**—eliminating what the student already knows and teaching new content at a faster pace

(Colangelo et al., 2004; Peters, 2022)

 Weighing the pros and cons of academic acceleration should always be done on an individual basis.

Although weighing the pros and cons of academic acceleration should always be done on an individual basis, decades of research has revealed the many benefits (Assouline et al., 2015). Peters (2022) describes academic acceleration as being "the most effective intervention in the advanced learning toolbox" (p. 164). For most students, the benefits of acceleration far outweigh the possible need for social-emotional adjustment that may concern adults (Colangelo et al., 2004).

Regardless of the method to support advanced needs (extended learning or acceleration, or both), differentiated programming within these approaches requires ongoing monitoring to ensure that it is sufficiently advanced and provides challenge (Dixson et al., 2020; VanTassel-Baska, 2023).

Further, for students who are economically disadvantaged, potential challenges such as lack of access to text or technology should be factored into program development (Cross et al., 2018; VanTassel-Baska, 2018; VanTassel-Baska et al., 2002). In the next sections, programming for advanced students in the context of reading and writing is addressed.

Learn More!

Thomas B. Fordham Institute. (2023). *Building a wider, more diverse pipeline of advanced learners: Final report of the national working group on advanced education.* https://fordhaminstitute.org/national/research/building-wider-more-diverse-pipeline-advanced-learners.

Plucker, J. &, Callahan, C. (Eds.) (2020). *Critical Issues and practices in gifted education: A survey of current research on giftedness and talent development.* Prufrock Press.

Acceleration Institute at the Belin-Blank Center. https://accelerationinstitute.org/.

PROGRAMMING FOR STUDENTS ADVANCED IN READING

Reading skills advance primarily by reading practice (Hoover & Tunmer, 2020). As such, students who are AIR need to keep reading! Unnecessary instruction for students who are AIR is likely to delay learning and may result in student frustration and boredom (Brighton et al., 2015; Reis & Fogarty, 2020). The following sections address some components underlying the systematic design of literacy programming for students who are AIR.

Data Measurement Tools

Literacy programming should always be informed by data, but what does that mean for students in the early grades who are already advanced in reading? For students who are AIR, the focus should be determining how best to support their continued climb up the Ladder and ensuring they are not spending time on unnecessary skill instruction (Hoover & Tunmer, 2020; Peters, 2022).

> Unnecessary instruction for students who are AIR is likely to delay learning and may result in student frustration and boredom.

Given that screeners and progress monitoring tools used in the early grades are primarily designed to identify and support students with reading challenges, widely used tools may be inappropriate to determine the needs of students already reading. For example, educators should be aware that the need to test the phonemic awareness skills of students who are AIR has not been validated by research. Assessing these students' phonemic awareness may generate inaccurate results that lead educators to inhibit progress by providing instruction that is unnecessary (see Scarborough et al., 1998).

Considerations When Assessing and Planning Programming for Students with AIR

- Decoding/encoding assessments should be used judiciously, taking into account that these students' ability to learn implicitly may result in atypical skill development sequences (see Treiman, 2017).

- Recognize that CBM assessments for spelling and writing may suggest less-developed skills (due to asynchronous development). However, this is not a reason to hold students back from an advanced reading program (Rimm et al., 2018).

- Standardized achievement tests (such as the Woodcock-Johnson®) enable above-level testing, which makes them appropriate choices for assessing the skills of students who are AIR.

- Integration of findings from giftedness testing, when available, may help to determine above grade-level skills. However, identification of giftedness should not be required to provide advanced programming for students who are AIR (see Peters, 2022).

- Informal assessment for students in the early grades who have not yet received formal testing to determine reading ability may include: listening to students read aloud and asking questions to evaluate comprehension, reviewing student portfolios or products (VanTassel-Baska, 2023), and interviewing families about their child's early development and current abilities.

Instruction for Reading

Students who are AIR must be permitted, and encouraged, to read (Reis & Fogarty, 2020) since reading practice advances reading skill (Hoover & Tunmer, 2020). The provision of instruction intended to strengthen specific skills must consider academically advanced students' need for intellectual challenge. Without engaging ways to extend their learning and higher-level thinking, students who are AIR may become bored and unmotivated (Rimm et al., 2018).

Keep in mind that what may be considered high-quality literacy instruction for students still learning to read is likely inappropriate for students who are AIR. For example, while systematic, explicit phonics instruction is critical for many students, phonics instruction may delay progress for students who are AIR (Brighton et al., 2015; Connor, 2014; Connor et al., 2004; Connor et al., 2014).

> ### Appropriate programming and reading materials for students who are AIR will:
>
> - align to their advanced abilities, and not restrict students to simpler texts (e.g., controlled or "decodable" texts) typically used for beginning readers (Gross, 1999)
>
> - not confine students to foundational reading programs or leveling systems (Brighton et al., 2015; Reis et al., 2011)
>
> - incorporate evidence-based programming frameworks and models specifically developed to provide complexity and high-level thinking while extending literacy skills (VanTassel-Baska, 2023)
>
> - systematically increase challenge to foster the development of deeper comprehension strategies and critical thinking skills using varying texts (Firmender et al., 2013; VanTassel-Baska, 2018)
>
> - include scaffolding, where appropriate, to support gradual acquisition of increasingly complex concepts and challenging tasks (Stambaugh, 2018)
>
> - make above grade-level reading materials readily available for both learning and enjoyment (Reis & Fogarty, 2020). Varied texts should accommodate students' interests and represent diverse cultures and backgrounds (Ford et al., 2019; VanTassel-Baska, 2018)

Instruction for Writing

There are many considerations when supporting the writing development of students who are AIR. As previously noted, students who are advanced in reading learn skills more implicitly. Thus, their need for intellectual challenge and higher-level thinking during skill mastery is critical. Without highly engaging ways to extend skills, academically advanced students may disengage (Rimm et al., 2018). The same is true for writing.

Transcription Skills

Transcription skills include letter formation and spelling. Students who are AIR may require little support, if any, in these areas. Others may benefit from specific instruction based on individual need. The following are essentials to consider when designing programming for students who are AIR and need support in developing transcription skills.

- **Letter Formation:** Asynchronous physical development (meaning that motor skills are not as developed as reading mastery and cognitive ability) can result in frustration and anxiety as students who are AIR master letter formation (Rimm et al., 2018). Engaging instruction and practice opportunities are key (see Chapter 8).

- **Spelling:** Frequent exposure to words and their patterns while reading enables many students who are AIR to develop spelling skills more implicitly (Pacton et al., 2013; Pacton et al., 2014; Treiman & Kessler, 2006). Spelling instruction deemed necessary for students who are AIR should carefully balance benefits with time spent on instruction and practice, considering learner motivation and intellectual engagement. For example, the study of morphological relationships between words can be an intriguing way for students who are AIR to strengthen spelling skills (Pacton et al., 2013; VanTassel-Baska, 2003). Spelling programming can also include learning through engaging games (Harris et al., 2017).

Check Your Understanding

Check all that apply. Students who are AIR:

___ should receive instruction based on reading skill, not age or grade

___ may begin Kindergarten reading at a level expected of an eight-year-old (or older)

___ require programming that reflects advanced abilities

___ may demonstrate handwriting skills that lag behind advanced cognitive abilities due to asynchronous development

Generation Skills

It is rare for students who are AIR to begin Kindergarten with writing skills that far surpass the norm (Noel & Edmunds, 2006). As such, some aspects of writing support for students who are AIR will be similar to that of other students climbing the Ladder. Examples include focusing on ideas rather than transcription skills during the drafting stage, teaching/modeling the revision process as needed, and providing feedback at all stages. Targeting generation skills for students who are AIR also requires certain program essentials.

- **Cognitive Engagement:** Writing support for students who are AIR needs to take into account their advanced cognitive abilities. This entails considering their need for intellectual engagement and ongoing opportunities for creative expression, as well as encouraging the inclusion of advanced concepts, such as metaphor, in their writing (Bass, 2020; Spanke & Paul, 2015).

- **Personalization:** Programming should allow for a nonlinear writing process and enable collaborative opportunities with a community of peers similarly advanced in language skills. Assignments should consider student interests, allow for critical thinking, and include opportunities to write for authentic audiences (Bass, 2020).

- **Organization:** Due to the perfectionism that is characteristic of many gifted children (Szymanski, 2020), some advanced students need boundaries around when to stop revising. Providing due dates for completion of stages during the writing process may help with this (Bass, 2020; Olthouse, 2012).

Advanced programming for reading and writing should support students' continued development of syntactical skills as delineated in established standards (i.e., parts of speech). However, skill development may be addressed at a much younger age (Hughes et al., 2014). Educators are encouraged to refer to the Pre–K to Grade 12 Gifted Education Programming Standards (National Association for Gifted Children, 2019).

Conclusion

The dark green area of the continuum on *The Ladder of Reading & Writing* infographic represents students who are advanced in reading (AIR), some of whom may be reading two or more years ahead. These students require differentiated programming and related materials enabling them to continue developing their literacy skills. Instruction should be delivered at a pace and in ways appropriate for their advanced abilities. Programming considerations include acceleration and extended learning. Cross-grade grouping is an effective way to provide appropriate instruction and support for students who are AIR. Educators should receive preservice education and ongoing professional learning that prepares them to teach all students, including students whose literacy skills are ahead of what would be expected for their age.

KEY TAKEAWAYS

- Students who are AIR (advanced in reading) require programming designed for their advanced abilities.

- When gathering data to inform programming for students who are AIR, use tools and methods appropriate for identifying above-level abilities, including family input.

- Instruction that fosters critical thinking and analysis, including texts aligned to advanced reading abilities, is paramount for students who are AIR.

- Ensure that students who are AIR have opportunities to read for enjoyment.

PART III

EXPLORING ADDITIONAL CONSIDERATIONS

OLDER STUDENTS

LISA was a new student *in my 7th grade science class who struggled with reading. When she attempted to read the lesson texts, Lisa often stumbled on multisyllabic words such as "atmosphere," "respiration," or "environmental." She didn't seem to have any strategy for breaking down longer words and quickly became frustrated. Of course, this affected her ability to comprehend what she was reading and her motivation. I overheard her saying, "These books are too hard. I hate science." I knew Lisa had just begun working with the school's reading specialist two days per week, so I reached out to see if he had any suggestions. He shared with me some strategies he'd taught Lisa during her intervention time.*

AUTHORS

Christy R. Austin

Assistant Professor
University of Utah
Salt Lake City, UT, USA

Elizabeth A. Stevens

Assistant Professor
The University of Kansas
Lawrence, KS, USA

Sharon Vaughn

Endowed Chair, The University of Texas
Executive Director, Meadows Center
for Preventing Educational Risk
Austin, TX, USA

I began using these strategies with Lisa during her small-group instruction. Not only did they seem to help her, but her fellow group members adopted them as well. I was soon using the strategy of identifying meaningful word parts as I introduced new science terms in all my classes. ⭐

In this chapter, we present a brief overview of the primary reasons why older students sometimes struggle in their climb up the Ladder. We describe how increasing text complexity impacts students who struggle with word reading. Many teachers in Grade 4 and up may be aware that some students struggle to read complex text but they don't know how to help these students. Therefore, we recommend instructional strategies that consider both the age of these students and the subject areas covered in the upper grades. We recognize older students may need ongoing support and advocate for instruction that focuses on both decoding and language comprehension.

OLDER STUDENTS WHO REQUIRE LITERACY SUPPORT

There can be a variety of reasons older students struggle to read and write, including severe (or inadequately addressed) dyslexia and/or dysgraphia, ADHD, developmental language disorder (DLD), specific reading comprehension disability (SRCD), etc. (An overview of these exceptionalities and ways teachers can offer support is provided in other chapters of this book.) Yet not all older students struggle due to an exceptionality. Some older students may be what has been described as "instructional casualties" (Fletcher et al., 2013, p. 47). In other words, it is possible that appropriate instruction or data-informed intervention during their formative years could have prevented the struggles they are now experiencing in upper grades.

 A significant number of older students who find reading and writing to be challenging have a combination of needs, and the impact of these needs has compounded over time.

Widely Varying Needs

The needs of older students vary widely, so interventions should be differentiated based on students' identified needs. Some may need a focus on handwriting and/or text composition skills. Others may need support in developing their receptive and expressive language skills. Some may need specific comprehension strategies. Many older students have learned to decode text with reasonable accuracy, but they lack sufficient fluency to support comprehension. Teachers may be surprised to realize some students require support at the very basic levels of learning the alphabetic principle (connecting sounds with letters and decoding simple words).

A significant number of older students who find reading and writing to be challenging have a combination of needs, and the impact of these needs has compounded over time. Sadly, the difficulty in mastering literacy skills often negatively affects these students' social and emotional well-being (Morgan et al., 2012; McArthur et al., 2022). Along with interventions specifically designed to successfully address their identified reading and writing concerns, many students can also benefit from the support of a counselor or therapist.

Clearly, planning appropriate intervention for older students is complex, and many teachers may not know where to start. Should the intervention focus on fluency? Should it focus on comprehension? If students are going to learn to read fluently and with comprehension, as well as demonstrate their knowledge in writing, they need to be able to read words accurately. By the upper grades, many of the words that students will encounter across subject areas are multisyllabic. For these students, teaching basic strategies about how to handle these longer words can be a first step on the road to success with reading and writing and a huge factor in building confidence.

Increased Text Complexity

As students transition from primary to upper elementary and secondary grades, the texts they are expected to read become increasingly complex (Toste et al., 2019; Vaughn, Roberts et al., 2019; Wanzek & Roberts, 2012). Early elementary texts typically contain a large percentage of single syllable words, such as *cat* and *house*, and simple, two-syllable words, such as *rabbit* and *swinging*. Texts in the upper elementary and secondary grades contain a larger number of complex, multisyllabic words, such as *archeology*, *photosynthesis*, or *atmosphere*. These multisyllabic words often convey important meanings in complex texts (Vaughn, Roberts et al., 2019). Therefore, accurate and efficient decoding of multisyllabic words is essential to support both accessing and understanding complex texts (Vaughn, Martinez et al., 2019; Vaughn, Roberts et al., 2019).

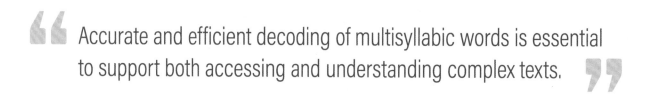

"Accurate and efficient decoding of multisyllabic words is essential to support both accessing and understanding complex texts."

Students with reading difficulties, compared to those who read on-grade-level, make different types of errors when reading multisyllabic words. Some students may successfully decode the initial sounds or syllable of a word but guess the rest of the word rather than decoding the entire word. For example, they might mistakenly read the word *transpiration* as *transportation*. In addition, many students have a difficult time determining the correct vowel pronunciation in multisyllabic words. For example, a student might encounter a long word without having the knowledge needed to determine the correct pronunciation of the vowels and might choose to skip the word due to feeling overwhelmed.

The English language is opaque and complex. Sounds are represented by more than one spelling (e.g., the **long a** sound can be written **a** as in *halo*, **a_e** as in *crate*, **ai** as in *rain*, **ay** as in *stay*, **eigh** as in *sleigh*, **ei** as in *vein*) and a given spelling may be pronounced in different ways (e.g., **ough** in *through, though, thought*). To determine the correct pronunciation, students often need to be flexible and try more than one sound when decoding. In addition, to recognize the correct pronunciation when they hear it, the word must be a part of the student's oral vocabulary (e.g., correctly pronouncing *epitome* is facilitated through knowing the meaning of the word; determining the correct vowel pronunciation for **ea** in *endeavor* would be impossible if the word was not a part of a student's oral vocabulary).

Students must be taught flexible approaches for decoding unfamiliar and challenging multisyllabic words (Vaughn, Martinez et al., 2019) and benefit from knowing the meaning of the complex, academic words they will encounter (Seidenberg, 2005; 2017). By successfully decoding multisyllabic words, students will read complex texts more accurately and efficiently, which will in turn support comprehension.

TEACHING STRATEGIES FOR READING COMPLEX WORDS

There are many instructional approaches for decoding multisyllabic words. We describe a flexible approach for breaking apart an unfamiliar word that requires students to acquire proficiency in a manageable number of rules. Working memory is often taxed when students are presented with a large number of rules and must first recall the rule before applying the rule to read an unfamiliar word. Even when approaches that use many rules support students in decoding a multisyllabic word accurately, they often do not facilitate sufficient reading fluency or efficiency for comprehension (LaBerge & Samuels, 1974).

> ## Instructional Recommendations for Accessing Multisyllabic Words
>
> **RECOMMENDATION #1** Teach students to identify affixes (prefixes and suffixes) to break apart a larger word into smaller, meaningful units to support decoding.
>
> **RECOMMENDATION #2** Teach students to identify the vowels in a word to break a larger word into syllables to support decoding.
>
> **RECOMMENDATION #3** Ensure that students know the meaning of complex, multisyllabic words, as semantic (word meaning) knowledge supports decoding and facilitates accurate and efficient word reading.

Let's explore each recommendation in greater detail.

Recommendation #1
Break Words into Meaningful Parts Using Affixes

Affixes are word parts that change the meaning of the words they are attached to; affixes include prefixes and suffixes. There are several steps to explicitly teach students to recognize affixes and use them to break multisyllabic words into smaller parts.

Step 1: Teach Prefixes and Suffixes

Make sure students know the terms *prefix* and *suffix*. A prefix appears at the beginning of a word and affects the meaning of the root word to which it is attached. For example, in the word *unsanitary*, the prefix **un-** means "not," so *unsanitary* means "not sanitary." A suffix appears at the end of a word and affects the meaning of the root word to which it is attached. For example, in the word *evaporation*, the suffix **-tion** means "a state of being." Therefore, the word *evaporation* means "the state of liquid evaporating." Before teaching the steps in the strategy, explicitly teach students the pronunciation and meaning of several target prefixes and/or suffixes (see examples in the chart on the following page).

"Before teaching the steps in the strategy, explicitly teach students the pronunciation and meaning of several target prefixes and/or suffixes."

Common Prefixes and Suffixes with Meanings

Prefix	Meaning of Prefix	Suffix	Meaning of Suffix
un-	not	-s, -es	plural
re-	again	-ed	past tense
in-, im-, il-, ir-	not	-ing	act of
dis-	not	-ly	having qualities of
en-, em-	to make or put into	-er, -or	person who
non-	not	-ion, -tion, -ation, -ition	state, quality of being
over-	too much	-able, -ible	capable of being
mis-	wrong	-al, -ial	related to
sub-	below	-y	characterized by
pre-	before	-ness	state of being
inter-	between	-ity, -ty	quality of
fore-	toward	-ment	condition of
de-	down	-ic	of, related to
trans-	across, changed	-ous	full of
super-	above, beyond	-en	made of
semi-	half	-er	comparative
anti-	against	-ive, -ative, -itive	having the nature of
mid-	middle	-ful	full of
under-	not enough	-less	without

Step 2: Teach the Strategy

Explain to students that identifying prefixes and suffixes can help them break multisyllabic words into smaller parts to support word reading. Make sure there is a list of steps students can follow each time they encounter a multisyllabic word with a prefix and/or suffix.

SAMPLE: Reading Complex Words Using Affixes

Step 1: Circle prefixes and suffixes in the word.

Step 2: Underline the remaining vowel sounds in the root word.

Step 3: Read the word part by part.

Step 4: Blend each part together and read the whole word fast.

*Watch me follow the steps with this word—**disappearing**.*

1. *First, I will circle the prefixes and suffixes in the word. I see the prefix **dis-** at the beginning of the word, and the suffix **-ing** at the end of the word.*

2. *Next, I will underline the remaining vowel sounds in the root word. I see the vowel **a** and the vowel pair **ea** in the root word.*

dis app<u>ea</u>r ing

3. *Next, I read the word part by part: **dis–a–pear–ing**.*

4. *The fourth step is to blend each part together and read the whole word fast: **disappearing**.*

Step 3: Model Application

Model following the steps to break apart a complex, multisyllabic word using prefixes and suffixes. Repeat the same procedure to provide students with guided practice decoding 2–3 additional words that follow the same pattern.

Step 4: Provide Practice with Feedback

Provide students with an opportunity to practice reading words independently with a partner, still following the steps posted in the classroom. Observe students' application of the steps to break apart words using prefixes and suffixes and offer feedback as needed.

Recommendation #2
Break Words into Syllables Using Vowels

You may also teach students to break apart multisyllabic words by separating the syllables using vowels. There are several steps to explicitly teach students this strategy to facilitate decoding.

Step 1: Review Common Vowel Sounds

To begin, ensure that students can identify the common vowel sounds that appear in words. Common vowel sounds include:

(a) single vowels that can make long vowel sounds (*native, protection*) and short vowel sounds (*canyon, navigate*);

(b) vowel-consonant-e, where the **e** makes the previous vowel sound long (*capsize, reptile*);

(c) vowel combinations—also referred to as vowel teams or within-word vowel patterns, where vowels work together to make one vowel sound (*steadfast, remains, approachable*);

(d) vowel diphthongs, where a sound begins as one vowel and moves toward another sound (*astounding, howling, joyful*); and

(e) r-controlled vowels, where the letter **r** follows a vowel and changes the vowel sound (*disturb, particle*)
(Vaughn et al., 2022).

Step 2: Teach the Strategy

Explain that students can use their knowledge of vowels to break long words into syllables, or smaller parts, that help them sound out words more easily. Make sure there is a list of steps students can follow to break apart any multisyllabic word into syllables using vowels.

Model how to follow the steps to break apart a complex, multisyllabic word using vowel sounds. Repeat the same procedure to provide students with guided practice decoding 2–3 additional words.

SAMPLE: Reading Complex Words Using Vowels

Step 1: Underline the vowel sounds in the word.

Step 2: Count the vowel sounds to identify how many syllables are in the word.

Step 3: Break the word into parts, making sure every part has a vowel sound.

Step 4: Blend each part together and read the word fast.

*Watch me follow the steps with this word—**momentum**.*

1. *First, I will underline the vowel sounds in the word. I see the vowels **o**, **e**, and **u**.*

<u>mo</u>m<u>e</u>nt<u>u</u>m

2. *Next, I will count the vowel sounds to identify the number of syllables. 1, 2, 3. This word has 3 syllables.*

3. *The third step is to break the word into parts, making sure each part has a vowel sound. I will use slash marks to break the work into parts, then check and make sure I have a vowel in each part.*

m<u>o</u>/m<u>e</u>n/t<u>u</u>m

4. *The fourth step is to blend each part together and read the whole word fast: **momentum**.*

Step 3: Provide Practice Opportunities

Provide students with an opportunity to practice reading words independently with a partner, following the steps posted in the classroom. Observe student practice and offer feedback as needed.

Recommendation #3
Integrate Word Meaning Instruction

Intervention research has shown that semantic knowledge (i.e., knowing the meaning of words) supports word reading (Austin et al., 2022; Nation & Snowling, 1998). For example, to read a word such as *pleasant*, a reader must determine the correct pronunciation for the vowel combination *ea* to accurately decode the word. It would be impossible to determine the correct pronunciation if this word was not part of the reader's oral vocabulary.

Evidence also suggests that despite having similar spellings and sounds, poor readers would be more likely to accurately and efficiently decode the word *hilarious* compared to the word *nefarious*, as the meaning of the word *hilarious* is more widely known. Finally, we know that some words have multiple meanings, and pronunciation varies based on the meaning of the word (e.g., the *wind* blew v. the *wind*-up toy); when students encounter a word with multiple possible meanings, reading fluency slows because they must determine the correct meaning before decoding the word.

Despite our understanding that semantic knowledge impacts word reading accuracy and fluency, instruction often targets word reading and word meaning as separate and distinct skills.

Despite our understanding that semantic knowledge impacts word reading accuracy and fluency, instruction often targets word reading and word meaning as separate and distinct skills. Many reading intervention programs focused on foundational reading skills provide extensive practice decoding words out of context; this fails to help students develop the semantic knowledge necessary for skilled reading and comprehension (Compton et al., 2014). We recommend ensuring that students know the meaning of the words they will be expected to read independently. One method for doing this is integrating word-meaning instruction within word-reading instruction.

Selecting Appropriate Words

For students with word-level reading difficulties and disabilities, we recommend using multisyllabic words that students will encounter in their content-area classes. For example, a science teacher might notice that the words *evaporation*, *condensation*, *transpiration*, *accumulation*, and *precipitation* all include the suffix **-tion** and are vocabulary words in an upcoming science unit about the water cycle. For this reason, an intervention teacher might use these words rather than selecting random multisyllabic words as the focus of instruction.

After appropriate words have been selected, it is important to match the most efficient step-by-step procedure for decoding the multisyllabic words—either focusing on prefixes and suffixes or vowel sounds to break words into syllables. Using the water cycle vocabulary listed above, a teacher would likely guide students to use prefixes and suffixes to break the multisyllabic words into smaller parts, since each word includes the suffix **-tion**.

After complex multisyllabic words are mastered, teachers can provide explicit vocabulary instruction before asking students to read a complex academic text independently. Explicit vocabulary instruction and multiple opportunities to process the meaning of each word during listening, speaking, reading, and writing activities will support effective independent word reading (Austin et al., 2022; Beck et al., 2013).

Check Your Understanding

Check all that apply.

Older students who have struggled to learn to read:

___ should focus only on fluency

___ may require both instruction and counseling support

___ benefit from learning strategies that apply to multisyllabic words

___ don't necessarily have a reading disability; they may not have been taught effective strategies

Learn More!

Austin et al. (2022). The relative effects of instruction linking word reading and word meaning compared to word reading instruction alone on the accuracy, fluency, and word meaning knowledge of 4th–5th grade students with dyslexia. *Scientific Studies of Reading, 26*(3), 204–222.

Vaughn et al. (2022). *Providing reading interventions for students in grades 4–9: Educator's practice guide.* (WWC 2022007). What Works Clearinghouse, National Center for Education Evaluation and Regional Assistance (NCEE), Institute of Education Sciences, U.S. Department of Education. https://ies.ed.gov/ncee/wwc/PracticeGuide/29.

Vaughn, Roberts et al. (2019). Efficacy of a word- and text-based intervention for students with significant reading difficulties. *Journal of Learning Disabilities, 52*(1), 31–44.

Using an Essential Words Routine

To provide explicit word meaning instruction, teachers can use an "essential words" routine, in which they preteach the meaning of each complex, multisyllabic vocabulary word using a semantic map and an explicit instructional routine.

First, the teacher names the target vocabulary word, provides a student-friendly definition of the word, and explains how the picture on the semantic map accurately represents the meaning of the word. During this instruction, students repeat the target word and the student-friendly definition. The teacher also invites students to elaborate how the picture represents the target vocabulary word.

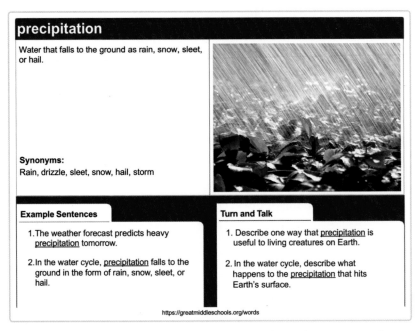

Sample Semantic Map. *Reprinted with permission from The University of Texas at Austin/The Meadows Center for Preventing Educational Risk.*

Next, the teacher presents synonyms or related words. As each synonym or related word is presented, the teacher can guide students to think about how the synonyms and related words are similar and different. Then, the teacher provides two examples of the vocabulary word used in context. The first example readily relates to the students' everyday lives. The second example relates directly to the content-area passage the students will read.

Finally, students practice using the vocabulary word in turn-and-talk prompts. During each prompt, both partners have a turn to use the word in a sentence. For students who appear to struggle, the teacher might model answering the question before students have a turn or provide students with a sentence stem to support accurate use of the word in a sentence.

Conclusion

For some older students, learning to read and write continues to be challenging even in the upper grades. Teaching these students to read and understand the meaning of complex, multisyllabic vocabulary words prepares them to tackle the complex texts they are expected to read independently. Teaching students to identify prefixes and suffixes and break a larger word into smaller, meaningful units or to identify vowel sounds and break long words into syllables supports students in decoding complex, multisyllabic words. Providing explicit vocabulary instruction targeting word meaning improves students' word reading and language comprehension. Word reading instruction in Grades 4–12 supports struggling readers to accurately and fluently read complex, multisyllabic words. Accurate and efficient reading is necessary to facilitate reading comprehension—the ultimate goal of reading.

KEY TAKEAWAYS

- Some students struggle with literacy in Grades 4 and beyond for a variety of reasons.

- Older readers need instruction specifically designed to address their identified concerns.

- Texts become increasingly complex as students progress through school and this complexity impacts students who struggle with word reading.

- Students benefit from learning specific strategies to identify and break apart multisyllabic words, which improves fluency and comprehension.

VARIATIONS OF ENGLISH

T**he first time I met Adrian,** *he was standing in the doorway of my new classroom. He was at least a foot taller than me, but it was the slouched posture and look* of defeat on his face that made the greatest impression. It was clear when Adrian spoke that he had a dense dialect. He was fifteen years old and in the eighth grade. As the newly hired middle school reading interventionist, I already knew that he had been retained twice. I was there to assess Adrian's reading skills and develop an intervention plan.

Adrian shared that he "hated reading" and was embarrassed to read in front of others. During the assessment, Adrian often dropped word endings and confused letter sounds like **/f/**, **/v/**, and **/th/**, but he demonstrated high comprehension levels when text was read to him.

AUTHORS

Kymyona Burk

Senior Policy Fellow, Early Literacy
Foundation for Excellence in Education
(ExcelinEd)
Tallahassee, FL, USA

Casey Sullivan Taylor

Policy Director, Early Literacy
Foundation for Excellence in Education
(ExcelinEd)
Tallahassee, FL, USA

After completing the assessment I asked Adrian, "What if I told you I believe you can become a better reader?" He looked up with a look of vulnerability on his face. "You think I could do that?" he asked. I replied, "I'm confident that we can do it together." This is where our journey began. ⭐

The colored continuum on *The Ladder of Reading & Writing* infographic represents the wide range of ease when learning to read and write, and the associated wording presents the instructional implications. The blue arrow on the side of the infographic draws attention to the potential impact of environmental factors on a students' climb up the Ladder, and a student's dialect is one of those factors.

The achievement gap between Caucasian students and students of color in the United States is longstanding (Children's Defense Fund, 2021). Do environmental factors such as dialect contribute to this gap? Brown et al. (2015) suggest they do and partly attribute the achievement gap to linguistic factors and curricular demands. This chapter considers the role of dialect and how this can be addressed in school settings to support the success of all students.

ENGLISH LANGUAGE FAMILY BACKGROUND

Language acquisition begins in infancy and continues throughout life. The foundations of oral language typically develop by age four and can have a substantial impact on a child's readiness for school and future academic performance. Families and caregivers are children's first teachers, and a child's dialect is heavily influenced by those with whom they spend the most time. Experiences such as being read to or engaging in conversation throughout everyday activities—asking and answering questions, narrating routines, and providing or receiving positive feedback—are activities that engage children and support language development.

Although learning to speak is a natural process for most children, learning to read is not. Literacy develops by applying spoken language knowledge to written language. Students who experience a language-rich environment in early childhood typically begin school with an advantage in oral language and vocabulary. Conversely, students with limited oral language ability are typically at a disadvantage upon Kindergarten entry (Fielding et al., 2007).

Converging evidence also indicates that students with delayed or poor language acquisition skills are likely to be poor readers and writers (Catts et al., 2006). Some students' home language is influenced by language variations that differ from school language, or Standard American English (SAE). The good news is that these students and those who enter school with limited language exposure can still become skilled readers and writers.

 Families and caregivers are children's first teachers, and a child's dialect is heavily influenced by those with whom they spend the most time.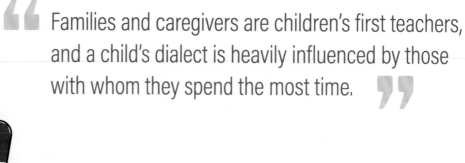

VALUING ALL CULTURES

What is Standard American English (SAE)? In Washington and Seidenberg's *Teaching Reading to African American Children* (2021), the authors caution against defining "Standard English" as a language, instead describing it as a variety of English that should not be considered "linguistically superior to other varieties." Why is this important? The world is made up of a vast number of cultures and languages. Within those languages are a variety of dialects. Chambers and Trudgill (1998) define dialect as "a variant of a language, spoken by people grouped by region, ethnicity, race, income, and other aspects."

Types of Dialects

Dialects may be described by their characteristics. For example, a regional dialect may be distinguished by geography while an ethnolect is a language unique to an ethnic group, like African American English (AAE) is to African Americans. The use of other dialects may be situational. Sociolect, or social dialect, is used in settings of the same social group, profession, or socioeconomic class, while idiolect represents an individual's language (Stoop & Bosch, 2014).

Learn More!

Washington, J. A., & Seidenberg, M. S. (2021). Teaching reading to African American children: When home and school language differ. *American Educator, 45*(2), 26–33, 40. [Key features Infographic, p. 27]

Catts, H. W., Adlof, S. M., & Weismer, S. E. (2006). Language deficits in poor comprehenders: A case for the simple view of reading. *Journal of Speech, Language, and Hearing Research, 49*(2), 278–293.

Fitton et al., (2021). Language variation in the writing of African American students: Factors predicting reading achievement. *American Journal of Speech-Language Pathology, 30*(5), 1–15.

VARIATIONS OF ENGLISH

Types of Dialects	
Type of Dialect	**Definition**
Regional Dialect	A regional variety of language distinguished by features of vocabulary, grammar, and pronunciation (*Merriam Webster*, n.d.-a)
Ethnolect	A variety of language spoken by an ethnic group (*The Concise Oxford Dictionary of Linguistics*, 2014)
Idiolect	The language or speech pattern of one individual at a particular period of life (*Merriam Webster*, n.d.-b)
Sociolect	A variety of a language that is used by a particular social group (*Merriam Webster*, n.d.-c)

One of the most studied English dialects is African American English (AAE), which has features of both ethnolect and sociolect. AAE differs from SAE in key areas such as phonology, morphology, syntax, pragmatics, and discourse (Green, 2002). According to Washington and Seidenberg (2021, p. 27), AAE is "significantly implicated in learning to read" because of its variations in spoken language through verb morphology, syntax, and phonology (see chart below).

Key Features of African American English

Verb Morphology	Description	Examples
Variable past tense	The **-ed** marker is variably attached to verb forms in past tense contexts.	*The cow jump__ over the moon.* *He fix__ the broken car.*
Variable plural	The **-s** marker is variably attached to nouns.	*She saw three cat_ in the window.* *A girl puttin' some glass__ on the table to drink.*
Variable third person -s	The **-s** marker is variably included on the verb in third-person singular contexts.	*My friend want_ to buy some candy when we get to the store.*
Variable possessive	The **-s** marker is variably included to mark possession, and possessive pronouns are variably marked.	*I rode in my uncle__ car.* *They waitin' for they car.*

Syntax	Description	Examples
Variable subject-verb agreement	Subject and verb do not agree in tense and number.	*My friends was runnin' fast to catch the bus.*
Variable inclusion of *to be* in copula (linking) and auxiliary forms.	Main and auxiliary forms of the verb *to be* are variably included.	*This _____ my red car.* *They _____ watchin' the girls jump rope.**

Phonology	Description	Examples
Consonant cluster reduction	Consonant clusters in the final position of words are reduced to one final consonant.	*col_/cold* *fiel_/field* *cas_/cast*
Dropped g	Variable inclusion of **g** in the final position of a word ending in **-ing**.	*jumpin_/jumping* *waitin_/waiting* *goin_/going*
Intervocalic and postvocalic positions for f/q, v/ð, and t/q	Following a vowel, voiceless (**q**) and voiced (**ð**) the sounds in medial and final positions of words are replaced by **/f/**, **/t/**, or **/v/**.	*wif/with* *wit/with* *bave/bathe*
Prevocalic positions for d/ð	Preceding a vowel, the voiced (**ð**) th sound in initial position of words is replaced with **/d/**.	*dis/this* *dem/them* *dat/that*
Consonant cluster movement	The **/sk/** consonant cluster is transposed, becoming **/ks/**.	*aks/ask* *ekscape/escape*

*These examples were taken from the transcripts of child speakers of African American English. Some examples include another AAE feature in addition to the feature being highlighted. In this sentence, for example, the child deletes the auxiliary form *are* and also drops the final **g**. Production of multiple AAE features in a single sentence is common. (Washington & Seidenberg, 2021).

Potential Impact of Dialect Variation

A study conducted by Brown et al. (2015) indicates that the achievement gap between African American and Caucasian students may be related to students' dialect, asserting that "children whose home and school dialects differ are at greater risk for reading difficulties because tasks such as learning to decode are more complex for them." Many practitioners and researchers believe that dialects which differ substantially in phonology or usage from SAE, or even the dialect of the teacher, can lead to interference in the educational environment. The impact may be greatest on phonological awareness, spelling correspondence, vocabulary, morphology, and syntax; however, there is little agreement among researchers across disciplines.

Dialect shifting, also known as a form of code-switching, occurs when individuals alternate between two languages or dialects based upon context and environment. Washington, Terry, and Seidenberg (2014) report that stronger metalinguistic skills including the ability to switch back and forth between SAE and AAE can be associated with better reading achievement.

> ## Check Your Understanding
>
> **Check all that apply.
> A student's dialect
> may impact:**
>
> ___ pronunciation of letter
> sounds or words
>
> ___ understanding of teacher
> directions or instruction
>
> ___ reading comprehension
>
> ___ academic achievement
>
> ___ self-esteem

 The achievement gap between African American and Caucasian students may be related to students' dialect.

Students who speak in a dialect which is substantially different from SAE can benefit from explicit and systematic instruction to compare dialect variations. It is essential to communicate and demonstrate the value and equality of all dialects. Every dialect is worthy of respect and represents the values, history, and identity of an individual, family, and community. The goal is not to change the language learned at home but to support the student's achievement in reading and writing. For example, in the southern part of the United States the words, *pin* and *pen* are often pronounced as "pin" and sound the same. In oral communication, context is critical to understanding which word meaning is intended. Explicitly examining the two words, their meaning, their pronunciation in Southern English and Standard American English, and their letter-sound correspondence will empower the learner to effectively differentiate the two words in the contexts of oral language, reading, and writing.

VARIATIONS OF ENGLISH

INSTRUCTIONAL CONSIDERATIONS

For students from a variety of backgrounds, their home language and the language used within the classroom may differ greatly. Teachers play a critical role in bridging that gap. However, teachers rarely receive the professional training needed to ensure that their literacy instruction meets students' diverse needs (Washington & Seidenberg, 2021).

As we learn more about the impact of dialect and other environmental factors on students' literacy, the following strategies may be considered as educators prepare to deliver reading and writing instruction to a diverse group of learners.

Instructional Considerations

- Communicate and maintain high expectations for all learners. It is important to believe that all students can learn.

- Demonstrate appreciation for each student's cultural and linguistic background; communicate and reflect appreciation in classroom materials and conversations.

- Differentiate literacy instruction to meet the needs of each learner. While dialect may be considered a risk factor for some, students with a different dialect may be the most advanced readers and writers in the class. Dialect is not an indicator of intelligence.

- Recognize that content mastery may vary widely depending on background and cognitive load requirements among students who need to reconcile multiple word forms and meanings between languages or dialects. Some learners may need additional time and repetition to achieve mastery.

- Engage in professional learning to enhance knowledge and skills on the impact dialects can have on reading proficiency. Explicit instruction in the differences between SAE and local dialects should be provided using an unbiased, neutral, and factual perspective that demonstrates the value of each dialect and culture.

- Utilize knowledge of SAE and dialects to interpret assessment results and refine instruction. Teachers who understand dialectical norms are better equipped to interpret assessments and adjust instruction to meet the needs of each learner.

Conclusion

Research suggests that there are predictable ways in which variation in language can affect reading, writing, and spelling, and that mismatches in spoken AAE and written SAE can slow a student's reading development (Brown et al., 2015; Terry, 2006; Washington et al., 2018). Additional research is needed to enhance and substantiate understanding of the impact dialect may have on reading and writing development. Further study would be most beneficial utilizing contemporary methods to examine each step in the acquisition of reading and writing skills and to what degree dialect, the density of dialect, and the instructional materials may impact reading and writing outcomes. Opportunities to look more closely at the development and application of code-switching may also provide deeper understanding to professionals in the fields of education, linguistics, and psychology.

The body of research around language and literacy continues to shed light on ways in which educators can intentionally address students' various needs. Now, now more than ever, there is hope for ensuring that all students receive effective support to successfully climb the Ladder, no matter where they are on the continuum of the infographic.

KEY TAKEAWAYS

- It is essential to communicate and demonstrate the value and equality of all dialects.

- Students whose home language is influenced by language variations that differ from school language can still become skilled readers and writers.

- Students who speak in a dialect which is substantially different from SAE can benefit from systematic and explicit instruction to compare dialect variations.

- Teachers who understand dialectical norms are better equipped to interpret assessments and adjust instruction to meet the needs of each learner.

MULTILINGUAL LEARNERS

I moved from Hong Kong to the U.S. *at seven years old. I already knew some English, but my pronunciation differed from my American classmates. In school, learning to spell new words* was easy since I had been trained in school in Hong Kong to memorize holistically. I was good at memorizing spellings!

*The most difficult part of lessons in the U.S. was identifying the individual letter-sounds in words. When I learned a new word, I could only identify the pronunciation of the whole word (e.g., **still**, **flask**) but not the individual speech sounds (phonemes) in a word (e.g., separating **s-t-i-ll** or **f-l-a-s-k**).*

AUTHORS

Gairan Pamei

Doctoral Student,
The Chinese University
of Hong Kong
Dept. of Psychology
Hong Kong, China

Zebedee Cheah

Doctoral Student,
The Chinese University
of Hong Kong
Dept. of Psychology
Hong Kong, China

Jing Tong Ong

Lab Manager,
Purdue University
Human Development &
Family Science
West Lafayette, IN, USA

Catherine McBride

Professor, Purdue University
Human Development &
Family Science
West Lafayette, IN, USA

*In Hong Kong, we had not been taught phonological skills such as segmenting words into letter-sounds. In addition, I had difficulty understanding where the stress should be in some words. For example, when reading, I had no idea that the stress is on the second syllable for **rehearsal** and the first for **dominate**. In English, syllable stress is never indicated in print, so you just have to know the word.* ⭐

Learning to read and write in English is standard practice in Canada, the U.S., the U.K., New Zealand, and Australia. Many students in other countries also learn to read in English, regardless of their home language, including India, Malaysia, Zambia, and the Philippines. How does a student's language background impact their English literacy learning? And what instructional supports best serve these students as they climb the Ladder to acquire fluency in English?

LEARNING TO READ AND WRITE IN ENGLISH

There are some language universals that all literate people understand, regardless of the language being taught. For example, all languages have some kind of structure that supports meaningful communication of ideas. Students learning to read in English as a second (ESL) or alternative language (EAL, third or beyond) bring their existing knowledge of how to read and write in their native language to the classroom. For example, they may learn to associate letter names with sounds in similar ways (McBride-Chang & Treiman, 2003).

First Language Influences

Teachers of multilingual learners should consider how similar or dissimilar the student's first language (L1) is to English (the second language, or L2). Does the student's native language use the same alphabetic system as English? Is the text read from right to left or left to right? Are there phonemes shared between the two languages?

It may be more difficult for non-native speakers to pick up on particular speech sounds that are not in their native language. Consonant clusters are not used in Chinese, for instance. In addition, lexical stress can differ markedly across languages. Syllable stress in French is a good example (Tremblay, 2008). In French, equal stress is placed on each syllable of a word. In contrast, in English, the stress of the syllable varies from word to word. In the word *table*, the stress is on the first syllable. In the word *report*, the stress is on the second syllable.

It may be more difficult for non-native speakers to pick up on particular speech sounds that are not in their native language.

Students may differ in their spelling accuracy or how they spell stressed versus unstressed syllables. Some studies indicate that English Learners spell more accurately than native speakers (Hong & Chen, 2011; Treiman et al., 1993), due in part to the way in which these students were taught to read and to write in their first language. For example, Wang and Geva (2003) demonstrated that Chinese students tended to be better spellers of English words than their native English-speaking peers from Canada. The explanation for this difference was that the students with Chinese backgrounds had been trained in literacy techniques involving rote memorization. Such skills were useful to them in recalling precise spellings of English words.

 Students with a nonalphabetic L1 script (e.g., Chinese) tend to rely less on their phonological skills for learning to spell and to read in English.

At the same time, these students were not as good as their native English-speaking peers at reading nonsense words. This phenomenon may be attributed to the fact that students with a nonalphabetic L1 script (e.g., Chinese) tend to rely less on their phonological skills for learning to spell and to read in English (L2).

English Alphabetic Orthography

Various features of English, in comparison to other languages and scripts, may also impact students' literacy acquisition. Across Indo-European languages, English stands out as being relatively opaque in letter-sound correspondences. For example, the phoneme /f/ could be spelled as **f** in *fan*, **ff** in *cuff*, or even **ph** as in *alphabet*. For this reason, students from diverse linguistic backgrounds might struggle with phonemic awareness in English (Lipka & Siegel, 2007).

Learning to read and write in English takes about 1–2 years longer to master than more phonologically transparent languages such as Spanish and German (McBride, 2015). Because English is a language that has evolved from various origins (including Latin, Greek and Anglo-Saxon), and integrates words from other languages (e.g., *safari* comes from Arabic), there is less consistency between the ways in which English words are sounded out and spelled as compared to other alphabetic languages. This makes learning to read and to spell in English more complex (McBride, 2015).

> **Learning to read and write in English takes about 1–2 years longer to master than more phonologically transparent languages such as Spanish and German.**

Some research suggests that learning to read and write in a more transparent alphabetic orthography first, before learning English, can be an advantage in literacy learning for English (Siegel, 2016). A student who already knows a more transparent language, such as Spanish, may be advantaged in this way. Learning to read and write in English requires attention to phonemes, letters, and letter units such as the rime **-ain** in *rain*, *pain*, and *grain*. It also requires some knowledge of stress patterns which are involved in phonological processing.

LITERACY SUPPORT FOR MULTILINGUAL LEARNERS

It would be erroneous to assume that all multilingual learners begin in the "red" or even "orange" areas of the continuum in *The Ladder of Reading & Writing* infographic. Like all students, these students' abilities vary widely based on multiple factors. However, some multilingual learners will need explicit instruction in the English sound-symbol system to become successful readers. In general, an effective program for multilingual learners will be sequenced in a way that starts with the most consistent English phoneme-grapheme relationships and builds toward less consistent ones. It is important to also consider how English consonant and vowel sounds are similar (or different) from the student's L1.

> Some multilingual learners will need explicit instruction in the English sound-symbol system to become successful readers.

When multilingual learners struggle, it is important that teachers understand the nature of their challenges and adjust instruction accordingly. To support L2 reading, strategy groups that focus on one strategy at a time can provide more time for collaborative conversation. Giving ample time on one concept or strategy before moving to another supports students' comprehension and application of skills.

Cross-Linguistic Transfer

When teachers understand the similarities and differences of students' L1 and L2, they can capitalize on cross-linguistic transfer. This refers to the positive, negative, or zero transfer of learning across languages.

Positive transfer means the known language supports acquisition of the learned language. For example, languages that share the same alphabetic orthography may have positive transfer, because students can use their existing knowledge of the alphabet in the second language. Negative transfer occurs when linguistic differences cause students to make errors in the second language. Words that look similar or identical but are not cognates (i.e., same or visibly similar orthography in both languages) are a good example. For example, *bin* means "is" in German, but in English it means a "receptacle"; the word is also pronounced differently in these two languages.

> " When teachers understand the similarities and differences of students' L1 and L2, they can capitalize on cross-linguistic transfer. "

Zero transfer occurs when prior linguistic knowledge has no effect on learning another language. Typically, this occurs when certain linguistic elements exist in one language but not the other. In French, for example, many vowels have distinct accents that are not used in English. These examples demonstrate how cross-linguistic transfer may facilitate or inhibit students as they climb the Ladder to speak, read, and write in English.

Cross-Linguistic Transfer	
Positive Transfer	Elements of the known language support acquisition of the learned language.
Negative Transfer	Linguistic differences cause students to make errors in the second language.
Zero Transfer	Prior linguistic knowledge has no effect on learning another language.

Asset-Based Strategies

Explicit instruction of cross-linguistic relationships builds upon students' existing linguistic knowledge. With languages that share significant similarities with English, students can be encouraged to think about words in their L1 that sound like or look similar to English words. Providing opportunities for students to share what they know in different languages is an important asset-based strategy that invites native English readers and writers to learn about these relationships as well.

Translated resources can also be helpful to build both vocabulary and comprehension toward fluency. Students can read a text in their L1 first, then read it again in English, comparing and contrasting linguistic elements, vocabulary, and content of both texts. Classroom teachers who can't read in a student's L1 may ask the student to read it aloud. This affirms students' prior linguistic knowledge and supports ongoing fluency development in both languages.

 Translated resources can also be helpful to build both vocabulary and comprehension toward fluency.

It should be noted that some research on cross-linguistic transfer suggests that transfer might be script-dependent (Cheah et al., 2022; Chung et al., 2022; Lui et al., 2022; Pasquarella et al., 2015). Therefore, it is important to include specific practice of English relevant skills and not solely rely on possible beneficial effects of cross-linguistic transfer.

Learn More!

McBride, C. (2015). *Children's literacy development: A cross-cultural perspective on learning to read and write.* Routledge.

McBride, C. (2019). *Coping with dyslexia, dysgraphia and ADHD: A global perspective.* Routledge.

McBride, C., Jue Pan, D., & Mohseni, F. (2022). Reading and writing words: A cross-linguistic perspective, *Scientific Studies of Reading, 26*(2), 125–138.

Teacher Preparation and Professional Learning

Across learning contexts, the salient common feature in student achievement is the potential impact of the teacher (Hattie, 2012; Lyon & Weiser, 2009). This is also true for multilingual learners. The professional preparation of teachers in multilingual teaching methods is essential, but unfortunately, it is not implemented consistently. One survey found that fewer than one sixth of teacher education programs in the United States require any undergraduate coursework in second language pedagogy (Menken & Antunez, 2001).

When prospective teachers do learn about second language teaching methods, it is often taught as part of a course on multilingual education but not in depth (Lucas & Grinberg, 2008). Therefore, teachers might be prepared for the cultural diversity of the classroom, but not the linguistic diversity or knowing how to teach students of linguistically diverse backgrounds. ESL credentialing requirements vary, which further contributes to the inconsistency of instructional practices (Fenner, 2013). For these reasons, continuing education and professional development for post-graduate teachers is advisable.

> " Across learning contexts, the salient common feature in student achievement is the potential impact of the teacher. "

ADDITIONAL FACTORS

Aside from cross-linguistic influences, there are additional factors that may affect students learning to read and write in English. Some of these factors are internal (e.g., exceptionalities and motivation) and others are external (e.g., family socioeconomic status and parental involvement).

L1 Exceptionalities

Having dyslexia (or other exceptionalities) in one's "mother tongue" may pose additional challenges for students learning to read and write in English. Reading and writing in both L1 and L2 share many similar cognitive resources and processes. As a result, it is not uncommon for poor readers of L1 to have problems with their L2 English learning. For example, Li et al. (2012) found that in Chinese-English bilinguals, their L1 Chinese and L2 English were strong correlates of corresponding spelling ability in each language. However, other studies indicate this may not always be the case. Some studies of native speakers of German, Swedish, and Chinese demonstrate that a substantial minority of students with dyslexia in their native language or script nevertheless excelled in reading and writing in English as L2 (e.g., McBride, 2019; Miller-Guron & Lundberg, 2000).

Students with dyslexia generally struggle with cognitive-linguistic skills such as rapid naming, phonological, orthographic, and morphological awareness. These skills play a vital role in literacy acquisition. Such L1 cognitive-linguistic skills often predict not only students' L1 word reading abilities but also their L2 word recognition skills (e.g., Chinese-English bilingual students: Chung & Ho, 2010; Spanish-English bilingual students: Durgunoğlu et al., 1993). For this reason, it is important to consider the influence of L1 on L2 exceptionalities when planning appropriate instruction or intervention.

 Having dyslexia (or other exceptionalities) in one's "mother tongue" may pose additional challenges for students learning to read and write in English.

Motivation

There is also a documented motivational aspect to learning an L2. Some students interviewed about learning to read in English noted specific reasons for learning L2 literacy skills that kept them persisting despite some difficulties. For example, the ability to play games online and dialogue with other players in English is one such motivation (Brevik, 2016). Interest in multimedia, including movies and YouTube© excerpts is another. Such informal, repeated exposure and engagement in exercising L2 reading and writing abilities can help to reduce students' anxiety and increase confidence with L2 English usage (Silseth, 2012). When planning instruction or practice, digital technology, such as gaming, (Sundqvist & Wikström, 2015) can be adapted to embed motivation that increases practice.

> " Informal, repeated exposure and engagement in exercising L2 reading and writing abilities can help to reduce students' anxiety and increase confidence with L2 English usage. "

Socioeconomic Status and Language Exposure

Finally, there are important interactions of socioeconomic status and literacy learning to consider for students who are linguistically diverse. Additional resources spent by families in the form of games or tutors or even parents who are skilled in understanding English, all facilitate English literacy skills (e.g., McBride, 2019); however, these additional resources are not readily available to all students. Studies of Chinese students learning to read and write in English highlight the importance of greater resources in the home for better performance in English reading and writing as early as Kindergarten (Yeung & King, 2016; Chow et al., 2010).

Early word recognition is significantly correlated with the socioeconomic status of the child's family, particularly for readers of English as a foreign language (Kahn-Horwitz et al., 2006). Specifically, for low-income immigrant families, the inability to read proficiently is compounded with sociocultural barriers (Li, 2003). When assessments are not available in languages spoken in the home environment, delayed identification of L1 exceptionalities may also influence L2 acquisition.

More Info!

For more information, on the impact of socioeconomic factors, see Chapter 17.

Furthermore, research has consistently indicated that English language exposure to young children is beneficial. Interestingly, Dulay et al. (2017) found that Hong Kong households with the presence of an English-speaking foreign domestic helper were found to have a beneficial effect to young Chinese children's English vocabulary skills. However, readers should note that young bilingual children's English ability is not negatively impacted with an increased exposure to non-English L1 home language input (see Hammer et al., 2009).

Parental Involvement

Parental involvement also contributes to students' L2 English learning. Apart from formal, explicit teaching of reading and writing L2 English, implicit teaching via shared book reading with children can be beneficial. Particularly, a specific approach of shared book reading known as *dialogic reading* has been found to reliably improve L2 English ability of students in English-speaking regions (e.g., US: Brannon & Dauksas, 2014) and across Asia (e.g., Hong Kong: Chow et al., 2010; Thailand: Petchprasert, 2014). Dialogic reading allows students to become active language users in storytelling and story sharing. With the use of prompts and appropriate support from parents or teachers, students' English acquisition is enhanced via shared reading activities.

> ## Check Your Understanding
>
> **Match each asset-based strategy to the correct description:**
>
> **a.** Explicit instruction/practice
>
> **b.** Discussion protocols
>
> **c.** Classroom resources
>
> **d.** Trans-adapted texts
>
> ___ routines that support peer-to-peer discussions and collaborative learning
>
> ___ students read texts in their L1 first, then L2, comparing and discussing the two texts
>
> ___ tools that support students' participation and vocabulary development
>
> ___ integrates all four language domains

 Parents should be mindful that their own literacy beliefs, attitudes, and expectations influence their children's levels of engagement in English literacy activities at school or at home.

Parents can also engage in home literacy activities such as singing alphabet songs or talking about literacy in everyday life (e.g., reading words on signs together) as these activities also benefit the development of children's English abilities. Overall, parents should be mindful that their own literacy beliefs, attitudes, and expectations influence their children's levels of engagement in English literacy activities at school or at home.

MULTILINGUAL LEARNERS

Instructional Strategies

As indicated, there are multiple factors that may influence students' L2 English acquisition and the role of teachers is paramount. Some multilingual learners will benefit from explicit instruction in reading and writing, as well as practice listening and speaking. All four of these language domains need to be addressed.

> Some multilingual learners will benefit from explicit instruction in reading and writing, as well as practice listening and speaking. All four of these language domains need to be addressed.

Developing oral language can be accomplished through discussion protocols that support peer-to-peer discussions and collaborative learning. Classroom resources like dictionaries, anchor charts, and word walls support students at various language acquisition levels. Graphic organizers and sentence stems also augment student participation and vocabulary development, helping students transfer their oral language understanding to print.

Providing students with abundant, authentic opportunities to practice speaking builds confidence. Regular read-aloud experiences help students learn to hear and mimic fluent speaking and reading rhythms and intonation. Shared reading experiences can also be helpful. When trans-adapted resources are available, shared reading may be preceded by having students read texts in their L1 first, then reread and discuss the same text in L2. Such activities support cross-linguistic transfer, vocabulary development, knowledge-building, and fluency.

Asset-Based Strategies to Support English Learners

- Integrate all four language domains during explicit instruction and practice (i.e., reading, writing, speaking, and listening).

- Use discussion protocols to support peer-to-peer conversations and collaborative learning.

- Provide classroom resources: dictionaries, anchor charts, and word walls.

- Utilize graphic organizers and sentence stems to support vocabulary development and use.

- Include read-aloud and shared reading experiences to model fluent speaking and reading.

- Access trans-adapted texts when available.

Conclusion

There are many factors which affect multilingual learners as they climb the Ladder to read and write in English. These factors may include the relative comparability of their L1 script to English, any L1 or script-dependent linguistic or cognitive exceptionalities, their level of motivation, and their family's socioeconomic status and/or parental involvement in L2 English learning.

While there is no "one size fits all" approach to supporting English Learners, teachers can support these students as they climb the Ladder by gathering information on significant aspects of students' L1 scripts, engaging discussion protocols and reading strategies to provide frequent and repeated exposures to language, and bolstering factors such as motivation and parental involvement wherever possible. It is important to highlight that students learning English may come from widely varying levels of L1 fluency which will affect the level at which they begin their climb toward English literacy.

KEY TAKEAWAYS

- Multilingual learners' needs depend on several factors including: L1/L2 compatibility, L1 linguistic or cognitive exceptionalities, socioeconomic family status, parental involvement, and motivation.

- Teachers can support multilingual learners by learning about script features and stress patterns in the student's L1 and exploring any identified L1 exceptionalities.

- Teachers should apply instructional strategies that support L2 language acquisition, including cross-linguistic transfer.

- Engaging family support for reading and language activities at home is also beneficial.

SOCIOECONOMIC FACTORS

Early in my teaching career, *I worked for several years as a reading specialist in a small rural community about 45 miles from my home. Many of the families who lived in this area faced numerous challenges due to economic struggles. Every day my colleagues and I saw the impact of poverty on our students' lives. We knew that some children came to school hungry. Some were experiencing housing situations that we worried were extremely uncomfortable and possibly unsafe. Many of the families seemed to live in constant stress.*

Of all the children I worked with during those years—and in the years since then—one really touched my heart. Benjy was a first grader who lived in an old trailer with his mother who was barely out of her teens. Benjy was clearly loved, but his mother simply was unable to provide many of the things that parents all hope to give to their children. While I couldn't solve the socioeconomic problems that Benjy faced, as his teacher I could give him one life-changing gift. I could teach him to read and write, and I did my very best to make that happen. ⭐

AUTHOR **Steven P. Dykstra**

Clinical Psychologist
Milwaukee County, WI, USA

> "It is well understood that students from less advantaged socioeconomic conditions are at higher risk for experiencing academic challenges."

On *The Ladder of Reading & Writing* infographic, the blue arrow draws attention to additional factors for educators to consider when supporting learners, no matter where they are on the continuum. One of the factors is environment, which includes both the school and the home environment. It is well understood that students from less advantaged socioeconomic conditions are at higher risk for experiencing academic challenges (Abadzi, 2006; Buckingham et al., 2013; Hernandez, 2012). The reasons for their struggles are numerous and complex. Without denying the value of deconstructing and studying the ways in which poverty, racism, and intergenerational disadvantage contribute to low literacy rates, we need not overly concern ourselves with all the mechanisms by which these students are disadvantaged. If our task is to educate the students in front of us now, we should focus our attention on the factors which are most under our control—namely, providing appropriate, differentiated literacy instruction that supports their climb up the Ladder.

BEYOND EARLY ACCESS

Among the most targeted factors for children raised in poverty is early access to books and literacy experiences within the home. Efforts to get books into the hands and homes of economically disadvantaged students has been a widespread and noble effort. However, if we are distributing books to poor families so that parents and others will read to children, and the children will thereby learn to read themselves, we are misguided. Unfortunately, it's not that simple. We must also focus on how we *teach* reading and writing, the details of *instruction*. All children benefit from this focus, but poor and vulnerable children absolutely require it.

> If we are distributing books to poor families so that parents and others will read to children, and the children will thereby learn to read themselves, we are misguided.

The Same Science of Learning to Read

Fortunately, an increasing number of teachers, schools, districts, and communities are becoming aware of the scientific explanation for how children learn to read, and the evidence-based approaches to reading instruction which emanate from that science. These scientific discoveries and the associated instructional methods can benefit all children, including those who are poor or disadvantaged. In other words, there is not a different science for children based on their socioeconomic status.

However, as indicated by the blue arrow on *The Ladder of Reading & Writing* infographic, environmental circumstances inarguably affect students' learning. Therefore, teachers need to be aware that the application of the science to children who struggle or are behind in their development as readers, and particularly in classrooms and schools where these children are numerous or in the majority, is different. It must be.

Too often, early instruction is designed based on a broad expectation for where students should be at a particular point in time, even when we know that many or most of the students in the class will not be there. The instruction proceeds in a scheduled way, based more on the calendar than the students in front of us. While more economically privileged families may have the time and other resources to keep their children moving along a successful instructional path, disadvantaged children are unlikely to be so fortunate.

Learn More!

Hernandez, D. J. (2012). *Double jeopardy: How third grade skills and poverty influence high school graduation.* The Annie E. Casey Foundation.

Abadzi, H. (2006). *Efficient learning for the poor: Insights from the frontier of cognitive neuroscience.* World Bank.

Olszewski-Kubilius, P., & Clarenbach, J. (2012). *Unlocking emergent talent: Supporting high achievement of low-income, high-ability students.* National Association for Gifted Children. https://cdn.ymaws.com/nagc.org/resource/resmgr/unlocking_emergent_talent.pdf.

FOCUSING ON WHAT WE CAN CONTROL

Students struggling to read need us to respond with instruction that is timely and precise. They need educators to recognize their struggles early and to categorize and understand those struggles in much greater detail than the vague recognition that things aren't going well. Time is of the essence! These students cannot afford delayed or generalized instruction that fails to meet their data-identified needs. Our response to their difficulties needs to focus primarily on those things which are under our control: providing differentiated instruction that is systematically designed, and informed by data.

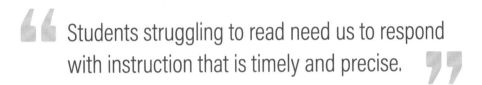

" Students struggling to read need us to respond with instruction that is timely and precise. "

While noting that a room full of students may be struggling to read because of poverty or other disadvantages may help drive long-needed policy changes, it does little or nothing for the students in the room now. For them, we need to focus on responsive instruction that is likely to benefit them. Fortunately, the growing abundance of knowledge provided by science, translated into practice by a growing body of skilled, supported, and dedicated teachers allows us to respond more effectively than was typical in the past. While all students benefit from instruction grounded in the science of learning, students who are struggling to read, particularly those who lack advantages, absolutely require it.

Early struggles to read can have a corrosive effect on a student's self-image and their ability to succeed academically across all subject areas. "

The Importance of Early Intervention

We must also acknowledge that while struggling to read is a bad thing that threatens the developmental path of any student who experiences it, it is more dangerous for some students than others. Early struggles to read can have a corrosive effect on a student's self-image and their ability to succeed academically across all subject areas (Abadzi, 2006; Lovett et al., 2017). This is particularly true when the struggles are persistent and insufficiently remediated. Like any burden we may heap upon students, it is more crushing to those who are already carrying a sizable load (McArthur et al., 2022).

While we wish every student came to school with an abundance of hope, and a wealth of success in a world they experienced as both safe and welcoming, we know that isn't the case. For students whose sense of safety and security is not as firm as we would like it to be, who are already navigating a world that seems not to value them, the early experience of school will either establish it as an oasis where they learn to reach for a future they might otherwise never imagine, or yet another voice that whispers in their ear telling them they are not good enough, or smart enough, or valued enough. The message comes across that school and success are just more things that are not for them.

In the first few years of education, nothing will benefit students more than an early experience of success with reading and writing. Not all students who face poverty struggle with learning to read and write, but many do. And those students who struggle know they struggle, just as students know they are poor, marginalized, or afraid.

Students need to see that our plan is something more than telling them to try harder, practice more, find more "grit." The research on systematic, explicit instruction gives teachers clear guidance, including benchmarks for assessing and intervening (Fletcher et al., 2019). Students who are struggling can rely on those same benchmarks to see that they are doing better, to assure them that they are making progress and moving forward to where they would like to be (Furey & Loftus-Rattan, 2021; Schunk, 2003).

A Series of Dilemmas

It is often and truthfully said that while listening and speaking are evolved skills for which the brain is well adapted, and which typically require no explicit instruction, reading and writing are modern extensions of language for which our brains are not nearly so well prepared (Seidenberg, 2017). While this is true, it obscures an essential truth: modern society requires adequate reading and writing skills as if they occurred naturally. It isn't enough to listen and speak well. To function successfully in the modern world, you must be able to read and write well enough (World Literacy Foundation, 2018).

Early or persistent struggle with reading and writing is often experienced by the individual as a crisis—more like failure at a core developmental task than difficulty with an optional skill. Reading and writing are no more natural for our brain than golfing, yet where the failure to be a good golfer will likely be of little significance, the failure to be a good reader and writer can be devastating. Furthermore, reading failure is very likely to begin accumulating at a young age, before an individual has a chance to amass other successes that might balance it out, or the cognitive wherewithal to fully understand it and put it in perspective.

 Modern society requires adequate reading and writing skills as if they occurred naturally.

We find ourselves and the students we teach ensnared in a series of dilemmas. The students who most need reading success to give them hope for a brighter future and protect them from the burdens of their current reality are too often the students who are more likely to struggle with reading (Reardon et al., 2012). The need to assess for reading difficulties at a young age may unwittingly serve to undermine the same students' self-confidence before they are old enough or experienced enough to withstand it. Recognizing difficulties early and responding urgently, even to the point of naming or labeling some students, runs the risk of sending the wrong message to vulnerable students; however, these efforts are essential to their long-term success. Educators must proceed with caution and empathy.

Check Your Understanding

Check all that apply. Supporting students living in poverty requires:

___ expectations of success and support to achieve success

___ timely and precise intervention if needed

___ early access to reading materials in the home

___ needs-based instruction that is systematically designed

___ positive school experiences that support self-esteem

THE NEED FOR URGENCY

Our response to these challenges has far too often been a tepid mixture of guidance to "wait and see," dangerously lowered expectations for too many of our students, and far too much worry over describing or labeling a problem than we have for failing to solve it. And while every student has paid a price for these approaches, as is always the case, poor, disadvantaged, and struggling students have paid more than their share.

If we are honest, these approaches have been more about protecting adults than students. "Wait and see" moves students along to someone else under cover of the unrealistic hope that problems might take care of themselves. Lowered expectations masquerade as sympathetic understanding for disadvantage, when they too often hide the fact that we simply don't know what to do.

 All students need to see themselves as capable of ongoing learning —whether their climb up the Ladder is easy or challenging. . . . Disadvantaged students, especially students living under the weight of multiple burdens, need this even more.

All students deserve needs-based instruction as they continue to move up the Ladder. They need us to be timely, precise, and effective. All students need to see themselves as capable of ongoing learning—whether their climb up the Ladder is easy or challenging—and experience the hope and success that literacy brings. Disadvantaged students, especially students living under the weight of multiple burdens, need this even more (Buckingham et al., 2013; Hernandez, 2012).

Conclusion

Like a canary in a mine who needs the same oxygen as the coal miners, students who are living in poverty need the same high-quality literacy instruction that every student needs. And like the dying canary, the struggles of students who are at-risk and economically disadvantaged should alert us to a problem with how we teach everyone. Unfortunately, we have been less alarmed by their failures because they are "poor." We are like miners who ignore the dying canary because it is just a bird.

KEY TAKEAWAYS

- Learning to read and write are complex processes that can be even more challenging for students from impoverished environments.

- The evidence from scientific research about effective instruction applies to all learners, including students facing environmental challenges like poverty.

- To help these students, we must focus on the factors we can control: The delivery of differentiated instruction that is systematically designed and sufficiently explicit so students feel successful and experience real progress.

HOME-SCHOOL CONNECTIONS

We always knew *our son, Charlie, was struggling to acquire reading and writing skills, but his 1st and 2nd grade teachers assured us he was learning. Charlie did not want to read at home and completing homework often included a meltdown. We tried hard to get someone at his school to listen to us, but they just kept saying "Charlie is so bright. He'll be fine."*

Before he entered 5th grade we moved to another district and enrolled Charlie in a new school. We noticed a difference right away! When we were registering him, the staff in the front office told us they valued partnering with their students' families and caregivers. They even had Parent Liaison office; their handout said "Call or email us with any concerns. We are here for you and your family!" Charlie's teacher had a checklist of questions to ask and really heard us about our concerns. Within one week Charlie had been assessed by a reading specialist and we had a plan to help Charlie at home. This made such a difference for our family. Now we volunteer at the Parent Liaison office!

AUTHORS

Amy Fleisher

General Education and Intervention Teacher
Seattle, WA, USA

Julie Bedell

Reading Specialist and General Education Teacher
Seattle, WA, USA

> "Decades of research confirms that family engagement improves school readiness, student academic achievement, and graduation rates."

Neither parenting nor teaching is for the faint of heart. Both noble pursuits come with the joys and frustrations of helping children become skilled, confident members of society. Parents and caregivers are their children's first teachers—helping them learn to talk, walk, think, and interact with others. Strong receptive and expressive language skills, developed through adult interaction and modeling, pave the way for learning to read and write.

Once formal education begins, ideally a partnership forms between home and school. Decades of research confirms that family engagement improves school readiness, student academic achievement, and graduation rates (Henderson & Mapp, 2002; Mapp & Kuttner, 2013; Weiss et al., 2010). Family involvement in a child's schooling helps not only the child but strengthens the entire school community. This chapter outlines steps that can be taken by districts, schools, teachers, and families to support this important connection.

HOME-SCHOOL CONNECTIONS

DISTRICT AND SCHOOL SUPPORT FOR FAMILIES

Students climbing the Ladder benefit from coordinated support that includes their teachers and families. For that reason, districts should set the expectation that schools develop both formal and informal ways to involve parents in their children's education. To increase involvement, districts can organize ways for families to have a voice in the decision-making, including the selection of literacy programs and materials, budget, schedules, and even staffing when appropriate.

School staff may need additional training on how to work with families to foster these relationships. When parents and caregivers understand how to support their children's academic learning at home and stay actively involved in their schooling, the children tend to do well in school and continue with their education (Weiss et al., 2010).

Leadership at the district and school levels can set a tone and create systems to support family engagement. Programs that effectively engage families require planning, time, and financial resources, including appropriate and sustained training for district staff and teachers. Research has shown that successful programs invite involvement, are welcoming, and address identified parent and community needs (Henderson & Mapp, 2002; Mapp & Bergman, 2019). Academic achievement should be a top priority. While the district plays a key role in establishing a culture and climate for family involvement, what is the role of the individual school?

 School staff may need additional training on how to work with families.

When we think of school outreach, we often think of curriculum night or jog-a-thons. However, research shows that family outreach needs to target specific components of academic skills and knowledge to improve student achievement. Workshops for parents and caregivers describing what students are learning and how to support them at home can lead to gains in achievement (Mapp, 2002). For example, teacher-delivered presentations help families understand how to increase their child's vocabulary, support letter-sound knowledge, or aid in handwriting effectively connect families to the development of their child's literacy skills.

TEACHER SUPPORT FOR FAMILIES

Learn More!

Mapp, K. L., & Kuttner, P. J. (2013). *Partners in education: A dual capacity-building framework for family-school partnerships.* SEDL.

Weiss, H. B., Lopez, M. E., & Rosenberg, H. (2010). *Beyond random acts: Family, school, and community engagement as an integral part of education reform.* National Policy Forum for Family, School and Community Engagement. Harvard Family Research Project.

Edutopia. (n.d.). *Home-to-School Connections Guide.* Reading Rockets. https://www.readingrockets.org/resources/resource-library/home-school-connections-guide.

While a school-wide approach to encouraging family involvement can be a starting point for forging relationships between home and school, a student's teacher is at the heart of that relationship and contributes to its success. Families are subject matter experts on their children and can often provide teachers with valuable insight into where the students may be on the continuum of *The Ladder of Reading & Writing* infographic. If a student struggles to master early literacy foundations, a parent or caregiver might be the first to bring attention to the issue. It is well known that early intervention is best, so investigating caregiver concerns about a child can save valuable time when addressing reading and writing challenges.

If parents are unaware that their child is behind in meeting established academic benchmarks, the first conversation between the teacher and the family can be anxiety-producing for both parties. Teachers can find comfort knowing that most caregivers, regardless of ethnicity, race, or social-economic status, want their children to do well in school and to help them succeed (Lemmer, 2012; Mapp, 2002). Addressing concerns about students who are advanced in skills (dark green area of the continuum) should also be given focused attention because these students also have specific learning needs. On the following page are some suggestions for teachers to foster positive relationships with parents and caregivers.

HOME-SCHOOL CONNECTIONS

Suggestions for Teachers

- Establish frequent communication about students' progress, including in-person conferences, phone calls, emails, and materials for at-home practice. In a 2022 Westat report, teacher outreach to families of low-performing students related to improved achievement in both reading and math.

- Have systems in place to address obstacles that can limit the ability of parents and caregivers to participate directly with the school. These can include difficulty taking time off from work to attend meetings, language or cultural barriers, transportation and financial challenges, etc. Teachers should understand that some families find interacting with schools intimidating or even traumatizing (Hornby & Lafaele, 2011).

- For families that request it, provide specific ideas to support students at home with targeted practice that includes explicit modeling or directions. Training caregivers to support children while completing homework can be beneficial to student achievement (Patall et al., 2008). For example, teachers could provide caregivers with brief coaching on how to sound out and blend unfamiliar words or how to offer corrective feedback and encouragement.

- Clarify unfamiliar terms and concepts. Caregivers who are not in the education field will likely be unfamiliar with terms like decoding, fluency, morphology, or graphemes. Curriculum nights provide opportunities to explain these terms. Use graphic visuals like *The Ladder of Reading & Writing* infographic, Scarborough's *Reading Rope* (1998), or Joan Sedita's *Writing Rope* (2023) during caregiver meetings. Visuals can help families understand their child's reading and writing development and why their child is working on specific skills: https://www.nancyyoung.ca/

- Collect and share formative data with families. Curriculum-based measurements are quick to administer and show immediate progress—or lack of progress (see Chapter 4). Share results from oral reading fluency measures, handwriting samples, or writing assessments.

- Connect families with online resources such as readingrockets.org, understood.org, parentcenterhub. org, and https://dyslexiaida.org/. The website colorincolorado.org is a bilingual website for educators and families of English Learners. For students in the light or dark green areas of the continuum, you may direct caregivers to nagc.org.

- Provide families with supplemental print resources as requested. Some curriculums provide activities for advanced readers and writers. The National Association for Gifted Children also provides resources, including Gifted Education Programming Standards. Classroom libraries are also resources, especially those that have breadth and depth in genre and reading complexity, and feature topics that are culturally inclusive and diverse.

HOME-SCHOOL CONNECTIONS

FAMILY SUPPORT FOR STUDENTS

Families know their children best, and educators must genuinely listen to their concerns and insights. While time limitations, language and cultural differences, and mobility challenges certainly affect some families' interaction with schools (Hornby & Lafaele, 2011), most parents are curious about what is going on in their child's classroom. For example, they may want to understand how reading and writing are being taught or what assessments are being administered. And the question parents most often ask: How is my child doing in learning to read and write? These are all excellent lines of inquiry that families should be asking of their child's school, and they deserve accurate and clear answers. Schools must support teachers to find ways to address these questions for all caregivers, including those who may not be able to connect directly with the school.

Some parents and families may also be concerned about their child's motivation or emotional needs. For many families, the first step is to check in with their child's teacher. This can begin the important process of assembling a team to best support the student.

> **“** Families know their children best, and educators must genuinely listen to their concerns and insights. **”**

Sometimes students need more evaluation than what can be accomplished in the classroom. If a parent or teacher suspects a learning disability, they should follow the required process that every public school in the U.S. must have for further testing. However, families who have the financial means may also decide to find a private psychologist to complete a comprehensive evaluation. Parents who suspect their child might be gifted should also raise that question with their school and identify the resources that might be available to support students who are highly capable.

On the following page are some suggestions for parents and caregivers to support children climbing the Ladder. These range from early learning activities to engage in with a typical toddler to strategies for supporting an older child who is struggling to become a skilled reader.

Check Your Understanding

Check all that apply. Teachers may encourage home-school connections by:

___ initiating frequent communications about students' progress

___ having systems in place to support family participation

___ empowering families with knowledge and resources to work with their children at home

___ using visuals to support families' understanding of unfamiliar terms or explain data

Suggestions for Families

- Talk! Talk! TALK! Oral language is the springboard for learning to read and write. As children learn to speak, they can also start to play with the sounds in the English language. Reciting nursery rhymes, singing songs, and playing rhyming games contribute to awareness of sounds in words before formal schooling begins.

- Help children build an expansive vocabulary through exposure to new background knowledge and complex text regardless of word reading skills. Audiobooks, age-appropriate podcasts, and documentaries can build prior knowledge for future comprehension of complex text.

- Read aloud to children—from birth to young adulthood. A family can share the experience of listening to an audiobook together. Talking about what is happening in the story, and predicting what might happen next, helps build comprehension skills. Book clubs are another great way to keep children reading and discussing text.

- Expose children to a variety of texts, for those who are already reading and those just starting their reading journey. Caregivers can model enjoyment of reading and books, including books from the library.

- Sound out words. Applying phonics knowledge to sound out unfamiliar words is an essential step in learning to read. Caregivers can help by providing opportunities for children to sound out new words using environmental print or reading texts together. Some children need to sound out words multiple times before the word is stored for automatic word recognition.

- Support homework. For those children whose climb up the Ladder is taking more time and effort, homework can be fraught with frustration even when the children are exceptionally bright (Orkin et al., 2017). While it may be tempting to provide help at every step, instead support with proximity and availability. For example, during designated homework time, a parent can sit at the same table as their child, completing tasks like answering emails or paying bills. When the need arises, they can provide support and quickly disengage. If a child is experiencing stress or excessive difficulties completing their homework, parents or caregivers should contact that teacher to see if modifications or adjustments can be made.

- Use appropriate technology at home (apps, devices, and websites). This supports children's climb up the Ladder (see Chapter 19). Many resources are free or low cost. Parents or caregivers may ask their child's teacher or school librarian for suggestions.

Conclusion

The involvement of families in academic life has the potential to affect a child's development and success as a confident reader and writer. It is one of the many variables that play a role as every child climbs the Ladder, whether that journey is difficult or occurs at a rapid pace. A strong partnership forged between school and home can support positive academic and social-emotional outcomes for not only individual children but the wider community. The form that these partnerships can take may vary but schools should make partnering a key goal and establish purposeful, integrated, and sustained systems to facilitate this process of collaboration.

KEY TAKEAWAYS

- Families play an important role in supporting the academic growth of children, and on-going family engagement strengthens the entire school community.

- Systems at the district, school, and classroom level encourage the involvement and contributions of families and should include support for the varying needs of some caregivers to participate.

- There are many ways that parents can support the success of their children as they climb the Ladder, wherever children are on the continuum.

TECHNOLOGY

How can two children *from the same parents be so different? Greer is 5 years old. She loves to listen as I read stories aloud. While not quite reading yet, she is on her way. If I pause in the middle of a sentence, she will finish it, pointing to each word. Her grandmother gave her a tablet for her birthday; Greer was delighted to see her favorite books, so she could read along on her own. Her brother Griffin, age 10, is a challenged reader who would rather play video games than read. He qualifies for free downloadable books, which he uses in the car and at home. Thank goodness for headphones!*

Griffin's class has 1 to 1 laptops and Google Classroom, which means he can use voice recognition and text-to-speech for many of his assignments. He doesn't use these tools all the time— but when he needs extra assistance or has a long assignment, they keep him from feeling frustrated. He has a vivid imagination and loves working with his friends to create action scenes to play out. Perhaps he'll be a film director? ⭐

AUTHOR **Kathleen Puckett**

Associate Professor, MLF Teachers College
Arizona State University
Tempe, AZ, USA

> The challenge for teachers, parents, and students is understanding how and when to use technology effectively.

As most parents know, children as young as two years old can navigate icon-driven apps on tablets and smartphones easily. Once they become familiar with the computers found in most schools, students quickly learn to use the keyboard and mouse or touch pad features. The challenge for teachers, parents, and students is understanding how and when to use technology effectively to support and enhance each student's reading and writing journey.

This chapter presents an overview of how technology may facilitate learning that is interactive and interesting in relevant ways for students climbing the Ladder, and particularly students for whom the climb is more challenging.

TECHNOLOGY

FRAMEWORKS UNDERPINNING TECHNOLOGY USE

Technology provides the opportunity for personalized learning that is self-paced and allows students to pursue areas of interest. Personalized learning requires more than simple exposure to technology tools that support literacy. Effective use of technology will enhance, rather than replace, explicit instruction. Some technology tools are designed to provide access to reading and writing by removing obstacles related to specific exceptionalities. For example, read-aloud software may support language acquisition for multilingual learners or reading comprehension for students with dyslexia by increasing opportunities for students to hear fluent reading. Similarly, transcription software may facilitate writing experiences for students who struggle with written expression difficulties, like dysgraphia.

> " Effective use of technology will enhance, rather than replace, explicit instruction. "

Appropriate use of technology may also boost students' motivation for practicing specific tasks or pursuing individual areas of interest. To maximize the value of technology for supporting students' learning and engagement, it is helpful for teachers and families to have some direction on how to accomplish this. Two frameworks can offer such guidance for determining how and when to use these tools purposefully and effectively.

Universal Design for Learning

Universal Design for Learning (UDL) is a framework for planning and designing inclusive instruction (CAST, 2018). The three principles of UDL are to provide options for engagement, expression, and representation of information. UDL guidelines provide leveled suggestions toward the ultimate goal of developing expert learners who are purposeful, motivated, resourceful, knowledgeable, strategic, and goal-directed (CAST, 2018). The UDL framework can support teacher planning of differentiated instruction to support students in all areas of the Ladder continuum. Digital tools can be used to support the principles of this framework.

PROVIDE MULTIPLE MEANS OF **ENGAGEMENT** Affective Networks The "WHY" of Learning	PROVIDE MULTIPLE MEANS OF **REPRESENTATION** Recognition Networks The "WHAT" of Learning	PROVIDE MULTIPLE MEANS OF **ACTION & EXPRESSION** Strategic Networks The "HOW" of Learning
ACCESS PROVIDE OPTIONS FOR **RECRUITING INTEREST (7)** • Optimize individual choice and autonomy (7, 1) • Optimize relevance, value, and authenticity (7, 2) • Minimize threats and distractions (7, 3)	PROVIDE OPTIONS FOR **PERCEPTION (1)** • Offer ways of customizing the display of information (1, 1) • Offer alternatives for auditory instruction (1, 2) • Offer alternatives for visual information (1, 3)	PROVIDE OPTIONS FOR **PHYSICAL ACTION (4)** • Vary the methods for response and navigation (4, 1) • Optimize access to tools and assistive technologies (4, 2)
BUILD PROVIDE OPTIONS FOR **SUSTAINING EFFORT & PERSISTENCE (8)** • Heighten salience of goals and objectives (8, 1) • Vary demands and resources to optimize challenge (8, 2) • Foster collaboration and community (8, 3) • Increase mastery-oriented feedback (8, 4)	PROVIDE OPTIONS FOR **LANGUAGE & SYMBOLS (2)** • Clarify vocabulary and symbols (2, 1) • Clarify syntax and structure (2, 2) • Support decoding of text, mathematical notation, and symbols (2, 3) • Promote understanding across languages (2, 4) • Illustrate through multiple media (2, 5)	PROVIDE OPTIONS FOR **EXPRESSION & COMMUNICATION (5)** • Use multiple media for communication (5, 1) • Use multiple tools for construction and composition (5, 2) • Build fluencies with graduated levels of support for practice and performance (5, 3)
INTERNALIZE PROVIDE OPTIONS FOR **SELF REGULATION (9)** • Promote expectations and beliefs that optimize motivation (9, 1) • Facilitate personal coping skills and strategies (9, 2) • Develop self-assessment and reflection (9, 3)	PROVIDE OPTIONS FOR **COMPREHENSION (3)** • Activate or supply background knowledge (3, 1) • Highlight patterns, critical features, big ideas, and relationships (3, 2) • Guide information processing and visualization (3, 3) • Maximize transfer and generalization (3, 4)	PROVIDE OPTIONS FOR **EXECUTIVE FUNCTIONS (6)** • Guide appropriate goal-setting (6, 1) • Support planning and strategy development (6, 2) • Facilitate managing information and resources (6, 3) • Enhance capacity for monitoring progress (6, 4)

GOAL

EXPERT LEARNERS who are…

Purposeful & Motivated	Resourceful & Knowledgeable	Strategic & Goal-Directed

TECHNOLOGY

Udlguidelines.cast.org © CAST, Inc 2018
CAST (2018). Universal design for learning guidelines version 2.2 [graphic organizer]. Wakefield, MA: Author.

Three Principles of Universal Design for Learning

Engagement

Options for engagement may be enhanced by providing choices in how a learning objective may be reached. This might mean encouraging students' interest areas in reading, even if the texts are above their assessed level, or in writing, using technology tools to provide independent support. Students in the green and light green areas of the continuum might be provided some independence or autonomy in selecting options for reading, learning advanced vocabulary, or engaging in inquiry-based writing activities. For students in the red or orange areas teachers can offer games or practice apps to support their targeted skill goals.

Expression

Options for expression include multiple ways that students may demonstrate what they have learned by using media, such as any combination of text, speech, drawing, or video. Digital media options can be selected to support the reading and writing of students in all areas of the continuum, for both independent and collaborative work.

Representation

Options for representation refers to making content accessible using a variety of means. Digital examples of this principle involve alternatives for visual information (such as text-to-speech software, illustrations, and manipulatives), for auditory information (captions and written transcripts), and for language understanding (linking key vocabulary to definitions or enabling translation software). This principle of UDL is especially valuable for teachers working with students in the red and orange areas of the continuum to find novel and effective ways to support students in their learning.

The UDL framework can support teacher planning of differentiated instruction to support students in all areas of the Ladder continuum. For students in the red and orange areas, this may mean providing options for expression and representation. For students in the light and dark green areas of the continuum, it may mean emphasizing or enhancing options for engagement by providing choices for inquiry-based or self-paced learning in students' interest areas.

Substitution, Augmentation, Modification, Redefinition (SAMR)

SAMR is a second framework for personalized learning that provides guidance for different uses of technology in progressive stages (Puentedura, 2013). In *substitution*, the digital tool replaces the traditional (such as reading a passage on the computer instead of in a book), but no functional change occurs. *Augmentation* refers to using technology as a direct tool substitute, but with functional improvements that incorporate useful scaffolding to support reading or writing tasks, such as voice typing to write a story or consulting the dictionary feature to look up a word.

> **SAMR guides the intensity of technology integration to support students' access to areas previously out of reach.**

In *modification*, the task is redesigned. For example, instead of traditional tools, you may choose to use collaborative tools (such as Google Docs) for students to write and share knowledge. Modification moves the task from something students do individually to something they do socially in a shared environment. In *redefinition*, students explore areas they may not be able to access otherwise; a new task is created with the computer supporting the learning. For example, a class might create a video that explores a particular concept, with smaller teams of students collaborating on subtopics and combining their work into a final product.

Teachers can use these two frameworks to guide the integration of technology in their classrooms and support students as they climb the Ladder. UDL offers suggestions for using technology in preplanning so that all or most students can participate and benefit from the added opportunities provided for accessibility or extended learning. SAMR guides the intensity of technology integration to support students' access to areas previously out of reach. In the next section, we'll consider how specific components of technology may support developing readers and writers.

DIGITAL TOOLS TO SUPPORT READERS AND WRITERS

Technology involves two distinct components: the hardware, or physical device, and the programs that operate within each device. Hardware is ever changing and improving, making it accessible to more individuals. Features that formerly were expensive add-ons for accessibility (e.g., touch screens and voice commands) are now built into most devices. Programs include the software (along with preloaded, customizable settings), websites, and apps that are stored within the device or accessed through the Internet.

Useful software applications are:

- cognitively accessible (easy to navigate)

- interactive (requires the user to do something)

- ubiquitous (readily available or in general use)

- free, nearly free, or supported by the educational organization through a subscription

The settings on most devices contain customizable features that may help some students with reading and writing. The ease of access folder (Windows) or accessibility folder (Apple products) contains controls for turning on speech recognition (enabling students to dictate text instead of typing). Other options include changing the size or shape of the mouse pointer or text cursor, turning on magnification, and changing color displays or mouse button configurations for right- or left-handed users. Keyboard settings (found in the devices folder) include providing text suggestions and autocorrecting misspelled words. Exploring the various settings in these folders helps you determine which features are most suitable for individual students.

> **The settings on most devices contain customizable features that may help some students with reading and writing.**

Other literacy tools are accessed within software programs, such as the suite of tools in Microsoft Office or Google. Spelling and grammar checks, thesaurus, language translation, and read-aloud are commonly used features. Graphics features include templates that teachers may use for prereading activation, such as KWL (what do I already *know*, what do I *want* to know, what did I *learn*) charts or Venn diagrams. And, of course, new hardware and software continue to be developed.

KWL Chart		
Know	**Want to Know**	**Learned**

Sample: KWL Chart

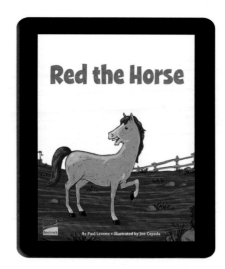

Sample: e-Book for beginning readers

Beginning Readers and Writers

As the colored continuum on the infographic makes clear, students vary in the ease in which they master skills. From early childhood, as they begin their climb, technology may be used in various ways to support skill development and exposure to text, no matter where students are on the continuum. The task for beginning readers is to acquire foundational reading skills of decoding sounds and words, developing fluency, expanding vocabulary, and comprehending what is read (Fletcher et al., 2019). A search online will result in a list of hundreds of early learning software programs, websites, and apps created with the intention of providing practice with foundational skills such as letter names and sounds, rhyming, syllables, and word families, as well as ways to build vocabulary and background knowledge appropriate for young learners.

> **Technology may be used in various ways to support skill development and exposure to text, no matter where students are on the continuum.**

Beginning readers may also enjoy early reader e-books or even just looking at the text while listening to the audio. These technology applications provide opportunities for variety in *representation* and *engagement* (UDL framework) and can be used to supplement or substitute for traditional paper and pencil tasks (SAMR framework) (Puentedura, 2013).

The choice of digital versus print-based texts and materials should be made carefully as there can be both positive and negative outcomes for young children (Reid Chassiakos et al., 2016; Wolf, 2018). Research indicates "very few of the commercially available apps found in the educational section of app stores have evidence-based design input with demonstrated learning effectiveness" (Reid Chassiakos et al., 2016, p. 35). Culatta et al. (2016) recommend asking specific questions during the selection process, including consideration of the quality of sound, the accuracy of concepts taught, and the complexity of skills being introduced. When selecting resources for young students, educators "first should consider what is best for healthy child development and then consider how technology can help early learners achieve learning outcomes" (US Department of Education, n.d.). Planning is key (Quesenberry et al., 2016).

> " The choice of digital versus print-based texts and materials should be made carefully as there can be both positive and negative outcomes for young children. "

TECHNOLOGY

Established Readers and Writers

As they continue to climb the Ladder and move beyond foundational skills for reading and writing, students build academic literacy by reading and writing increasingly complex narrative and expository texts found in literature, science, math, social studies, and other content areas. While digital tools can scaffold this development, the process is reciprocal; reading and writing further support the skills needed to use digital technologies effectively (Janssen et al., 2013). When considering technology for established readers and writers, UDL provides teachers with a framework for designing instruction that includes opportunities for choice, while SAMR supports purposeful development and growing intensity.

For example, within the UDL framework, students may use technology for highly personalized learning that involves self-selected topics for research and reporting. Technology tools provide new avenues for discovering knowledge and simultaneously, multiple options for students to *represent* their growing understanding (e.g., online poster, slideshow, vlog, podcast, website, animated cartoon). These features also support using technology for *augmentation*, or the "incorporating useful tools" aspect of SAMR.

Helpful Websites

The IRIS Center provides teachers and parents with an overview of how Tier 3 supports are designed and a comprehensive discussion of areas of intervention in reading (https://iris.peabody.vanderbilt.edu/module/rti03-reading/).

Khan Academy Kids (https://learn.khanacademy.org/khan-academy-kids/) is a comprehensive early learning resource that can be used to help students get individual practice with important foundational learning material.

Starfall (Starfall Education Foundation, (https://www.starfall.com/h/index.php) is a website with research-based activities that align with Individual and Common Core State Standards in English language arts. The website features games and books that provide audiovisual interactivity in phonemic awareness, phonics, and common sight words.

Storyline Online https://storylineonline.net/about-us/ is a children's literacy website that streams videos featuring celebrated actors reading children's books along with the text and illustrations.

Teacher guidance is needed to ensure that online resources for knowledge-building are appropriate for each student's age and reading ability. However, for students in the dark green area of the Ladder continuum, technology enables extended and interest-based learning through access to multiple sources of information, including primary documents (US Department of Education, 2017), as well as the ability to "publish their work to a broad global audience regardless of where they go to school" (p. 9).

In other words, as students' literacy skills continue to develop, their use of technology also progresses from merely viewing content to actively engaging with and providing their own. Using collaborative tools for writing and other forms of expression moves the purpose of technology to a shared environment (*modification* in the SAMR framework and options for *engagement* in the UDL framework).

Learn More!

Puckett, K., & O'Bannon, B. (2011). Technology applications for students with dyslexia. In N. Mather & B. Wendling (Eds.), *Essentials of dyslexia assessment and intervention* (pp. 199–222). John Wiley & Sons, Inc.

Rao, K., Torres, C., & Smith, S. J. (2021). Digital tools and UDL-based instructional strategies to support students with disabilities online. *Journal of Special Education Technology, 36*(2), 105–112.

U.S. Department of Education Office of Educational Technology (n.d.). Advancing digital equity for all: Community-based recommendations for developing effective digital equity plans to close the digital divide and enable technology-empowered learning. https://tech.ed.gov/advancing-digital-equity-for-all/.

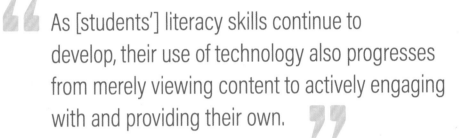

> As [students'] literacy skills continue to develop, their use of technology also progresses from merely viewing content to actively engaging with and providing their own.

© Benchmark Education Company LLC | **269**

Challenged Readers and Writers

As discussed in Chapter 3, students in the red and orange areas of the Ladder continuum require more explicit instruction in the fundamentals of understanding how language works for both reading and writing (Fletcher et al., 2019; Seidenberg, 2017). Technology can support interventions based on results from diagnostic assessments to improve students' reading, writing, test taking, and study skills.

To support these students, computer-based reading intervention programs are often used as differentiated Tier 2 and Tier 3 intervention within a Multi-Tiered System of Support. If computer-based supports are used as Tier 2 and 3 interventions, they should be applied strategically to enhance but not supplant teacher-provided, systematically designed programming that includes explicit instruction. Reed (2018) suggests taking specific steps to "ensure the digital activities remain the complement and not the core of their literacy instruction" including:

- making sure materials align to the assistive technology documented in the student's IEP or 504 plan;

- ensuring that the activity provided by the technology supports the learning and practice the student actually needs;

- preparing teacher-led lessons to include or extend from the digital text or activity; and

- balancing intentional time on the device, time with peers, and time with teacher-led instruction and support.

Check Your Understanding

Match each word or phrase to the correct description.

a. Universal Design for Learning (UDL)

b. Substitution, Augmentation, Modification, Redefinition (SAMR)

c. Digital tools

d. Literacy tools

___ the hardware and software features that support students' access to information and learning

___ KWL charts or other graphic organizers that support reading and writing practice

___ a framework that guides different uses of technology in progressive stages

___ a framework that supports teachers to plan and design inclusive instruction

While students are engaged in intervention, their involvement with the rest of the academic world does not stop. The challenge for these students is twofold: how to keep up with and access the content that their classmates are learning and how to demonstrate their knowledge. Technology tools can help them address these challenges that support multiple means of *representation* in UDL and the "functional use of technology" from the SAMR framework.

Tech Tools for Accessibility

Text-to-Speech

Text-to-Speech (TTS) technology supports read-aloud options and is available with many eBooks, web-based text, or text converted from print by scanning. Struggling readers may need support to use TTS features strategically and effectively. For example, you may directly teach interactive comprehension strategies, such as highlighting key words or grammatical features, and if allowed by the software, adding simple definitions or annotations to support students as they work through a text.

Speech-to-Text

Speech-to-Text (sometimes called dictation or voice typing) can reduce the written expression barriers experienced by some students when completing writing tasks. To support its use, teachers can provide a quiet place to dictate, model speaking clearly, and show students how to correct and edit words that were not recognized or were misspelled.

Microsoft Office Tools—Immersive Reader (IR)

A built-in feature of all MS Office programs that groups literacy tools together for easy access. Websites accessed with Edge, Microsoft's web browser, will display the Immersive Reader icon in the address bar. IR features are also available in other Office tools, such as Word and PowerPoint, to a limited extent.

Accessing IR changes the view by eliminating ads and sidebar links, and adding these tools:

- **Read-aloud** (reads the text with options for adjusting the voice and speed)
- **Text preferences** (personalizes text size, font, and columns to make it easier to read)
- **Grammar tools** (settings that split words into syllables and highlight parts of speech)
- **Reading preferences** (offers language translation options, line focus for displaying 1–5 lines of text at a time, and a picture dictionary based on 45,000 symbols)

Google Tools

This tool set gives teachers and students the means to collaborate on projects and assignments in real time, or even offline, uploading edits and changes when Internet connection is restored. Google tools provide literacy support including voice typing, spelling and grammar checks, translation, and a dictionary.

eBooks

Electronic versions of traditional books are becoming established parts of personal and academic learning environments. Their advantages are numerous: one device can hold many books, the view can be customized for one's reading preferences, a dictionary is always available, and most offer read-aloud capabilities. Many e-textbooks have built-in study features, such as highlighting and note taking, bookmarking, and flashcards.

Bookshare

An eBook library with a collection of more than one million titles, including most textbooks used in K–12 schools and popular press items. Bookshare is available to individuals who have a qualifying reading or perceptual disability, a visual impairment, or a physical disability that affects their ability to read printed works. A professional with appropriate expertise (such as a special education teacher, school psychologist, reading specialist, or librarian) must certify that an individual meets one of these qualifications. This service is free for U.S. students. Bookshare e-books can be read directly from an Internet browser or on tablets and smartphones with a compatible app. The text-to speech feature is a computerized voice. (https://www.bookshare.org/cms/)

Learning Ally

A subscription-based e-book program with a human-read text-to-speech voice. It is available to individuals, families, and school districts on behalf of individuals who have a demonstrated learning disability, visual impairment, or physical disability that makes it difficult to read using print-based materials. Learning Ally requires certifying documentation for each member from a qualified professional (such as a special education teacher, school psychologist, reading specialist, or librarian). Books can be read directly from Internet browsers or smartphones. (https://learningally.org/)

Conclusion

This chapter has provided an overview of ways technology can be used to support students as they learn to read and write. For all learners, technology can support differentiated or personalized learning and practice. With the many tools (and variations within the tools) available, the opportunities to make the learning journey interactive and interesting seem limitless.

Providing support for accessibility and effective application is essential. This includes reducing barriers to access wherever possible. Educators and families are encouraged to exercise caution as the research continues to examine the benefits and best use of technology for students in all grades (Reid Chassiakos et al., 2016). Technology changes quickly; websites, apps, and devices come and go. This presents a significant challenge for researchers to carry out studies amidst the fast pace of change (Hassigner-Das, 2017). Moving forward, students and their teachers need to know more than just how to use basic literacy and writing technology tools, but how to embrace technology as an evolving repertoire of resources that offer many opportunities for students to master the skills of reading and writing.

KEY TAKEAWAYS

- For students who experience challenges in learning to read and write, technology can support their learning journey in many effective ways.

- Instructional frameworks (UDL and SAMR) can guide how and when to use technological tools purposefully and effectively to support personalized learning and differentiated instruction based on need.

- Established readers may also benefit from technology to extend learning and provide challenging and collaborative learning opportunities.

- Any use of technology needs to be done carefully, with awareness there may be positive and/or negative outcomes.

TEACHER DEVELOPMENT

grew up knowing *I wanted to be a teacher. I was lucky that the college I attended enabled me to learn research-supported teaching methods and provided practice opportunities in school settings with helpful feedback. However, when I started teaching, I quickly realized I had so much more to learn!*

As I watched my more experienced colleagues manage their classrooms, or plan wonderful lessons, I understood that teaching was more complex and challenging than I had anticipated. I was hungry to learn more, but also to zero in on how to apply my learning to the wide range of needs in my classroom—especially to support students' literacy development. While some of the in-service experiences I received were beneficial and I was able to incorporate new practices into my teaching, others seemed like a waste of time. When my principal offered the support of an instructional coach, I jumped at the chance! I have come to realize that while teaching is complicated, so is providing high-quality professional development to hard-working and busy teachers! ⭐

AUTHORS

Tiffany Peltier

Lead Learning and Delivery
Specialist in Literacy at
NWEA, a division of HMH
Boston, MA, USA

Erin K. Washburn

Associate Professor
of Reading Education
University of North Carolina
Charlotte, NC, USA

> **To effectively teach all readers and writers … professional learning should be aligned with the most current research.**

The purple arrow on *The Ladder of Reading & Writing* infographic emphasizes the need for all students to receive systematically designed and data-informed instruction that is differentiated based on needs. Differentiation is essential to ensure that every student thrives as a skilled, strategic, and knowledgeable literacy learner. To equip teachers with the knowledge and skills to effectively teach all readers and writers, both initial teacher preparation and ongoing professional learning should be aligned with the most current research. Additionally, providing continued opportunities to engage in research-based practices for adult learning is critical for teachers, regardless of experience, to bridge new knowledge to classroom practice. This chapter addresses the need for research-informed teacher preparation and ongoing professional learning to help teachers support every student in their pursuit of reading and writing mastery.

A FRAMEWORK FOR PROFESSIONAL KNOWLEDGE-BUILDING

In this chapter, we work from Dr. Lee Shulman's (1986) seminal framework outlining the different types of knowledge teachers need to continue to reflectively grow expertise throughout their professional education and career. These types of knowledges include content knowledge, pedagogical knowledge (or knowledge of teaching methods), and knowledge of the curriculum.

Content Knowledge

Building strong content knowledge, or a teacher's personal and deep understanding of the topics, concepts, and skills related to reading and writing, through professional learning is essential for preparing and equipping educators to meet the needs of all literacy learners. Teacher content knowledge must be much deeper than what students are expected to know. For example, although students themselves need to understand how to form the sound /mmmm/, they do not need to know terms such as "continuant consonant." However, teachers need to understand the differences in terminology and the articulatory gestures used to form various consonants and vowels and, when working with multilingual students, how these graphemes and phonemes compare to a student's first language (if applicable). The level of detail in content knowledge provided to teachers in professional learning situations should be much more in-depth than the curriculum presented to students.

 Teacher content knowledge must be much deeper than what students are expected to know.

Methods and Curricular Knowledge

Professional learning must also grow a teacher's knowledge of methods, or how to effectively teach general routines for classroom and behavior management, as well as specific routines and strategies for reading and writing. For example, a first-grade teacher needs to have knowledge of how to differentiate content for small groups of students learning initial letter sounds or letter formation, as well as groups of students already reading chapter books and writing fluently.

Methods also include general knowledge of how to use data to guide instructional decision-making (see Chapter 4), how to organize a classroom to support differentiated instruction (see Chapter 5), how to foster home-school connections (see Chapter 18), and how to include appropriate technology to support instruction (see Chapter 19). All of these methods should be represented in a well-prepared teacher's toolkit.

Finally, an expert teacher must continue to develop deep curricular knowledge to leverage the specific resources and assessment materials available within their own context and to align these materials for the assessed needs of the student population they serve.

REFINING THE FRAMEWORK

Teaching is a complex and highly skilled profession that requires a dynamic cycle of professional learning and reflective practices to grow expertise throughout a career. Building on Dr. Shulman's original 1986 framework, we attempt to summarize research-based practices that specifically improve two broad and essential realms of teacher knowledge through continued professional learning experiences: content knowledge and knowledge of methods.

Content Knowledge

- Deep Teacher Content Knowledge

- Knowledge of Curricular and Assessment Materials

Knowledge of Methods

- Knowledge of General Teaching Procedures

- Knowledge of Methods for Teaching Literacy Skills

Teacher Expertise

Three recommendations from research to improve teacher expertise are clear.

Professional learning experiences must:

- connect theory to practical applications

- dispel myths

- integrate best practices

Connect Theory to Practical Applications

To promote effective classroom literacy practices, professional learning experiences need to include both evidence-aligned theory (content knowledge) and practical, classroom application of that theory (general and specific pedagogical knowledge or methods). We have heard too many teachers leave professional learning experiences with the lingering question, "But what does this look like in the classroom?" The following sections will summarize the importance of anchoring practices in theory.

Content Knowledge for Reading and Writing

Anchoring content knowledge in theoretical, research-based findings is key. Within the realm of scientific understanding about reading and reading development, the *Simple View of Reading* (SVR; Gough & Tunmer, 1986; Hoover & Tunmer, 2018) is a particularly helpful tool for building teachers' content knowledge about this complex topic.

 **x** **=**

| **Word Recognition** | **Language Comprehension** | **Reading Comprehension** |

 We have heard too many teachers leave professional learning experiences with the lingering question, "But what does this look like in the classroom?"

|

Learn More!

International Dyslexia Association. (2018, April 3). *Knowledge and practice standards for teachers of reading.* https://dyslexiaida.org/knowledge-and-practices.

Kirschner, P. A., Hendrick, C., & Heal, J. (2022). *How teaching happens: Seminal works in teaching and teacher effectiveness and what they mean in practice.* Routledge.

Hasbrouck, J., & Michel, D. (2022). *Student-focused coaching: The instructional coach's guide to supporting student success through teacher collaboration.* Brookes.

The SVR model provides an overarching schema for professionals to think about how skilled reading develops. By simplifying the multifaceted process of reading comprehension into two broad categories—word recognition and language comprehension—teachers can better build their mental model of reading instruction, assessment, and reading difficulties.

Word recognition combines the ability to decode (using knowledge of letter sounds—phonemes, and letter formations—graphemes, to identify a word) with instantaneously identifying words by sight. Language comprehension is the understanding of spoken language, processing the linguistic features of sentence grammar and text structure with the meaning of words. The product of these two components is reading comprehension, the ability to accurately and completely understand the meaning of written text.

Paired with the SVR, both the detailed "Cognitive Foundations Framework" (Hoover & Tunmer, 2020) and Scarborough's "Reading Rope" (2001) provide visuals that can help teachers break down the complex reading process to determine which specific areas within word recognition and language comprehension should be targeted for assessment and instruction. *The Ladder of Reading & Writing* infographic can then be used to help teachers understand the need for differentiating the assessment and instruction for all students across the continuum.

By simplifying the multifaceted process of reading comprehension into two broad categories—word recognition and language comprehension—teachers can better build their mental model of reading instruction, assessment, and reading difficulties.

Pedagogical Knowledge for Reading and Writing

If specific content knowledge (the *what*) is like the skeleton of a body, pedagogical knowledge (the *how*) is like the muscles. Both are necessary and important to the expert teacher's body of knowledge.

Researchers agree teachers must possess deep and accurate knowledge of the subject being taught in order to be effective (Piasta et al., 2009). This includes an understanding of not only the content itself, but also how to teach the content in an effective and efficient way.

> " If specific content knowledge (the *what*) is like the skeleton of a body, pedagogical knowledge (the *how*) is like the muscles. "

Effective teaching methods include:

- Having multiple ways to explain and model the content to students, including concise, explicit, student-friendly definitions or procedural steps;

- Knowing common misconceptions of students at each stage of their learning and having explicit and implicit ways to dispel these misconceptions;

- Having a repertoire of analogies that connect new knowledge to students' linguistic and cultural background experiences;

- Using strategies to help students connect new and previous knowledge into a coherent, expanded, and personalized "web of knowledge" in their minds;

- Knowing tactics to support students' retention of new knowledge in long-term memory;

- Knowing how to appropriately use technology to assist and support learning.

DISPELLING MYTHS

If teachers hold misconceptions in their own knowledge structures of how students learn to read, professional learning around research-based concepts won't be as effective. It would be like trying to fit a square peg into a round hole. First, the square peg (in this case, the previously misconceived ideas) needs to be restructured. Then, the new content knowledge can be better understood and connected to previous knowledge, as well as retained and generalized by the learner for future use.

Posner and colleagues' (1982) seminal theory of conceptual change, or the process of moving from a misconception to an evidence-supported conclusion, suggests that change is most likely to happen when individuals are dissatisfied with their current (mis)conception. Furthermore, the new conception must be presented in a way that is:

- intelligible to understand

- plausible to believe

- useful to their future endeavors

As an example of how to use this process to help dispel educational myths, Peltier and colleagues (2020) have used a refutation text to assist preservice teachers in better understanding the term *dyslexia* that is frequently misrepresented in the media and misconceived by teachers, school administrators, and the general public. A refutation text directly addresses widespread misconceptions, refutes them, provides an alternative, scientifically supported conception, explained in an intelligible, plausible, and productive way. The diagram on the following page outlines how a refutation text can be used to dispel misunderstandings about dyslexia.

> " If teachers hold misconceptions in their own knowledge structures of how students learn to read, professional learning around research-based concepts won't be as effective. "

State the misconception	"Many people think dyslexia is a visual difficulty that includes seeing words or letters backwards on the page."
Refute the misconception directly	"This is a common misconception."
State the scientific conception	"Instead, researchers use the term *dyslexia* to describe individuals who experience great difficulty learning to decode text."
Present the new conception in an intelligible and plausible way	"Students with dyslexia need more explicit instruction and repetition to connect sounds to symbols. According to research, they need more opportunities to practice decoding and fluency with a high rate of success."

Organization of a Refutation Text

Professional learning experiences should ensure that common myths are directly addressed for participants to begin disentangling myth from fact, build accurate knowledge structures or schema around key concepts, and move toward a better understanding of reading and writing development, instruction, assessment, and difficulties.

INTEGRATING BEST PRACTICES

Decades of research have identified characteristics of effective professional learning for both novice and seasoned teachers.

Effective Professional Learning

- has a content-specific focus
  (e.g., teaching reading, reading assessment)

- is aligned with instructional goals

- incorporates active engagement

- promotes collaboration with colleagues

- provides opportunities for ongoing support
  through job-embedded coaching or mentoring

(Darling-Hammond et al., 2017)

Rehearsal Plus Microteaching

Practice-based teaching has been a particularly effective pedagogy for providing professional learning that embodies the aforementioned best practices for both preservice and in-service teachers (Forzani, 2014). One effective practice-based method is rehearsal plus microteaching. By experiencing the new method as modeled by an expert, then having a chance to practice in a low-stake setting, teachers can better understand the challenges for implementation and ask questions to clarify understanding.

These activities are particularly helpful for acquiring new teaching methods as both techniques involve opportunities to practice learned information with peers or colleagues under the guidance of an expert before application in a classroom setting (Grossman et al., 2009). This provides an opportunity to clarify the teaching method and become more fluent using it before applying the new method in a higher-stakes environment affecting students.

Analysis of Work Samples and Case Studies

Another effective practice-based method has been the analysis of student work samples, case studies, and/or videos of classroom instruction to help teachers make connections to real-world application and teaching practice. These activities can move beyond the acquisition of new content knowledge to applying the content knowledge through the use of simulated student samples. This supports transfer of the professional learning to the classroom setting and helps teachers plan targeted instruction for their students.

Instructional Coaching

Key to any practice-based approach is the inclusion of modeling from an expert combined with specific feedback to the teacher during practice. Positive, immediate, targeted feedback helps to promote teacher self-efficacy, or a teacher's confidence in their ability to promote students' learning, which has been reported as an important factor in effective reading instruction by Spear-Swerling et al., (2005). In addition to practice-based opportunities embedded in teacher education or professional learning opportunities, high-quality instructional coaching can play an important role in the continued development of teacher expertise (Hasbrouck & Michel, 2022).

The general purpose of instructional coaching is to provide support to teachers as they learn new methods or implement new strategies to optimize student learning. Coaching has been shown to be especially effective when it is both sustained and individualized (Kraft et al., 2018). There are several models of instructional coaching, each of which has some unique processes meant to address a particular need of teachers.

> ### Check Your Understanding
>
> **Check all that apply.**
> **Effective professional learning:**
>
> ___ has a content-specific purpose
>
> ___ is aligned with instructional goals
>
> ___ incorporates active engagement
>
> ___ promotes collaboration with colleagues
>
> ___ provides ongoing support through job-embedded coaching or mentoring

> Key to any practice-based approach is the inclusion of modeling from an expert combined with specific feedback to the teacher during practice.

> **Preservice Teacher Preparation Resources**
>
> - TeachingWorks at the University of Michigan, and the Collaboration for Effective Educator Development, Accountability, and Reform (CEEDAR) Center at the University of Florida provide vetted resources for integrating high-leverage practices and practice-based pedagogies into preservice teacher preparation and in-service professional development.
>
> - The Institute for Education Sciences Regional Educational Laboratories (IES RELs) also provides resources aligned with the science of reading such as instructional videos and lesson plans that can be used to implement a practice-based approach to teacher professional learning.

Conclusion

To help teachers develop expertise in literacy knowledge across their career, teacher educators and professional learning providers should connect theory to practical application, dispel instructional myths, integrate hands-on practice, and include coaching to support change.

To ensure that all students succeed, teacher training and ongoing professional learning must engender the understanding that reading and writing can be taught to *all* students using different amounts of teacher-led and student-led differentiated learning, as appropriate for each student no matter where they are on the continuum. For teachers to successfully differentiate instruction, they should be informed about two areas of professional literacy learning: content knowledge (the *what*) and knowledge of methods (the *how*).

Along with opportunities to engage in hands-on learning, the goal of any professional learning should always be to foster curiosity, support openness to new ideas and evolving research, and provide tools enabling teachers to be critical consumers and expert thinkers within their unique educational contexts.

KEY TAKEAWAYS

- Teachers play a crucial role in providing high-quality instruction in reading and writing that is appropriately differentiated for all students.

- Teachers develop expertise by learning about the content and methodology of teaching through high-quality preparation and continued professional learning.

- The most effective teacher learning experiences will connect theory to classroom practice, dispel myths about teaching and learning, and integrate applied practice opportunities.

CONCLUSION

The Ladder of Reading & Writing infographic represents the wide range of ease in becoming literate, along with the instructional implications. Throughout this book about the infographic, our focus has been presenting ways to better serve all students through effective programming based on need.

Our intended audience is broad, given our passionate belief that teamwork is essential to support students as they successfully climb the Ladder. We are confident that the wealth of knowledge and practical ideas shared by our wonderful chapter authors will support the work you do as an educator, caregiver, or leader.

To address such a broad and thought-provoking topic as reading and writing instruction, the process of deciding what content to include was one of the hardest tasks we faced as co-editors. We believe many important themes are now visible:

- When students are provided with evidence-based instruction that addresses their identified needs, their climb up the Ladder can be ongoing and successful—no matter their challenges, age, or background.

- Students climb the Ladder at different rates based on various learning needs so there cannot be only "one right way" to teach literacy.

- Implicit learning opportunities are essential to enable literacy development. What should be taught more explicitly varies depending on each student's needs.

- Differentiated programming that effectively addresses the wide range of needs across the continuum may necessitate the shifting of perspectives and procedures.

While those messages are important, underpinning them is a crucial point we believe is integral: our students can—and should be—*enjoying* the learning journey. Although every word on the infographic has been carefully chosen to deliver important information, it is the images of the joyful, smiling faces of the climbing students that we want to ensure do not get lost.

We recognize, however, that the climb up the Ladder will require extraordinary effort for some students. The hard work needed to reach a higher rung may not feel joyful at every step. Nonetheless, the responsibility of educators is to teach needed skills as effectively and efficiently as we can, and to make that process as affirming and positive as possible at each step along the way. Only then can every student ultimately experience the powerful joys of literacy.

Whatever your role, may this book provide not only knowledge fundamentals and implementation guidance, but enthusiasm to collaboratively shape a learning environment in which all students master the life-changing skills of reading and writing successfully—and joyfully.

Nancy & Jan

Scan this QR code for additional book resources

REFERENCES

Why We Created This Book

Hasbrouck, J. (2020). *Conquering dyslexia: A guide to early detection and intervention for teachers and families.* Benchmark Education.

Chapter 1

Aizer, A., & Doyle, J. J. (2015). Juvenile incarceration, human capital, and future crime: Evidence from randomly assigned judges. *The Quarterly Journal of Economics, 130*(2), 759–803.

The Annie E. Casey Foundation. (2012). *Double jeopardy: How third grade reading skills and poverty influence high school graduation.* Retrieved from www.aecf.org

Dehaene, S. (2009). *Reading in the brain: The science and evolution of a human invention.* Viking.

Goldberg, M., & Goldenberg, C. (2022). Lessons learned? Reading wars, Reading First, and a way forward. *The Reading Teacher, 75*(5), 621–630.

Lyon, G., & Weiser, B. (2009). Teacher knowledge, instructional expertise, and the development of reading proficiency. *Journal of Learning Disabilities, 42*(5), 475–480.

Moats, L. (2011). Knowledge and practice standards for teachers of reading: A new initiative by the International Reading Association. *Perspectives on Language and Literacy, 37*(2), 51–52.

Moats, L. C. (2020). Teaching reading is rocket science: What expert teachers of reading should know and be able to do. *American Educator, 44*(2), 1–29.

National Center for Educational Statistics (NCES). (2022). *National assessment of educational progress: The nation's report card.* U.S. Department of Education.

National Early Literacy Panel (2008). *Developing early literacy: Report of the national early literacy panel.* National Institute for Literacy.

National Institute of Child Health and Human Development (NICHD). (2000). *Report of the national reading panel: Teaching children to read: An evidence-based assessment of the scientific research literature on reading and its implications for reading instruction: Reports of the subgroups* (NIH publication No. 00–4754). U.S. Government Printing Office.

Noble, K. (2017). Brain trust; poverty affects the size, shape, and functioning of a young child's brain, would a cash stipend to parents help prevent harm? *Scientific American, 316*(3), 44–49.

Petscher, Y., Cabell, S., Catts, H. W., Compton, D., Foorman, B., Hart, S. A., Lonigan, C., Phillips, B., Schatschneider, C., Steacy, L., Terry, N., & Wagner, R. (2020). How the science of reading informs 21st century education. *Reading Research Quarterly, 55*(S1).

Rose, J. (2006). *Independent review of the teaching of early reading. Final report*. Great Britain: Department for Education and Skills.

Rowe, K., & National inquiry into the teaching of literacy. (2005). *Teaching reading: Report and recommendations*. Canberra, Australia: Department of Education, Science, and Training.

Seidenberg, M. (2017). *Language at the speed of sight. How we read, why so many can't, and what can be done about it*. Basic Books.

Solari, E. J., Patton Terry, N., Gaab, N., Hogan, T. P., Nelson, N. J., Pentimonti, J. M., Petscher, Y., Sayko, S. (2020). Translational science: A road map for the science of reading. *Reading Research Quarterly, 55*(1), 347–360.

Vaughn, S., & Fletcher, J. M. (Winter 2020–2021). Identifying and teaching students with significant reading problems. *American Educator, 44*(4), 4–11, 40.

Wolf, M. (2007). *Proust and the squid: The story and science of the reading brain*. Harper Collins.

Young, N. (2021). Personal Website. https://www.nancyyoung.ca.

Chapter 2

Boada, R., Willcutt, E. G., & Tunick, R. A., Chabildas, N. A., Olson, R. K., DeFries, J. C., & Pennington, B. F. (2002). A twin study of the etiology of high reading ability. *Reading and Writing, 15*(7–8), 683–707.

Castles, A., Rastle, K., & Nation, K. (2018). Ending the reading wars: Reading acquisition from novice to expert. *Psychological Science in the Public Interest, 19*(1), 5–51.

Fletcher, J. M., Lyon, G. R., Fuchs, L. S., & Barnes, M. A. (2019). *Learning disabilities: From identification to intervention* (2nd ed.). Guilford Press.

Fletcher, J. M., & Miciak, J. (2019). *The identification of specific learning disabilities: A summary of research on best practices*. Texas Center for Learning Disabilities.

Gentry, R., & Graham, S. (2010). *Creating better readers and writers: The importance of direct, systematic spelling and handwriting instruction in improving academic performance*. [White paper] Saperstein Associates.

Graham, S. (2020). The sciences of reading and writing must become more fully integrated. *Reading Research Quarterly, 55*(S1), S35–S44.

Graham, S., Bollinger, A., Booth Olson, C., D'Aoust, C., MacArthur, C., McCutchen, D., & Olinghouse, N. (2018). *Teaching elementary school students to be effective writers: Educator's practice guide* (NCEE 2012–4058). What Works Clearinghouse, National Center for Education Evaluation and Regional Assistance, Institute of Education Sciences, U.S. Department of Education.

Graham, S., & Hebert, M. (2010). *Writing to read: Evidence for how writing can improve reading. Carnegie Corporation Time to Act Report.* Alliance for Excellent Education.

Hoover, W. A., & Tunmer, W. E. (2020). *The cognitive foundations of reading and its acquisition: A framework with applications connecting teaching and learning* (Vol. 20, pp. 85–88). Springer Cham.

Lyon, R. (2002). *Testimonies to Congress*. Center for the Development of Learning. https://files.eric.ed.gov/fulltext/ED475205.pdf

National Institute of Child Health and Human Development (NICHD). (2000). *Report of the national reading panel: Teaching children to read: An evidence-based assessment of the scientific research literature on reading and its implications for reading instruction: Reports of the subgroups* (NIH publication No. 00–4754). U.S. Government Printing Office.

Reis, S., & Fogarty, E. (2020). Reading and talented readers. In J. Plucker & C. Callahan, (Eds.), *Critical issues and practices in gifted education: A survey of current research on giftedness and talent development* (pp. 361–375). Prufrock Press.

Seidenberg, M. (2017). *Language at the speed of sight. How we read, why so many can't, and what can be done about it.* Basic Books.

Shanahan, T. (2016, June 26). *Further explanation of teaching students with challenging text.* Shanahan on Literacy. https://www.shanahanonliteracy.com/blog/further-explanation-of-teaching-students-with-challenging-text#sthash.r5T4Xzum.dpbs

Shaywitz, S. E., Escobar, M. D., Shaywitz, B. A., Fletcher, J. M., & Makuch, R. (1992). Evidence that dyslexia may represent the lower tail of a normal distribution of reading ability. *New England Journal of Medicine, 326*(3), 145–150.

Smith, R., Snow, P., Serry, T., & Hammond, L. (2021). The role of background knowledge in reading comprehension: A critical review. *Reading Psychology, 42*(3), 214–240.

Spear-Swerling, L. (2018). Structured literacy and typical literacy practices: Understanding differences to create instructional opportunities. *Teaching Exceptional Children, 51*(3), 201–211.

Vaughn, S., & Fletcher, J. M. (Winter 2020–2021). Identifying and teaching students with significant reading problems. *American Educator, 44*(4), 4–11, 40.

Chapter 3

Archer, A. L., & Hughes, C. A. (2010). *Explicit instruction: Effective and efficient teaching (what works for special-needs learners)*. Guilford Press.

Bass, E. (2020). Writing and the gifted learner. In J. Plucker & C. Callahan (Eds.), *Critical issues and practices in gifted education: A survey of current research on giftedness and talent development* (pp. 361–376). Prufrock Press.

Brighton, C. M., Moon, T. R., & L Huang, F. H. L. (2015). Advanced readers in reading first classrooms: Who was really "left behind"? Considerations for the field of gifted education. *Journal for the Education of the Gifted, 38*(3), 257–293.

Carnine, D. W., Silbert, J., Kame'enui, E. J., & Tarver, S. G. (2010). *Direct instruction reading* (5th ed.). Merrill.

Connor, C., Alberto, P. A., Compton, D. L., & O'Connor, R. E. (February 2014). *Improving reading outcomes for students with or at risk for reading disabilities: A synthesis of the contributions from the Institute of Education Sciences Research Centers*. National Center for Special Education Research.

Connor, C. M. (2014). Individualizing teaching in beginning reading. In *Better: Evidence-based education* (pp. 4–7). Institute for Effective Education at the University of York and the Center for Research and Reform in Education at Johns Hopkins School of Education.

Connor, C. M., Morrison, F. J., Fishman, B., Giuliani, S., Luck, M., Underwood, P. S., Bayraktar, A., Crowe, E. C., & Schatschneider, C. (2011). Testing the impact of child characteristics × instruction interactions on third graders' reading comprehension by differentiating literacy instruction. *Reading Research Quarterly, 46*(3), 189–221.

Connor, C. M., Morrison, F. J., & Katch, L. E. (2004). Beyond the reading wars: Exploring the effect of child-instruction interactions on growth in early reading. *Scientific Studies of Reading, 8*(4), 305–336.

Connor, C. M., Piasta, S. B., Fishman, B. J., Glasney, S., Schatschneider, C., Crowe, E. C., Underwood, P. S., & Morrison, F. J. (2009). Individualizing student instruction precisely: Effects of child x instruction interactions on first graders' literacy development. *Child Development, 80*(1), 77–100.

Crumbaugh, C., Frye, B., Schlagal, B., Schram, P., & Trathen, W. (2001). *Instructional grouping: Examples and issues*. www.reasearchgate.net

Dehaene, S. (2011). The massive impact of literacy on the brain and its consequences for education. Human Neuroplasticity and Education. *Scripta Varia* (117), 19–32.

Fiedler, E., Lange, R., & Winebrenner, S. (2002). In search of reality: Unraveling the myths about tracking, ability grouping, and the gifted, *Roeper Review*, *24*(3), 108–111.

Fletcher, J. M., Lyon, G. R., Fuchs, L. S., & Barnes, M. A. (2019). *Learning disabilities: From identification to intervention* (2nd ed.). Guilford Press.

Fletcher, J. M., Stuebing, K. K., Morris, R. D., & Lyon, G. R. (2013). Classification and definition in learning disabilities: A hybrid model. In H. L. Swanson, K. R. Harris, & S. Graham (Eds.), *Handbook of learning disabilities* (2nd ed., Ch. 3, pp. 33–50). Guilford Press.

Graham, S. (2020). The sciences of reading and writing must become more fully integrated. *Reading Research Quarterly*, *55*(S1), S35–S44.

Harris, K. R., Graham, S., Mason, L. H., & Friedlander, B. (2008). *Powerful writing strategies for all students*. Brookes.

Hasbrouck, J., & Glaser, D. (2019). *Reading fluency: Understand, assess, teach*. Benchmark Education.

Hoover, W. A., & Tunmer, W. E. (2020). *The cognitive foundations of reading and its acquisition: A framework with applications connecting teaching and learning* (Vol. 20, pp. 85–88). Springer Cham.

Hughes, C. E., Kettler, T., Shaunessy-Dedrick, E., & VanTassel-Baska, J. (2014). *A teacher's guide to using the common core state standards with gifted and advanced learners in the English language arts*. National Association for Gifted Children. Prufrock Press.

National Institute of Child Health and Human Development (NICHD). (2000). *Report of the national reading panel: Teaching children to read: An evidence-based assessment of the scientific research literature on reading and its implications for reading instruction: Reports of the subgroups* (NIH publication No. 00–4754). U.S. Government Printing Office.

Reis, S., & Fogarty, E. (2020). Reading and talented readers. In J. Plucker & C. Callahan, (Eds.), *Critical issues and practices in gifted education: A survey of current research on giftedness and talent development* (pp. 361–376). Prufrock Press.

Seidenberg, M. (2017). *Language at the speed of sight. How we read, why so many can't, and what can be done about it*. Basic Books.

Seidenberg, M. (2021, September 26). *Part 3: Reading, learning and instruction*. [Webinar] Reading Meetings with Mark and Molly: Conversations bridging science & practice. https://www.youtube.com/watch?v=adeSgFJ6fkQ

Seidenberg, M. S,. Cooper Borkenhagen, M., & Kearns, D. M. (2020). Lost in translation? Challenges in connecting reading science and educational practice. *Reading Research Quarterly*, *55*(S1), S119–S130.

Shanahan, T. (2010). *What about cross-grade or cross-class grouping?* Shanahan on Literacy. https://www.shanahanonliteracy.com/blog/what-about-cross-grade-or-cross-class-grouping

Slavin, R. (2013, September 13). *What are the pros and cons of grouping kids for reading instruction based on test results?* Literacy Now, International Literacy Association.

Spear-Swerling, L. (2018). Structured literacy and typical literacy practices: Understanding differences to create instructional opportunities. *Teaching Exceptional Children, 51*(3), 201–211.

Steenbergen-Hu, S., Makel, M. C., & Olszewski-Kubilius, P. (2016). What one hundred years of research says about the effects of ability grouping and acceleration on K–12 students' academic achievement: Findings of two second-order meta-analyses. *Review of Educational Research, 86*(4), 849–899.

Templeton, S., & Morris, D. (2000). Spelling. In M. L. Kamil, P. B. Mosenthal, P. D. Pearson, & R. Barr (Eds.), *Handbook of reading research* (Vol. 3, pp. 525–543). Routledge.

Treiman, R., & Kessler, B. (2022). Statistical learning in word reading and spelling across languages and writing systems, *Scientific Studies of Reading, 26*(2), 139–149.

VanTassel-Baska, J. (2023). The case for content-based curriculum for advanced learners. *Gifted Child Today, 46*(2), 142–145.

Wolf, M. (2007). *Proust and the squid: The story and science of the reading brain.* Harper Collins.

Wolf, M. (2013). How the reading brain resolves the reading wars. *A Literate Nation.* https://www.decodingdyslexiaiowa.org/wp-content/uploads/2014/05/How-the-Reading-Brain-Resolves-the-Reading-Wars-Maryann-Wolf.pdf

Chapter 4

Bambrick-Santoyo, P. (2019). *Driven by data 2.0: A practical guide to improve instruction.* Wiley.

Burns, M. K., & Symington, T. (2002). A meta-analysis of prereferral intervention teams: Student and systemic outcomes. *Journal of School Psychology, 40*(5), 437–447.

Deno, S. L. (1993). Curriculum-based measurement. In J. J. Kramer (Ed.), *Curriculum-Based Measurement* (pp. 1–23). Burros Center for Testing.

Fuchs, L. (2016). Curriculum-based measure as the emerging alternative—Three decades later. *Learning Disabilities Research & Practice, 32*(1), 5–7.

Grissom, J. A., Egalite, A. J., & Lindsay, C. A. (2021). *How principals affect students and schools: A systematic synthesis of two decades of research.* The Wallace Foundation.

Hasbrouck, J., & Tindal, G. (2017). An update to compiled ORF norms (Technical Report No. 1702). *Behavioral Research and Teaching,* University of Oregon.

Hoover, W. A., & Tunmer, W. E. (2018). The simple view of reading: Three assessments of its adequacy. *Remedial and Special Education, 39*(5), 304–312.

Hosp, M. K., Hosp, J. L., & Howell, K. W. (2016). *The ABCs of CBM: A practical guide to curriculum-based measurement* (2nd ed.). Guilford Press.

McDougal, J. L., Moody Clonan, S., & Martens, B. K. (2000). Using organizational change procedures to promote the acceptability of prereferral intervention services. *School Psychology Quarterly, 15*(2), 149–171.

Nellis, L. M. (2012). Maximizing the effectiveness of building teams in response to intervention implementation. *Psychology in the Schools, 49*(3), 245–256.

Seidenberg, M. (2021, September 26). *Part 3: Reading, learning and instruction.* [Webinar] Reading Meetings with Mark and Molly: Conversations bridging science & practice. https://www.youtube.com/watch?v=adeSgFJ6fkQ

St. Martin, K., Vaughn, S., Troia, G., Fien, & H., Coyne, M. (2020). *Intensifying literacy instruction: Essential practices.* MiMTSS Technical Assistance Center, Michigan Department of Education.

Chapter 5

Connor, C. M., Morrison, F. J., Fishman, B., Crowe, E. C., Al Otaiba, S., & Schatschneider, C. (2013). A longitudinal cluster-randomized controlled study on the accumulating effects of individualized literacy instruction on students' reading from first through third grade. *Psychological Science, 24*(8), 1408–1419.

Fisher, D., & Frey, N. (2015). *Unstoppable learning: Seven essential elements to unleash student potential (Using systems thinking to improve teaching practices and learning outcomes).* Solution Tree Press.

Fisher, D., Frey, N., & Hattie, J. (2016). *Visible learning for literacy, grades K–12: Implementing practices that work best to accelerate student learning.* Corwin Literacy.

Gibson, V. (2019a). *Classroom management: Routines for flexible grouping and collaboration (Early Learning): Professional learning guide for leaders.* Benchmark Education.

Gibson, V. (2019b). *Classroom management: Routines for flexible grouping and collaboration (Elementary School): Professional learning guide for leaders.* Benchmark Education.

Hattie, J. (2009). *Visible learning: A synthesis of over 800 meta-analyses relating to achievement.* Routledge.

Marzano, R. J. (2003). *Classroom management that works: Research-based strategies for every teacher.* Association for Supervision and Curriculum Development.

McLeod, J, Fisher, J., & Hoover, G. (2003). *The key elements of classroom management: Managing time and space, student behavior, and instructional strategies.* Association for Supervision and Curriculum Development.

Rogers, K. B. (2002). *Grouping the gifted and talented: Questions and answers. Roeper Review, 24*(3), 103–107.

Tomlinson, C. (2014). *The differentiated classroom: Responding to the needs of all learners* (2nd ed.). Association for Supervision and Curriculum Development, ASCD.

Vaughn, S., Bos, C., & Schumm, J. S. (2018). *Teaching students who are exceptional, diverse, and at risk in the general education classroom* (7th ed.). Pearson.

Chapter 6

Berninger, V. W., & Wolf, B. (2009). *Teaching students with dyslexia and dysgraphia: Lessons from teaching and science.* Brookes.

Burns, M. K., VanDerHeyden, A. M., Duesenberg-Marshall, M. D., Romero, M. E., Stevens, M. A., Izumi, J. T., & McCollom, E. M. (2022, June 3). Decision accuracy of commonly used dyslexia screeners among students who are potentially at-risk for reading difficulties. *Learning Disability Quarterly.*

Elliott, J. G. (2020). It's time to be scientific about dyslexia. *Reading Research Quarterly, 55*(S1), S61–S75.

Fletcher, J. M., Lyon, G. R., Fuchs, L. S., & Barnes, M. A. (2019). *Learning disabilities: From identification to intervention* (2nd ed.). Guilford Press.

Haft, S. L., Duong, P. H., Ho, T. C., Hendren, R. L., & Hoeft, F. (2019). Anxiety and attentional bias in children with specific learning disorders. *Journal of Abnormal Child Psychology, 47*(3), 487–497.

Hall, C., & Vaughn, S. (2021). Current research informing the conceptualization, identification, and treatment of dyslexia across orthographies: An introduction to the special series. *Learning Disability Quarterly 2021, 44*(3), 140–144.

Hasbrouck, J. (2020). *Conquering dyslexia: A guide to early detection and intervention for teachers and families.* Benchmark Education.

Hasbrouck, J., & Glaser, D. (2019). *Reading fluency: Understand, assess, teach.* Benchmark Education.

Hendren, R. L., Haft, S. L., Black, J. M., White, N. C., & Hoeft, F. (2018). Recognizing psychiatric comorbidity with reading disorders. *Frontiers in Psychiatry, 9*, 1–10.

International Dyslexia Association (2002). *Definition of dyslexia.* International Dyslexia Association. Retrieved 2022, October 16 from https://dyslexiaida.org/definition-of-dyslexia/

Livingston, E. M., Siegel, L. S., & Ribary, U. (2018). Developmental dyslexia: emotional impact and consequences. *Australian Journal of Learning Disabilities, 23*(2), 107–135.

Maddocks, D. L. (2020). Cognitive and achievement characteristics of students from a national sample identified as potentially twice exceptional (gifted with a learning disability). *Gifted Child Quarterly, 64*(1), 3–18.

Odegard, T. N. (2019). Dyslexia defined: Historical trends and the current reality. *Perspectives on Language and Literacy, 45*(1), 11–14.

Chapter 7

Barnes, M. A., Dennis, M., & Haefele-Kalvaitis, J. (1996). The effects of knowledge availability and knowledge accessibility on coherence and elaborative inferencing in children from six to fifteen years of age. *Journal of Experimental Child Psychology, 61*(3), 216–241.

Beck, I. L., McKeown, M. G., & Kucan, L. (2013). *Bringing words to life: Robust vocabulary instruction.* Guilford Press.

Best, R. M., Floyd, R. G., & McNamara, D. S. (2008). Differential competencies contributing to children's comprehension of narrative and expository texts. *Reading Psychology, 29*(2), 137–164.

Boudah, D. J. (2013). The main idea strategy: A strategy to improve reading comprehension through inferential thinking. *Intervention in School and Clinic, 49*(3), 148–155.

Brasseur-Hock, I. F., Hock, M. F., Kieffer, M. J., Biancarosa, G., & Deshler, D. D. (2011). Adolescent struggling readers in urban schools: Results of a latent class analysis. *Learning and Individual Differences, 21*(4), 438–452.

Cirino, P. T., Romain, M. A., Barth, A. E., Tolar, T. D., Fletcher, J. M., & Vaughn, S. (2013). Reading skill components and impairments in middle school struggling readers. *Reading and Writing, 26*(7), 1059–1086.

Coxhead, A. (2000). A new academic word list. *TESOL Quarterly, 34*(2), 213–238.

Filderman, M. J., Austin, C. R., Boucher, A. N., O'Donnell, K., & Swanson, E. A. (2022). A meta-analysis of the effects of reading comprehension interventions on the reading comprehension outcomes of struggling readers in third through 12th grades. *Exceptional Children, 88*(2), 163–184.

Fletcher, J. M., Lyon, G. R., Fuchs, L. S., & Barnes, M. A. (2019). *Learning disabilities: From identification to intervention* (2nd ed.). Guilford Press.

Gardner, D., & Davies, M. (2014). A new academic vocabulary list. *Applied Linguistics, 35*(3), 305–327.

Hebert, M., Bohaty, J. J., Nelson, J. R., & Brown, J. (2016). The effects of text structure instruction on expository reading comprehension: A meta-analysis. *Journal of Educational Psychology, 108*(5), 609–624.

Jitendra, A. K., & Gajria, M. (2011). Main idea and summarization instruction to improve reading comprehension. In R. E. O'Connor & P. F. Vadasy (Eds.), *Handbook of reading interventions* (pp. 198–219). Guilford Press.

Joseph, L. M., Alber-Morgan, S., Cullen, J., & Rouse, C. (2016). The effects of self-questioning on reading comprehension: A literature review. *Reading & Writing Quarterly, 32*(2), 152–173.

Kinnunen, R., & Vauras, M. (1995). Comprehension monitoring and the level of comprehension in high-and low-achieving primary school children's reading. *Learning and Instruction, 5*(2), 143–165.

Klingner, J. K., Vaughn, S., & Schumm, J. S. (1998). Collaborative strategic reading during social studies in heterogeneous fourth-grade classrooms. *The Elementary School Journal, 99*(1), 3–22.

Roehling, J. V., Hebert, M., Nelson, J. R., & Bohaty, J. J. (2017). Text structure strategies for improving expository reading comprehension. *The Reading Teacher, 71*(1), 71–82.

Schmitt, N., Jiang, X., & Grabe, W. (2011). The percentage of words known in a text and reading comprehension. *The Modern Language Journal, 95*(1), 26–43.

Stevens, E. A., Murray, C. S., Fishstrom, S., & Vaughn, S. (2020). Using question generation to improve reading comprehension for middle-grade students. *Journal of Adolescent & Adult Literacy, 64*(3), 311–322.

Stevens E. A., Park S., Vaughn S. (2019). A review of summarizing and main idea interventions for struggling readers in grades 3 through 12: 1978–2016. *Remedial and Special Education, 40*(3), 131–149.

Swanson, E., Wanzek, J., McCulley, L., Stillman-Spisak, S., Vaughn, S., Simmons, D., Fogarty, M., & Hairrell, A. (2016). Literacy and text reading in middle and high school social studies and English language arts classrooms. *Reading & Writing Quarterly, 32*(3), 199–222.

Vaughn, S., Gersten, R., Dimino, J., Taylor, M. J., Newman-Gonchar, R., Krowka, S., Kieffer, M. J., McKeown, M., Reed, D., Sanchez, M., St. Martin, K., Wexler, J., Morgan, S., Yañez, A., & Jayanthi, M. (2022). *Providing reading interventions for students in grades 4–9: Educator's practice guide* (WWC 2022007). What Works Clearinghouse, National Center for Education Evaluation and Regional Assistance (NCEE), Institute of Education Sciences, U.S. Department of Education.

Chapter 8

Applebee, A., & Langer, J. (2011). A snapshot of writing instruction in middle schools and high schools. *English Journal, 100,* 14–27.

Bass, E. (2020). Writing and the gifted learner. In J. Plucker & C. Callahan (Eds.), *Critical issues and practices in gifted education: A survey of current research on giftedness and talent development* (pp. 361–376). Prufrock Press.

Berninger, V. W., Vaughan, K., Abbott, R. D., Brooks, A., Begay, K., Curtin, G., Byrd, K., & Graham, S. (2000). Language-based spelling instruction: Teaching children to make multiple connections between spoken and written words. *Learning Disability Quarterly, 23*(2), 117–134.

Berninger, V. W., & Wolf, B. (2009). *Teaching students with dyslexia and dysgraphia: Lessons from teaching and science.* Brookes.

Fletcher, J. M., Lyon, G. R., Fuchs, L. S., & Barnes, M. A. (2019). *Learning disabilities: From identification to intervention* (2nd ed.). Guilford Press.

Graham, S. (2019). Changing how writing is taught. *Review of Research in Education, 43*(1), 277–303.

Graham, S. (2020). The sciences of reading and writing must become more fully integrated. *Reading Research Quarterly, 55*(S1), S35–S44.

Graham, S., Bollinger, A., Booth Olson, C., D'Aoust, C., MacArthur, C., McCutchen, D., & Olinghouse, N. (2018). *Teaching elementary school students to be effective writers: Educator's practice guide* (NCEE 2012-4058). What Works Clearinghouse, National Center for Education Evaluation and Regional Assistance, Institute of Education Sciences, U.S. Department of Education.

Graham, S., & Harris, K. R. (2013). Common core state standards, writing, and students with LD: recommendations. *Learning Disabilities Research & Practice, 28*(1), 28–37.

Graham, S., Harris, K. R., & Adkins, M. (2018). The impact of supplemental handwriting and spelling instruction with first grade students who do not acquire transcription skills as rapidly as peers: A randomized control trial. *Reading and Writing, 31*(6), 1273–1294.

Graham, S., Harris, K. R., & Santangelo, T. (2015). Research-based writing practices and the common core: Meta-analysis and meta-synthesis. *The Elementary School Journal, 115*(4), 498–522.

Harris, K. R., Graham, S., Mason, L. H., & Friedlander, B. (2008). *Powerful writing strategies for all students.* Brookes.

Hebert, M., Kearns, D. M., Hayes, J. B., Bazis, P., & Cooper, S. (2018). Why children with dyslexia struggle with writing and how to help them. *Language, Speech, and Hearing Services in Schools, 49*(4), 843–863.

Hendren, R. L., Haft, S. L., Black, J. M., White, N. C., & Hoeft, F. (2018). Recognizing psychiatric comorbidity with reading disorders. *Frontiers in Psychiatry, 9,* 1–10.

Hosp, M. K., Hosp, J. L., & Howell, K. W. (2016). *The ABCs of CBM: A practical guide to curriculum-based measurement* (2nd ed.). Guilford Press.

Joshi, R. M., Treiman, R., Carreker, S., & Moats, L. (2008–2009). How words cast their spell. *American Educator, 32*(4), 6–16.

Kiuhara, S. A., Graham, S., & Hawken, L. S. (2009). Teaching writing to high school students: A national survey. *Journal of Educational Psychology, 101*(1), 136–160.

Madelaine, A. (2022). Weekly spelling lists—are they a good idea? *Nomais, 14,* 35–37.

Madelaine, A. (2023). Spelling. In K. Wheldall, R. Wheldall, & J. Buckingham (Eds.), *Effective instruction in reading and spelling* (pp. 183–213). MRU Press.

Pacton, S., Foulin, J. N., Casalis, S., & Treiman, R. (2013). Children benefit from morphological relatedness when they learn to spell new words. *Frontiers in Psychology, 4,* 696.

Saddler, B. (2012). *Teacher's guide to effective sentence writing.* Guilford Press.

Saddler, B., & Asaro-Saddler, K. (2009). Writing better sentences: Sentence-combining instruction in the classroom. *Preventing School Failure: Alternative Education for Children and Youth, 54*(3), 159–163.

Saddler, B., & Graham, S. (2005). The effects of peer-assisted sentence-combining instruction on the writing performance of more and less skilled young writers. *Journal of Educational Psychology, 97*(1), 43–54.

Schwellnus, H., Cameron, D., & Carnahan, H. (2012). Which to choose: Manuscript or cursive handwriting? A review of the literature. *Journal of Occupational Therapy, Schools, & Early Intervention, 5*(3–4), 248–258.

Sedita, J. (2023). *The Writing Rope: A framework for explicit writing instruction in all subjects.* Brookes.

Treiman, R., & Kessler, B. (2006). Spelling as statistical learning: Using consonantal context to spell vowels. *Journal of Educational Psychology, 98*(3), 642–652.

Troia, G. A., Brehmer, J. S., Glause, K., Reichmuth, H. L., & Lawrence, F. (2020). Direct and indirect effects of literacy skills and writing fluency on writing quality across three genres. *Education Science, 10,* 297.

Truckenmiller, A. J., & Chandler, B. W. (2023). Writing to read: Parallel and independent contributions of writing research to the science of reading. *The Reading League Journal, 4*(1), 5–11.

Truckenmiller, A. J., McKindles, J. V., Petscher, Y., Eckert, T. L., & Tock J. (2020). Expanding curriculum-based measurement in written expression for middle school. *The Journal of Special Education, 54*(3), 133–145.

Chapter 9

Adolf, S. M., & Hogan, T. P. (2019). If we don't look, we won't see: Measuring language development to inform literacy instruction. *Policy Insights from the Behavioral and Brain Sciences, 6*(2), 210–217.

Alonzo, C. N., McIlraith, A. L., Catts, H. W., & Hogan, T. P. (2020). Predicting dyslexia in children with developmental language disorder. *Journal of Speech, Language, and Hearing Research, 63*(1), 151–162.

Bishop, D., Snowling, M., Thompson, P., Greenhalgh, T. & the CATALISE Constortium (2016), CATALISE: a multinational and multidisciplinary Delphi consensus study. Identifying language impairments in children. *PLOS One, 11*(12).

Brownlie, E. G., Jabber, A., Beitchman, J., Vida, R., & Atkinson, L. (2007). Language impairment and sexual assault of girls and women: Findings from a community sample. *Journal of Abnormal Psychology, 35*(4), 618–626.

Catts, H., Adlof, S., Hogan, T., & Ellis Weismer, S. (2005). Are specific language impairment and dyslexia distinct disorders? *Journal of Speech, Language, and Hearing Research, 48*(6), 1378–1396.

Chow, J. C. (2018). Comorbid language and behavior problems: Development, frameworks, and intervention. *School Psychology Quarterly, 33*(3), 356–360.

Dickinson, D. K. (2011). Teachers' language practices and academic outcomes of preschool children. *Science, 333*(6045), 964–967.

Donolato, E., Cardillo, R., Mammarella, I. C., & Melby-Lervag, M. (2022). Research review: Language and specific learning disorders in children and their co-occurrence with internalizing and externalizing problems: a systematic review and meta-analysis. *Journal of Child Psychology and Psychiatry, 63*(5), 507–518.

Hendricks, A. E., Adlof, S. M., Alonzo, C. N., Fox, A. B., & Hogan, T. P. (2019). Identifying children at risk for developmental language disorder using a brief, whole-classroom screen. *Journal of Speech, Language, and Hearing Research, 62*(4), 896–908.

Hogan, T. P., Bao, X., & Komesidou, R. (2022, November 23). *Developmental Language Disorder Screening Tests Fact Sheet.*

Joffe, V. L., Rixon, L., & Hulme, C. (2019). Improving storytelling and vocabulary in secondary school students with language disorder: A randomized controlled trial. *International Journal of Language & Communication Disorders, 54*(4), 656–672.

Leonard, L. (2014). *Children with specific language impairment.* MIT Press.

McGregor, K. K. (2020). How we fail children with developmental language disorder. *Language, Speech, & Hearing Services in Schools, 51*(4), 981–992.

McGregor, K. K., Van Horne, A. O., Curran, M., Cook, S. W., & Cole, R. (2021). The challenge of rich vocabulary instruction for children with developmental language disorder. *Language, Speech, and Hearing Services in Schools, 52*(2), 467–484.

Nippold, M. A., Mansfield, T. C., Billow, J. L., Tomblin, J. B. (2008). Expository discourse in adolescents with language impairments: Examining syntactic development. *American Journal of Speech Language Pathology, 17*(4), 356–366.

Novogrodsky, R., & Friedmann, N. (2006). The production of relative clauses in syntactic SLI: A window to the nature of the impairment. *Advances in Speech Language Pathology, 8*(4), 364–375.

Rice, M. L., & Hoffman, L. (2015). Predicting vocabulary growth in children with and without specific language impairment: A longitudinal study from 2;6 to 21 years of age. *Journal of Speech, Language, and Hearing Research, 58*(2), 345–359.

Snowling, M. J., Hulme, C., & Nation, K. (2020). Defining and understanding dyslexia: Past, present and future. *Oxford Review Education, 46*(4), 501–513.

Tomblin, J. B., Records, N. L., Buckwalter, P., Zhang, X., Smith, E., & O'Brien, M. (1997). Prevalence of specific language impairment in kindergarten children. *Journal of Speech, Language, and Hearing Research, 40*(6), 1245–1260.

Wittke, K., & Spaulding, T. J. (2018). Which preschool children with specific language impairment receive language intervention? *Language, Speech, and Hearing Services in Schools, 49*(1), 59–71.

Chapter 10

Barkley, R. A. (2020). *Taking charge of ADHD: The complete, authoritative guide for parents* (4th ed.). Guilford Press.

Denton, C. A., Tamm, L., Schatschneider, C., & Epstein, J. N. (2020). The effects of ADHD treatment and reading intervention on the fluency and comprehension of children with ADHD and word reading difficulties: A randomized clinical trial. *Scientific Studies of Reading, 24*(1), 72–89.

DuPaul, G. J., & Stoner, G. (2014). *ADHD in the schools: Assessment and intervention strategies* (3rd ed.). Guilford Press.

Mayes, S. D., Breau, R. P., Calhoun, S. L., Fry, S. S. (2019). High prevalence of dysgraphia in elementary through high school students with ADHD and autism. *Journal of Attention Disorders, 23*(8), 787–796.

Pliszka, S., & AACAP Work Group on Quality Issues. (2007). Practice parameter for the assessment and treatment of children and adolescents with attention-deficit/hyperactivity disorder. *Journal of the American Academy of Child & Adolescent Psychiatry, 246*(7), 894–921.

Tamm, L., Denton, C. A., Epstein, J. N., Schatschneider, C., Taylor, H., Arnold, L. E., Bukstein, O., Anixt, J., Koshy, A., Newman, N. C., Maltinsky, J., Brinson, P., Loren, R. E. A., Prasad, M. R., Ewing-Cobbs, L., & Vaughn, A. (2017). Comparing treatments for children with ADHD and word reading difficulties: A randomized clinical trial. *Journal of Consulting and Clinical Psychology, 85*(5), 434–446.

Chapter 11

Afacan, K., Wilkerson, K. L., & Ruppar, A. L. (2018). Multicomponent reading interventions for students with intellectual disability. *Remedial and Special Education, 39*(4), 229–242.

Ahlgrim-Delzell, L., Browder, D. M., Wood, L., Stanger, C., Preston, A. I., & Kemp-Inman, A. (2016). Systematic instruction of phonics skills using an iPad for students with developmental disabilities who are AAC users. *The Journal of Special Education, 50*(2), 86–97.

Allor, J., Kearns, D., Ortiz, M., & Conner, C. (2022). An examination of the text characteristics of an early reading book series: Implications for providing intensive practice with connected text. In M. Tankersley, B. G. Cook, & T. J. Landrum (Eds.), *Delivering intensive, individualized interventions to children and youth with learning and behavioral disabilities* (Vol. 32, pp. 131–152). Emerald Publishing Limited.

Allor, J. H., Gifford, D. B., Jones, F. G., Otaiba, S. A., Yovanoff, P., Ortiz, M. B., & Cheatham, J. P. (2018). The effects of a text-centered literacy curriculum for students with intellectual disability. *American Journal on Intellectual and Developmental Disabilities, 123*(5), 474–494.

Allor, J. H., Mathes, P. G., Champlin, T., & Cheatham, J. P. (2009). Research-based techniques for teaching early reading skills to students with intellectual disabilities. *Education and Training in Developmental Disabilities*, 356–366.

Allor, J. H., Mathes, P. G., Roberts, J. K., Cheatham, J. P., & Otaiba, S. A. (2014). Is scientifically based reading instruction effective for students with below-average IQs? *Exceptional Children*, 80(3), 287–306.

Browder, D., Gibbs, S., Ahlgrim-Delzell, L., Courtade, G. R., Mraz, M., & Flowers, C. (2009). Literacy for students with severe developmental disabilities: What should we teach and what should we hope to achieve? *Remedial and Special Education*, 30(5), 269–282.

Browder, D. M., Ahlgrim-Delzell, L., Courtade, G., Gibbs, S. L., & Flowers, C. (2008). Evaluation of the effectiveness of an early literacy program for students with significant developmental disabilities. *Exceptional Children*, 75(1), 33–52.

Browder, D. M., Wakeman, S. Y., Spooner, F., Ahlgrim-Delzell, L., & Algozzinexya, B. (2006). Research on reading instruction for individuals with significant cognitive disabilities. *Exceptional Children*, 72(4), 392–408.

Conner, C., G Jones, F., Ahlgrim-Delzell, L., Walte, S., & H Allor, J. (2022). What teachers know about teaching reading to students with developmental disabilities: A survey of special educators. *Journal of Policy and Practice in Intellectual Disabilities*, 19(3), 300–310.

Gadd, M., Berthen, D., & Lundgren, L. (2021). Helping students with intellectual disabilities become better writers: an inquiry into writing instruction. *International Journal of Disability, Development and Education*, 68(3), 395–413.

Joseph, L. M., & Konrad, M. (2009). Teaching students with intellectual or developmental disabilities to write: A review of the literature. *Research in Developmental Disabilities*, 30(1), 1–19.

Katims, D. S. (2001). Literacy assessment of students with mental retardation: An exploratory investigation. *Education and Training in Mental Retardation and Developmental Disabilities*, 36(4), 363–372.

Lemons, C. J., Allor, J. H., Al Otaiba, S., & LeJeune, L. M. (2016). 10 research-based tips for enhancing literacy instruction for students with intellectual disability. *Teaching Exceptional Children*, 49(1), 18–30.

Lemons, C. J., Kearns, D. M., & Davidson, K. A. (2014). Data-based individualization in reading: Intensifying interventions for students with significant reading disabilities. *Teaching Exceptional Children*, 46(4), 20–29.

Lemons, C. J., King, S. A., Davidson, K. A., Puranik, C. S., Al Otaiba, S., Fulmer, D., Mrachko, A. A., Partanen, J., & Fidler, D. J. (2017). Developing an early reading intervention aligned with the Down syndrome behavioral phenotype. *Focus on Autism and Other Developmental Disabilities*, 32(3), 176–187.

Lemons, C. J., King, S. A., Davidson, K. A., Puranik, C. S., Fulmer, D., Mrachko, A. A., & Fidler, D. J. (2015). Adapting phonological awareness interventions for children with Down syndrome based on the behavioral phenotype: A promising approach? *Intellectual and Developmental Disabilities*, 53(4), 271–288.

Schalock, R. L., Luckasson, R., & Tassé, M. J. (2021). *Intellectual disability: Definition, diagnosis, classification, and systems of supports* (12th ed.). American Association on Intellectual and Developmental Disabilities.

Chapter 12

American Academy of Pediatrics (AAP). 1999. Newborn and infant hearing loss: Detection and intervention. *Pediatrics, 103*(2), 527–530.

Ilari, B. (2002). Music and babies: A review of research with implications for music educators. *Update: Applications of Research in Music Education, 21*(2), 17–26.

McCreery, R. W., & Walker, E. A. (2022). Variation in auditory experience affects language and executive functioning skills in children who are hard of hearing. *Ear and Hearing, 43*(2), 347–360.

Rollins Center for Language & Literacy at The Atlanta Speech School. (2023). *Talk With Me Baby: TWMB @ Birthing Centers.* Cox Campus. https://learn.coxcampus.org/courses/talk-with-babies-make-a-difference/

Schafer, E. C., Kirby, B., & Miller, S. (2020). Remote microphone technology for children with hearing loss or auditory processing issues. *Seminars in Hearing, 41*(4), 277–290.

Vaccari, C., & Marsharck, M. (2006). Communication between parents and deaf children: Implications for social-emotional development. *Journal of Child Psychology and Psychiatry, 38*(7), 793–801.

Zauche, L. H., Mahoney, A. E. D., Thul, T. A., Zauche, M. S., Weldon, A. B., & Stapel-Wax, J. L. (2017). The power of language nutrition for children's brain development, health, and future academic achievement. *Journal of Pediatric Health Care, 31*(4), 493–503.

Zauche, L. H., Thul, T. A., Mahoney, A. E. D., & Stapel-Wax, J. L. (2016). Influence of language nutrition on children's language and cognitive development: An integrated review. *Early Childhood Research Quarterly, 36*, 318–333.

Assouline, S., Colangelo, N., VanTassel-Baska, J., & Lupkowski-Shoplik, A. (Eds.). (2015). *A nation empowered: Evidence trumps the excuses holding back America's brightest students* (Vols. 1 & 2). The Connie Belin & Jacqueline N. Blank International Center for Gifted Education and Talent Development.

Bass, E. (2020). Writing and the gifted learner. In J. Plucker & C. Callahan (Eds.), *Critical issues and practices in gifted education: A survey of current research on giftedness and talent development* (pp. 361–376). Prufrock Press.

Brighton, C. M., Moon, T. R., & Huang, F. H. L. (2015). Advanced readers in reading first classrooms: Who was really "left behind"? Considerations for the field of gifted education. *Journal for the Education of the Gifted, 38*(3), 257–293.

Colangelo, N., Assouline, S., & Gross, M. (2004). *A nation deceived: How schools hold back America's brightest students*. The Connie Belin & Jacqueline N. Blank International Center for Gifted Education and Talent Development.

Connor, C., Alberto, P. A., Compton, D. L., & O'Connor, R. E. (February 2014). *Improving reading outcomes for students with or at risk for reading disabilities: A synthesis of the contributions from the Institute of Education Sciences Research Centers*. National Center for Special Education Research.

Connor, C. M. (2014). Individualizing teaching in beginning reading. In *Better: Evidence-based education* (pp. 4–7). Institute for Effective Education at the University of York and the Center for Research and Reform in Education at Johns Hopkins School of Education.

Connor, C. M., Morrison, F. J., & Katch, L. E. (2004). Beyond the reading wars: Exploring the effect of child-instruction interactions on growth in early reading. *Scientific Studies of Reading, 8*(4), 305–336.

Cross, J. R., Frazier, A. D., Kim, M., & Cross, T. L. (2018). A comparison of perceptions of barriers to academic success among high-ability students from high-and low-income groups: Exposing poverty of a different kind. *Gifted Child Quarterly, 62*(1), 111–129.

Davis, J., & Douglas, D. (2021). *Empowering underrepresented gifted students: Perspectives from the field*. Free Spirit Press.

Dixson, D. D., Peters, S. J., Makel, M. C., Jolly, J. L., Matthews, M. S., Miller, E. M., Rambo-Hernandez, K. E., Rinn, A. N., Robins, J. H., & Wilson, H. E. (2020). A call to reframe gifted education as maximizing learning. *Phi Delta Kappan, 102*(4), 22–25.

Firmender, J. M., Reis, S. M., & Sweeny, S. M. (2013). Reading comprehension and fluency levels range across diverse classrooms: The need for differentiated reading instruction and content. *Gifted Child Quarterly, 57*(1), 3–14.

Flowers, T. (2016). Teaching a gifted kindergarten student using a literature-based approach: A personal reflection. *Illinois Schools Journal, 95*(2), 57–69.

Ford, D. Y., Walters, N. M., Byrd, J. A., & Harris, B. N. (2019). I want to read about me: Engaging and empowering gifted Black girls using multicultural literature and bibliotherapy. *Gifted Child Today, 42*(1), 53–57.

Gross, M. U. (1999). Small poppies: Highly gifted children in the early years. *Roeper Review, 21*(3), 207–214.

Harris, K. R., Graham, S., Aitken, A. A., Barkel, A., Houston, J., & Ray, A. (2017). Teaching spelling, writing, and reading for writing: Powerful evidence-based practices. *Teaching Exceptional Children, 49*(4), 262–272.

Henderson, S. J., Jackson, N. E., & Mukamal, R. A. (1993). Early development of language and literacy skills of an extremely precocious reader. *Gifted Child Quarterly, 37*(2), 78–83.

Hockett, J., & Doubet, K. (2020). Differentiated instruction. In J. Plucker & C. Callahan (Eds.), *Critical issues and practices in gifted education: A survey of current research on giftedness and talent development* (pp. 157–168). Prufrock Press.

Hoover, W. A., & Tunmer, W. E. (2020). *The cognitive foundations of reading and its acquisition: A framework with applications connecting teaching and learning* (Vol. 20, pp. 85–88). Springer Cham.

Hughes, C. E., Kettler, T., Shaunessy-Dedrick, E., & VanTassel-Baska, J. (2014). *A teacher's guide to using the common core state standards with gifted and advanced learners in the English language arts*. National Association for Gifted Children. Prufrock Press.

Kulik, J. A., & Kulik, C. L. C. (1992). Meta-analytic findings on grouping programs. *Gifted Child Quarterly, 36*(2), 73–77.

National Association for Gifted Children (n.d.). *Myths about gifted children*. https://www.nagc.org/myths-about-gifted-students

National Association for Gifted Children (2008). *The role of assessment in the identification of gifted students* [Position Statement]. https://cdn.ymaws.com/nagc.org/resource/resmgr/knowledge-center/position-statements/the_role_of_assessments_in_t.pdf

National Association for Gifted Children (2019). *Pre–K to Grade 12 gifted programming standards*. https://dev.nagc.org/resources-publications/resources/national-standards-gifted-and-talented-education/pre-k-grade-12

Noel, K., & Edmunds, A. L. (2006). Constructing a synthetic-analytic framework for precocious writing. *Roeper Review, 29*(2), 125–131.

Olthouse, J. M. (2012). Why I write: What talented creative writers need their teachers to know. *Gifted Child Today, 35*(2), 116–121.

Pacton, S., Borchardt, G., Treiman, R., Lété, B., & Fayol, M. (2014). Learning to spell from reading: General knowledge about spelling patterns influences memory for specific words. *Quarterly Journal of Experimental Psychology, 67*(5), 1019–1036.

Pacton, S., Foulin, J. N., Casalis, S., & Treiman, R. (2013). Children benefit from morphological relatedness when they learn to spell new words. *Frontiers in Psychology, 4*, 696.

Papadopoulos, T. C., Spanoudis, G., Ktisti, C., & Fella, A. (2020). Precocious readers: a cognitive or a linguistic advantage? *European Journal of Psychology of Education, 36*, 63–90.

Peters, S. J. (2022). Where does gifted education go from here: Chaos or community? *Gifted Child Quarterly, 66*(2), 163–168.

Reis, S. M., & Boeve, H. (2009). How academically gifted elementary, urban students respond to challenge in an enriched, differentiated reading program. *Journal for the Education of the Gifted, 33*(2), 203–240.

Reis, S., & Fogarty, E. (2020). Reading and talented readers. In J. Plucker & C. Callahan (Eds.), *Critical issues and practices in gifted education: A survey of current research on giftedness and talent development* (pp. 361–375). Prufrock Press.

Reis, S. M., McCoach, D. B., Little, C. A., Muller, L. M., & Kaniskan, R. B. (2011). The effects of differentiated instruction and enrichment pedagogy on reading achievement in five elementary schools. *American Educational Research Journal, 48*(2), 462–501.

Renzulli, J. S., Reis, S., & Brigandi, C. (2020). Enrichment theory, research, and practice. In J. Plucker & C. Callahan (Eds.), *Critical issues and practices in gifted education: A survey of current research on giftedness and talent development* (pp. 185–199). Prufrock Press.

Rimm, S., Siegle, D., & Davis, G. (2018). *Education of the gifted and talented* (7th ed.). Pearson Education.

Rogers, K. B. (2007). Lessons learned about educating the gifted and talented: A synthesis of the research on educational practice. *Gifted Child Quarterly, 51*(4), 382–396.

Scarborough, H. S., Ehri, L. C., Olson, R. K., & Fowler, A. E. (1998). The fate of phonemic awareness beyond the elementary school years. *Scientific Studies of Reading 2*, 115–142.

Shanahan, T. (2015, 19 January). *Why does he want to hurt kindergartners?* Shanahan on Literacy. https://www.shanahanonliteracy.com/blog/why-does-he-want-to-hurt-kindergartners

Spanke, J., & Paul, K. A. (2015). From the pens of babes: Authentic audiences for talented, young writers. *Gifted Child Today, 38*(3), 177–186.

Stambaugh, T. (2018). Scaffolding of instruction is necessary for gifted students too. *Teaching for High Potential*, 10–13. Vanderbilt University.

Steenbergen-Hu, S., Makel, M. C., & Olszewski-Kubilius, P. (2016). What one hundred years of research says about the effects of ability grouping and acceleration on K–12 students' academic achievement: Findings of two second-order meta-analyses. *Review of Educational Research, 86*(4), 849–899.

Szymanski, A. (2020). Social and emotional issues in gifted education. In J. Plucker & C. Callahan (Eds.), *Critical issues and practices in gifted education: A survey of current research on giftedness and talent development* (pp. 417–429). Prufrock Press.

Treiman, R. (2017). Learning to spell words: Findings, theories, and issues. *Scientific Studies of Reading, 21*(4), 265–276.

Treiman, R., & Kessler, B. (2006). Spelling as statistical learning: Using consonantal context to spell vowels. *Journal of Educational Psychology, 98*(3), 642–652.

VanTassel-Baska, J. (2003). *Differentiating the language arts for high ability learners, K–8: ERIC Digest.* ERIC Clearinghouse on Disabilities and Gifted Education.

VanTassel-Baska, J. (2018). Achievement unlocked: Effective curriculum interventions with low-income students. *Gifted Child Quarterly, 62*(1), 68–82.

VanTassel-Baska, J. (2023). The case for content-based curriculum for advanced learners. *Gifted Child Today, 46*(2), 142–145.

VanTassel-Baska, J., Zuo, L., Avery, L. D., & Little, C. A. (2002). A curriculum study of gifted-student learning in the language arts. *Gifted Child Quarterly, 46*(1), 30–44.

Chapter 14

Austin, C. R., Vaughn, S., Clemens, N. H., Pustejovsky, J. E., & Boucher, A. N. (2022). The relative effects of instruction linking word reading and word meaning compared to word reading instruction alone on the accuracy, fluency, and word meaning knowledge of 4th–5th grade students with dyslexia. *Scientific Studies of Reading, 26*(3), 204–222.

Beck, I. L., McKeown, M. G., & Kucan, L. (2013). *Bringing words to life: Robust vocabulary instruction.* Guilford Press.

Compton, D. L., Miller, A. C., Elleman, A. M., & Steacy, L. M. (2014). Have we forsaken reading theory in the name of "quick fix" interventions for children with reading disability? *Scientific Studies of Reading, 18*(1), 55–73.

Fletcher, J. M., Stuebing, K. K., Morris, R. D., & Lyon, G. R. (2013). Classification and definition of learning disabilities. A hybrid model. In H. L. Swanson, K. R. Harris, & S. Graham (Eds.), *Handbook of learning disabilities* (2nd ed., pp. 33–50). Guilford Press.

LaBerge, D., & Samuels, S. J. (1974). Toward a theory of automatic information processing in reading. *Cognitive Psychology, 6*(2), 293–323.

McArthur, G., Badcock, N., Castles, A., & Robidoux, S. (2022). Tracking the relations between children's reading and emotional health across time: Evidence from four large longitudinal studies. *Reading Research Quarterly, 57*(2), 555–585.

Morgan, P. L., Farkas, G., & Wu, Q. (2012). Do poor readers feel angry, sad, and unpopular? *Scientific Study of Reading, 16*(4), 360–381.

Nation, K., & Snowling, M. J. (1998). Individual differences in contextual facilitation: Evidence from dyslexia and poor reading comprehension. *Child Development, 69*(4), 996–1011.

Seidenberg, M. (2017). *Language at the speed of sight: How we read, why so many can't, and what can be done about it*. Basic Books.

Seidenberg, M. S. (2005). Connectionist models of word reading. *Current Directions in Psychological Science, 14*(5), 238–242.

Toste, J. R., Capin, P., Williams, K. J., Cho, E., & Vaughn, S. (2019). Replication of an experimental study investigating the efficacy of a multisyllabic word reading intervention with and without motivational beliefs training for struggling readers. *Journal of Learning Disabilities, 52*(1), 45–58.

Vaughn, S., Gersten, R., Dimino, J., Taylor, M. J., Newman-Gonchar, R., Krowka, S., Kieffer, M. J., McKeown, M., Reed, D., Sanchez, M., St. Martin, K., Wexler, J., Morgan, S., Yañez, A., & Jayanthi, M. (2022). *Providing reading interventions for students in grades 4–9: Educator's practice guide* (WWC 2022007). What Works Clearinghouse, National Center for Education Evaluation and Regional Assistance (NCEE), Institute of Education Sciences, U.S. Department of Education.

Vaughn, S., Martinez, L. R., Williams, K. J., Miciak, J., Fall, A. M., & Roberts, G. (2019). Efficacy of a high school extensive reading intervention for English learners with reading difficulties. *Journal of Educational Psychology, 111*(3), 373–386.

Vaughn, S., Roberts, G. J., Miciak, J., Taylor, P., & Fletcher, J. M. (2019). Efficacy of a word- and text-based intervention for students with significant reading difficulties. *Journal of Learning Disabilities, 52*(1), 31–44.

Wanzek, J., & Roberts, G. (2012). Reading interventions with varying instructional emphases for fourth graders with reading difficulties. *Learning Disability Quarterly, 35*(2), 90–101.

Brown, M. C., Sibley, D. E., Washington, J. A., Rogers, T. T., Edwards, J. R., MacDonald, M. C., & Seidenberg, M. S. (2015). Impact of dialect use on a basic component of learning to read. *Frontiers in Psychology, 6*(196), 1–17.

Catts, H. W., Adlof, S. M., & Weismer, S. E. (2006). Language deficits in poor comprehenders: A case for the simple view of reading. *Journal of Speech, Language, and Hearing Research, 49*(2), 278–293.

Chambers J. K., & Trudgill P. (1998). *Dialectology* (2nd ed.). Cambridge University Press.

Children's Defense Fund (2021). *The State of America's Children 2021.* https://www.childrensdefense.org/wp-content/uploads/2021/04/The-State-of-Americas-Children-2021.pdf

Fielding, L., Kerr, N., & Rosier, P. (2007). *Annual growth for all students, catch-up growth for those who are behind.* The New Foundation Press, Inc.

Green, L. J. (2002). *African American English: A linguistic introduction.* Cambridge University Press.

Merriam-Webster. (n.d.-a). Dialect. In *Merriam-Webster.com dictionary.* Retrieved from: https://www.merriam-webster.com/dictionary/dialect

Merriam-Webster. (n.d.-b). Idiolect. In *Merriam-Webster.com dictionary.* Retrieved from: https://www.merriam-webster.com/dictionary/idiolect

Merriam-Webster. (n.d.-c). Sociolect. In *Merriam-Webster.com dictionary.* Retrieved from: https://www.merriam-webster.com/dictionary/sociolect

Oxford University Press. (2014). Ethnolect. In *The concise Oxford dictionary of linguistics.* Retrieved from: https://www.oxfordreference.com/view/10.1093/acref/9780199675128.001.0001/acref-9780199675128-e-1109?rskey=sURwzi&result=1

Stoop, W., & Bosch, A. (2014). Using idiolects and sociolects to improve word prediction. In *Proceedings of the 14th Conference of the European Chapter of the Association for Computational Linguistics* (pp. 318–327). Association for Computational Linguistics.

Terry, N. (2006). Relations between dialect variation, grammar, and early spelling skills. *Reading and Writing, 19*(9), 907–931.

Washington, J. A., Branum-Martin, L., Sun, C., & Lee-James, R. (2018). The impact of dialect density on the growth of language and reading in African American Children. *Language, Speech, and Hearing Services in Schools, 49*(2), 232–47.

Washington, J. A., & Seidenberg, M. S. (2021). Teaching reading to African American children: When home and school language differ. *American Educator, 45*(2), 26–33, 40.

Washington, J. A., Terry, N. P., & Seidenberg, M. S. (2014). Language variation and literacy learning: The case of African American English. In C. A. Stone, B. J. Ehren, E. R. Silliman, & G. P. Wallach (Eds.), *Handbook of language and literacy development and disorders* (2nd ed., pp. 204–222). Guilford Press.

Chapter 16

Brevik, L. M. (2016). The gaming outliers. In E. Elstad (Ed.), *Educational technology and polycontextual bridging* (pp. 39–61). SensePublishers Rotterdam.

Brannon, D., & Dauksas, L. (2014). The effectiveness of dialogic reading in increasing English language learning preschool children's expressive language. *International Research in Early Childhood Education, 5*(1), 1–10.

Cheah, Z. R. E., Ye, Y., Lui, K. F. H., McBride, C., & Maurer, U. (2022). Spelling as a way to classify poor Chinese-English literacy skills in Hong Kong Chinese children. *Annals of Dyslexia*.

Chow, B. W.-Y., McBride-Chang, C., & Cheung, H. (2010). Parent-child reading in English as a second language: Effects on language and literacy development of Chinese kindergarteners. *Journal of Research in Reading, 33*(3), 284–301.

Chung, K. K. H., & Ho, C. S. H. (2010). Second language learning difficulties in Chinese children with dyslexia: What are the reading-related cognitive skills that contribute to English and Chinese word reading? *Journal of Learning Disabilities, 43*(3), 195–211.

Chung, K. K. H., Li, X., Lam, C. B., Fung, W. K., & Liu, C. (2022). What predicts first-and second-language difficulties? Testing language and executive functioning skills as correlates. *Learning Disabilities Research & Practice, 37*(2), 85–99.

Dulay, K. M., Tong, X., & McBride, C. (2017). The role of foreign domestic helpers in Hong Kong Chinese children's English and Chinese skills: A longitudinal study. *Language Learning, 67*(2), 321–347.

Durgunoğlu, A. Y., Nagy, W. E., & Hancin-Bhatt, B. J. (1993). Cross-language transfer of phonological awareness. *Journal of Educational Psychology, 85*(3), 453–465.

Fenner, D. S. (2013). Implementing the common core state standards for English learners: The changing role of the ESL teacher. TESOL.

Hammer, C. S., Davison, M. D., Lawrence, F. R., & Miccio, A. W. (2009). The effect of maternal language on bilingual children's vocabulary and emergent literacy development during Head Start and kindergarten. *Scientific Studies of Reading, 13*(2), 99–121.

Hattie, J. (2012). *Visible learning for teachers: Maximizing impact on learning.* Routledge.

Hong, S. C., & Chen, S. H. (2011). Roles of position, stress, and proficiency in L2 children's spelling: A developmental perspective. *Reading and Writing, 24*(3), 355–385.

Kahn-Horwitz, J., Shimron, J., & Sparks, R. L. (2006). Weak and strong novice readers of English as a foreign language: Effects of first language and socioeconomic status. *Annals of Dyslexia, 56*(1), 161–185.

Li, G. (2003). Literacy, culture, and politics of schooling: Counternarratives of a Chinese Canadian family. *Anthropology and Education Quarterly, 34*(2), 182–206.

Li, T., McBride-Chang, C., Wong, A., & Shu, H. (2012). Longitudinal predictors of spelling and reading comprehension in Chinese as an L1 and English as an L2 in Hong Kong Chinese children. *Journal of Educational Psychology, 104*(2), 286–301.

Lipka, O., & Siegel, L. S. (2007). The development of reading skills in children with English as a second language. *Scientific Studies of Reading, 11*(2), 105–131.

Lucas, T., & Grinberg, J. (2008). Responding to the linguistic reality of mainstream classrooms: Preparing all teachers to teach English language learners. In M. Cochran-Smith, S. Feiman-Neuser, D. J. McIntyre, & K. E. Demers (Eds.), *Handbook of research on teacher education: Enduring questions in changing contexts* (pp. 606–636). Routledge.

Lui, K. F. H., Cheah, Z. R. E., McBride, C., & Maurer, U. (2022). Testing the script-relativity hypothesis: Expertise in reading Chinese versus English is associated with better arithmetic skills. *Reading and Writing, 35*(6), 1359–1379.

Lyon, G. R., & Weiser, B. (2009). Teacher knowledge, instructional expertise, and the development of reading proficiency. *Journal of Learning Disabilities, 42*, 475–480.

McBride, C. (2015). *Children's literacy development: A cross-cultural perspective on learning to read and write.* Routledge.

McBride, C. (2019). *Coping with dyslexia, dysgraphia and ADHD: A global perspective.* Routledge.

McBride-Chang, C., & Treiman, R. (2003). Hong Kong Chinese Kindergartners learn to read English analytically. *Psychological Science, 14*(2), 138–143.

Menken, K., & Antunez, B. (2001). An overview of the preparation and certification of teachers working with limited English proficient (LEP) students. National Clearinghouse for Bilingual Education.

Miller-Guron, L., & Lundberg, I. (2000). Dyslexia and second language reading: A second bite at the apple? *Reading and Writing, 12*(1), 41–61.

Pasquarella, A., Chen, X., Gottardo, A., & Geva, E. (2015). Cross-language transfer of word reading accuracy and word reading fluency in Spanish-English and Chinese-English bilinguals: Script-universal and script-specific processes. *Journal of Educational Psychology, 107*(1), 96–110.

Petchprasert, A. (2014). The influence of parents' backgrounds, beliefs about English learning, and a dialogic reading program on Thai kindergarteners' English lexical development. *English Language Teaching, 7*(3), 50–62.

Siegel, L. (2016). Bilingualism and dyslexia: The case of children learning English as an additional language. In L. Peer & G. Reid (Eds.), *Multilingualism, literacy and dyslexia: Breaking down barriers for educators* (2nd ed., pp. 137–147). Routledge.

Silseth, K. (2012). The multivoicedness of game play: Exploring the unfolding of a students' learning trajectory in a gaming context at school. *International Journal of Computer-Supported Collaborative Learning 7*, 63–84.

Sundqvist, P., & Wikström, P. (2015). Out-of-school digital gameplay and in-school L2 English vocabulary outcomes. *System 51*, 65–76.

Treiman, R., Berch, D., & Weatherston, S. (1993). Children's use of phoneme-grapheme correspondences in spelling: Roles of position and stress. *Journal of Educational Psychology, 85*(3), 466–477.

Tremblay, A. (2008). Is second language lexical access prosodically constrained? Processing of word stress by French Canadian second language learners of English. *Applied Psycholinguistics, 29*(4), 553–584.

Wang, M., & Geva, E. (2003). Spelling performance of Chinese children using English as a second language: Lexical and visual-orthographic processes. *Applied Psycholinguistics, 24*(1), 1–25.

Yeung, S. S., & King, R. B. (2016). Home literacy environment and English language and literacy skills among Chinese young children who learn English as a second language. *Reading Psychology, 37*(1), 92–120.

Chapter 17

Abadzi, H. (2006). *Efficient learning for the poor: Insights from the frontier of cognitive neuroscience*. World Bank.

Buckingham, J., Wheldall, K., & Beaman-Wheldall, R. (2013). Why poor children are more likely to become poor readers: The school years. *Australian Journal of Education, 57*(3), 190–213.

Fletcher, J. M., Lyon, G. R., Fuchs, L. S., & Barnes, M. A. (2019). *Learning disabilities: From identification to intervention* (2nd ed.). Guilford Press.

Furey, J., & Loftus-Rattan, S. M. (2021). Actively involving students with learning disabilities in progress monitoring practices. Intervention in *School & Clinic, 57*(5), 329–337.

Hernandez, D. J. (2012). *Double jeopardy: How third-grade reading skills and high poverty influence high-school graduation*. The Annie E. Casey Foundation.

Lovett, M. W., Frijters, J. C., Wolf, M., Steinbach, K. A., Sevcik, R. A., & Morris, R. D. (2017). Early intervention for children at risk for reading disabilities: The impact of grade at intervention and individual differences on intervention outcomes. *Journal of Educational Psychology, 109*(7), 889–914.

McArthur, G., Badcock, N., Castles, A., & Robidoux, S. (2022). Tracking the relations between children's reading and emotional health across time: Evidence from four large longitudinal studies. *Reading Research Quarterly, 57*(2), 555–585.

Reardon, S. E., Valentino, R. A., & Shores, K. A. (2012). Patterns of literacy among U.S. students. *Future Child, 22*(2), 17–37.

Schunk, D. H. (2003). Self-efficacy for reading and writing: Influence of modeling, goal setting, and self-evaluation. *Reading & Writing Quarterly, 19*(2), 159–172.

Seidenberg, M. (2017). *Language at the speed of sight: How we read, why so many can't, and what can be done about it*. Basic Books.

World Literacy Foundation. (2018). *The economic & social costs of illiteracy*. https://worldliteracyfoundation.org

Chapter 18

Henderson, A., & Mapp, K. (2002). *A new wave of evidence: The impact of school, family, and community connections on student achievement: Annual synthesis 2002*. Southwest Educational Development Laboratory. https://sedl.org/connections/resources/evidence.pdf

Hornby, G., & Lafaele, R. (2011). Barriers to parental involvement in education: an explanatory model, *Educational Review, 63*(1), 37–52.

Lemmer, E. M. (2012). Who's doing the talking? Teacher and parent experiences of parent-teacher conferences. *South African Journal of Education, 32*(1), 83–96.

Mapp, K. (2002). Having their say: Parents describe how and why they are involved in the children's education [Paper]. Annual Meeting of the American Educational Research Association, New Orleans, LA.

Mapp, K. L., & Bergman, E. (2019). Dual capacity-building framework for family-school partnerships (Version 2). Retrieved from: www.dualcapacity.org

Mapp, K. L., & Kuttner, P. J. (2013). *Partners in education: A dual capacity-building framework for family-school partnerships.* SEDL.

Orkin, M., May, S., & Wolf, M. (2017). How parental support during homework contributes to helpless behaviors among struggling readers. *Reading Psychology, 38*(5), 506–541.

Patall, E. A., Cooper, H., & Robinson, J. C. (2008). Parent involvement in homework: A research synthesis. *Review of Educational Research, 78*(4), 1039–1101.

Weiss, H. B., Lopez, M. E., & Rosenberg, H. (2010). *Beyond random acts: Family, school, and community engagement as an integral part of education reform.* National Policy Forum for Family, School and Community Engagement, Harvard Family Research Project.

Westat and Policy Studies Associates (2001). *The Longitudinal Evaluation of School Change and Performance (LESCP) in Title I Schools, Highlights.* http://www.ed.gov/offices/OUS/PES/esed/lescp_highlights.html

Chapter 19

CAST (2018). Universal design for learning guidelines version 2.2 [Graphic organizer]. Retrieved from http://udlguidelines.cast.org

Culatta, B., Hall-Kenyon, K., & Bingham, G. (2016, January 7). *Five questions everyone should ask before choosing early literacy apps.* Sesame Workshop: Joan Ganz Cooney Center. https://joanganzcooneycenter.org/2016/01/07/five-questions-everyone-should-ask-before-choosing-early-literacy-apps/

Fletcher, J. M., Lyon, G. R., Fuchs, L. S., & Barnes, M. A. (2019). *Learning disabilities: From identification to intervention* (2nd ed.). Guilford Press.

Hassigner-Das, B. (2017, February 8). The pace of digital media development and academic research. *BOLD.* https://bold.expert/the-pace-of-digital-media-development-and-academic-research/

Janssen, J., Stoyanov, S., Ferrari, A., Punie, Y., Pannekeet, K., & Sloep, P. (2013). Experts' views on digital competence: Commonalities and differences. *Computers & Education, 68,* 473–481.

Puentedura, R. (2013). *SAMR: Moving from enhancement to transformation* [Presentation slides]. AIS ICT Management and Leadership Conference. http://www.hippasus.com/rrpweblog/archives/000095.html

Quesenberry, A. C., Mustian, A. L., & Clark-Bischke, C. (2016). Tuning in: Strategies for incorporating technology into social skills instruction in preschool and kindergarten. *Young Children, 71*(1), 74–80.

Reed, D. K. (2018). Responsibly incorporating technology into literacy instruction. *Iowa Reading Research Center.* https://iowareadingresearch.org/blog/incorporating-technology-literacy-instruction

Reid Chassiakos, Y. L., Radesky, J., Christakis, D., Moreno, M. A., Cross, C., Council on Communications and Media, Hill, D., Ameenuddin, N., Hutchinson, J., Levine, A., Boyd, R., Mendelson, R., & Swanson, W. S. (2016). Children and adolescents and digital media. *Pediatrics, 138*(5).

Seidenberg, M. (2017). *Language at the speed of sight: How we read, why so many can't, and what can be done about it.* Basic Books.

U.S. Department of Education Office of Educational Technology (n.d.). *Guiding principles for use of technology with early learners.* https://tech.ed.gov/earlylearning/principles/

US Department of Education Office of Educational Technology (2017). *Reimagining the role of technology in education.* https://tech.ed.gov/files/2017/01/NETP17.pdf

Wolf, M. (2018). *Reader come home: The reading brain in a digital world.* Harper Collins.

Chapter 20

Darling-Hammond, L., Hyler, M. E., & Gardner, M. (2017). Effective teacher professional development [Research Brief] *Learning Policy Institute.*

Forzani, F. M. (2014). Understanding "core practices" and "practice-based" teacher education: Learning from the past. *Journal of Teacher Education, 65*(4), 357–368.

Gough, P. B., & Tunmer, W. E. (1986). Decoding, reading, and reading disability. *Remedial and Special Education, 7*(1), 6–10.

Grossman, P., Hammerness, K., & McDonald, M. (2009). Redefining teaching, re-imagining teacher education. *Teachers and Teaching: Theory and Practice, 15*(2), 273–289.

Hasbrouck, J., & Michel, D. (2022). *Student-focused coaching: The instructional coach's guide to supporting student success through teacher collaboration.* Brookes.

Hoover, W. A., & Tunmer, W. E. (2018). The simple view of reading: Three assessments of its adequacy. *Remedial and Special Education, 39*(5), 304–312.

Hoover, W. A., & Tunmer, W. E. (2020). *The cognitive foundations of reading and its acquisition: A framework with applications connecting teaching and learning* (Vol. 20, pp. 85–88). Springer Cham.

Kraft, M., Blazar, D., & Hogan, D. (2018). The effect of teacher coaching on instruction and achievement: A meta-analysis of the causal evidence. *Review of Educational Research, 88*(4), 547–588.

Peltier, T. K., Heddy, B. C., & Peltier, C. (2020). Using conceptual change theory to help preservice teachers understand dyslexia. *Annals of Dyslexia, 70*(1), 62–78.

Piasta, S. B., Connor, C. M., Fishman, B. J., & Morrison, F. J. (2009). Teachers' knowledge of literacy concepts, classroom practices, and student reading growth. *Scientific Studies of Reading, 13*(3), 224–248.

Posner, G. J., Strike, K. A., Hewson, P. W., & Gertzog, W. A. (1982). Toward a theory of conceptual change. *Science Education, 66*(2), 211–227.

Scarborough, H. S. (2001). Connecting early language and literacy to later reading (dis)abilities: Evidence, theory, and practice. In S. Neuman & D. Dickinson (Eds.), *Handbook for Research in Early Literacy* (pp. 97–110). Guilford Press.

Shulman, L. (1986). Those who understand: Knowledge growth in teaching. *Educational Researcher, 15*(2), 4–14.

Spear-Swerling, L., Brucker, P. O., & Alfano, M. P. (2005). Teachers' literacy-related knowledge and self-perceptions in relation to preparation and experience. *Annals of Dyslexia, 55*, 266–296.